TAKING CAPTIVITY Captive

A Bible Study based on the Book of Jeremiah
SECOND EDITION

Carrie Neal

Copyright © 2013, Second Edition 2014 - Carrie Neal

All rights reserved. No part of this book may be reproduced or transmitted in any form or by any means, electronic or mechanical, including photocopying and recording, or by any information storage or retrieval system, except as may be expressly permitted in writing by the publisher. Requests for permission should be sent to Carrie Neal at carrie@grassandflowers.org.

ISBN -13: 978-0-9888136-1-8

Unless otherwise noted, Scripture quotations are from the New American Standard Bible, copyright ©1960, 1962, 1963, 1968, 1972, 1973, 1975, 1977, by The Lockman Foundation. Used by permission.

Scripture quotations marked NLT are taken from the Holy Bible, New Living Translation, copyright © 1996, 2004. Used by permission of Tyndale House Publishers, In., Wheaton, Illinois. All rights reserved.

Scripture quotations marked NIV are from the Holy Bible, New International Version, copyright © 1973, 1978, 1984, by International Bible Society.

Scripture quotations marked KJV are from the King James Version of the Bible.

The Chronological Study Bible NKJV, copyright © 2008, by Thomas Nelson, Nashville, Tennessee.

To order additional copies of this resource, please contact the publisher through www.grassandflowers.org.

Printed in the United States of America

DEDICATION

I dedicate this book to three people:

In memory of my Mom – who lived a life full of God's joy and grace. She radiated the love of Christ to not only my family, but to everyone she met. She was a gift given to us by God and my closest friend for the first 15 years of my life.

My Dad – who taught me how to work hard, think critically and instilled in me a love to learn. He encouraged me to move beyond the status quo. He pushes me to examine what I believe in thoroughly, even and especially when we have differences of opinion. He is a good man.

My husband, Rob – who has faithfully stood by my side through it all – the joys and the sorrows. He has been like a rock, helping me through difficult times. I couldn't have done it without him. He is my best friend and I will be forever grateful to him for all he has done and continues to do through our life's journey together.

This verse was given to me and my mom on separate occasions, 12 years apart. We each knew exactly what God was saying to us in this verse and it was the same message to us both, although given at different times.

> *"...weeping may endure for a night,*
>
> *but joy comes in the morning."*
>
> *Psalms 30:5*
>
> *(American King James Version)*

Mom, I'm looking forward to this verse being fulfilled in its entirety!

TABLE OF CONTENTS

WEEK ONE

DAY 1	Set Apart	9
DAY 2	Created for a Purpose	12
DAY 3	The Almond Rod & The Boiling Pot	17
DAY 4	King Josiah – A Reformer	20
DAY 5	Lost Treasures	26

WEEK TWO

DAY 1	Guard Against Sin	33
DAY 2	Temple Sermon	37
DAY 3	Temple Sermon (Continued)	41
DAY 4	You Must Die!	44
DAY 5	The Babylonians	49

WEEK THREE

DAY 1	The Linen Sash	55
DAY 2	The Scroll	58
DAY 3	The Drought & Jeremiah's Ministry Crisis	64
DAY 4	The Rechabites – Lives of Integrity	70
DAY 5	Jeremiah's Lifestyle & The Sabbath Day	75

WEEK FOUR

DAY 1	Garbage!	83
DAY 2	The Kings	91
DAY 3	A Good Leader	96
DAY 4	The Coming Righteous Branch	100
DAY 5	False Prophets	105

WEEK FIVE

DAY 1	A Turning Point	115
DAY 2	The Yoke of Babylon	124
DAY 3	Oracles to the Nations	130
DAY 4	Oracles to the Nations (Continued)	138
DAY 5	Babylon's Future	145

WEEK SIX

DAY 1	Message to the Exiles	151
DAY 2	The Famous Verse	157
DAY 3	Seeking God with all our Hearts	162
DAY 4	A Few Duds & Another Godly Prophet	166
DAY 5	Put No Confidence in the Flesh	170

WEEK SEVEN

DAY 1	Obstinate People	177
DAY 2	The Pit	182
DAY 3	Nothing is Too Difficult for God	188
DAY 4	Call to Me	194
DAY 5	Restoration	201

WEEK EIGHT

DAY 1	The Fall of Jerusalem	211
DAY 2	A Chance for a New Beginning	217
DAY 3	Egypt & Jeremiah's Last Words	223
DAY 4	Wrapping It Up	229
DAY 5	Hope	234

Carrie Neal

About the Author

Carrie Neal is a Bible teacher, author, and a Family Nurse Practitioner. Carrie loves to teach the Word of God and is passionate for others to know Jesus intimately and live the abundant life Christ speaks of in John 10:10. Carrie has taught at women's conferences, mom's groups, in adult Sunday school, in women's and teenage girl's classes, and served on a Women's Ministry Team at church. She currently works at a family medical practice and has so for the last 9 years. Carrie recently founded Grass and Flowers Ministry, where she is dedicated to empowering women to understand the Scriptures and enable them to fulfill Christ's ultimate purpose for their lives. Carrie, her husband Rob, their two lovely children, Aaron and Rachel, along with their three crazy cats, happily reside in Knoxville, Tennessee.

INTRODUCTION

If you had asked me a few years ago if I knew anything about the Old Testament prophet Jeremiah, I would have laughed and said I know he's called "the weeping prophet" and his book is located near the center of the Bible. I had read the book before, but with little interest. I found the book of Jeremiah to be difficult to understand. I considered the book of Lamentations, also thought to be written by Jeremiah, to be depressing and irrelevant.. I had no inclination or burning desire to tackle either of these books ever again. Then eight years ago, I attended a Bible Study Fellowship (BSF) Bible Study that radically changed my outlook on the Old Testament. Through BSF, I studied almost every minor and major prophet in the Old Testament and began to understand the prophets' teachings within a historical context. What's more, I began to understand how relevant every book of the Bible is as I daily gleaned practical application to my personal life. A hunger for God's Word ignited a passion for deeper study and investigation of God's Word. What I had previously glossed over casually now came fully alive. This stirring has not ceased and gradually led to a far deeper walk with the Lord.

About two years ago, I felt the Lord urging me to develop a Bible Study on the book of Jeremiah. I began to research books that spoke about him. The NKJV Chronological Study Bible helped me to understand how the book flowed chronologically. As I placed Jeremiah within the historical period he lived, I came to understand the incredible challenges Jeremiah faced. He carried a tremendous burden for his people, as well as, carried the weight of being God's mouthpiece to a stubborn people who did not want to listen.

There are many parallels between Jeremiah's times and the times in which we now live. God tried to wake up His people back then just as He is trying to wake us up now. God used not only the prophet Jeremiah, but also natural disasters, political events, and economic and social instability to capture the Jews attention. God's wakeup call didn't work initially though, so after 40 years God used another tactic. God broke through the hard heartedness of the Judeans, but it came at a high price. They lost everything they held dear and were taken into captivity to Babylon for 70 years. They lost their homeland, their temple, family and friends, their jobs, and their way of life. Yet, through their captivity they came to know God intimately and be forever changed. Our world is not much different from theirs. We say we trust in God, but do we really? I'm afraid our approach to sin in our lives individually and in our nation is as casual as the Jews in Jeremiah's times. I pray God opens our eyes to any hardness in our hearts towards sin. Let's readily apply to ourselves what God spoke to a stubborn, self-sufficient nation 2,500 years ago. This book is a rich treasure house of truth. Truths, that if applied, will forever change you.

God teaches us through the Judean people and directly through Jeremiah's life. It is perhaps my understanding of Jeremiah, as a man which brought me to a greater depth spiritually. He is so much more than a weeping prophet (although he did cry on occasion). Instead, he stands as a great example of how every Christian should live - totally sold out for Christ. He willingly walked away from every pleasure and comfort offered in this life to deliver the message God gave without compromise. As he took a stand against the sins of his day, he lost his reputation with his family, friends, and the nation of Judah. He chose to remain faithful to the purposes of God and walked the narrow road. Jeremiah disclosed himself emotionally more than any other prophet. His inner struggles with God and God's people were dispersed throughout his writings. Jeremiah addressed and spoke to the last five kings of Judah. For 40 years, God's message was delivered through Jeremiah. He faced opposition on every side. Yet, he did not give up.

Jeremiah is the second largest book of the Bible. The largest book is the Psalms. God dedicated an enormous part of Scripture to this book. While the book reveals the messages Jeremiah spoke to his contemporaries, it was more than a message just for that time. The message was written down to remind those in exile of the hope and the future God had in store for them, but it was also written for future generations to remind us of what God had done and still wants to do with His chosen ones.

As you walk through this study, may you slowly take it in and reflect deeply on every encouragement, exhortation, and truth God lays on your heart. May we all become less like the Judeans before they went into exile and more like Jeremiah. Ultimately, let's become more like Jesus Christ, as we take this journey together for the next 8 weeks.

Bible Study Structure

The study is divided into 8 weeks with 5 lessons per week. Each lesson takes about 30-45 minutes. One lesson should be completed daily versus trying to complete five in one day. While the lessons will be completed individually at home during the week, it's intended for the Bible study to be discussed weekly with a group of women. This encourages accountability in your walk with Christ and motivation to finish the Bible study. The Bible study format allows you to draw out valuable truths from God's Word on your own (with a little help) and then directs you to apply it to your life. Also, group discussion questions will be identified each day with . These questions are meant to help guide your discussion in your weekly Bible study group. Weekly video sessions can be done as well, one video session per week. The video session will cover material that is not in the weekly lessons.

The Bible study was written using the NASB (New American Standard Bible) translation of the Bible. It is recommended you use the NASB translation of the Bible while you do this study to make it easier to understand. On occasion, I will use a different translation, but I will always note it next to the verse. Know that unless otherwise stated, all Bible verses listed are from the NASB translation.

The purpose of this Bible study is two-fold: first and foremost is for you to learn about the character of Jeremiah and the secondary purpose is to see the consequences a nation faces that refuses to follow God. We will examine the courageous acts of Jeremiah, his perseverance, as well as observe a nation who refused to obey God despite the clear warnings and consequences laid out before them.

As you delve into this often unexplored book of the Bible, I pray your eyes will be opened to understand how just like a nation, we as God's chosen people, can also fall into the same trap nationally and individually. We face the same bondages as the Judeans. If you serve God faithfully, this study will show you how to avoid falling into sin. If you are not following God faithfully, you will see clearly the consequences of your disobedience and how He wants to free you from sin's grasp. Whether you find yourself captive to particular sins or want to avoid captivity to sin in general, this book is for you.

The book of Jeremiah will teach you about a man who stood up against all odds and did not give in to the culture of his day. Instead, he spoke the truth even when it seemed he was not being heard. It also teaches how God allows a nation to fall into captivity because of their disobedience, but then compassionately brings them back to their homeland as they turn back to Him.

Let's dive in and discover what God has in store for us.

WEEK ONE
TAKING CAPTIVITY CAPTIVE

DAY ONE
Set Apart

DAY TWO
Created for a Purpose

DAY THREE
The Almond Rod & The Boiling Pot

DAY FOUR
King Josiah – A Reformer

DAY FIVE
Lost Treasures

DAY 1

Set Apart

Welcome! I look forward to going through this Bible study with you. I can't think of anyone in the Old Testament I'd rather study than Jeremiah. He is real and doesn't hold back in telling us how he feels. He shares his excitement, his difficult questions to God, and even his down times. You name it, he talks about it. He is more personal than any other Old Testament prophet. The only other person that opens up more than Jeremiah in the Old Testament would have to be David, who wrote the majority of the Psalms. Jeremiah is the largest prophetic book in the Bible.

Let's begin by praying, asking God to open our hearts and minds to what He has in store for us. This promises to be a memorable journey gals!

Before you open to the book of Jeremiah, write down what you already know about Jeremiah. You may be like I was and know very little. That's okay. By the end of this study, you will know much more.

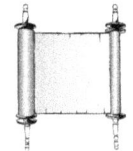

_____

_____

_____

Now let's dig in by reading Jeremiah 1:1-3. Who was Jeremiah's father and what was his occupation?

_____

Jeremiah's father, Hilkiah, was a priest. The priests in Jeremiah's times didn't preach often, like "priests" do today. Instead, priests attended to the ceremonial rituals in the temple and the prophets preached to the people. The prophets were considered God's mouthpiece, exposing the sins of the people and bringing them back to God when they strayed. "Priests were supported from the sacrifice and offerings of the people, but prophets had no guaranteed income."[1]

It was expected that Jeremiah would be a priest because of his family lineage. He was undoubtedly being trained to be a priest by his father since early childhood. Imagine what Jeremiah's father must have felt like when he learned God had called Jeremiah to be a prophet. Hilkiah probably felt a mixture of joy and sorrow concerning his son's new vocation. Joyful knowing that God called Jeremiah personally to be a prophet, but sad knowing his son would not be by his side working along with him in the priesthood. Also, Hilkiah understood prophets were not treated kindly by others, because their message typically was contrary to what people wanted to hear. Hilkiah must have mourned deeply for this loss.

I imagine Hilkiah's reaction was like a parent receiving the news that their child is going to serve as a missionary in an unsafe mission field. As God-fearing parents, they would be thrilled their child heard and obeyed God, but nervous of the inevitable dangers they would face.

Maybe you are in the same situation as Jeremiah. Your parents raised you to take on their trade. However, you know in your heart this is not the plan God has for your life.

Have you ever been expected to take on a family occupation, but then God called you to do something different? How did you and your family handle it?

_____

_____

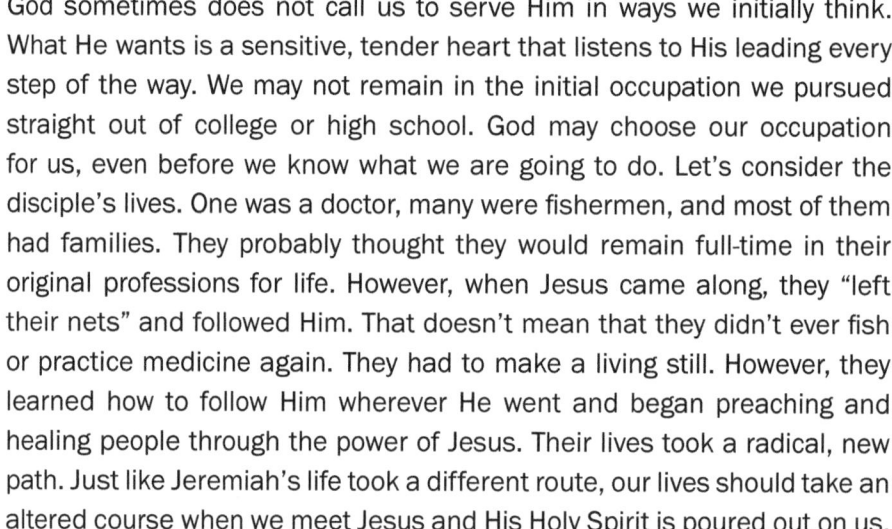

Sometimes God does not call us to serve Him in ways we initially think.

God sometimes does not call us to serve Him in ways we initially think. What He wants is a sensitive, tender heart that listens to His leading every step of the way. We may not remain in the initial occupation we pursued straight out of college or high school. God may choose our occupation for us, even before we know what we are going to do. Let's consider the disciple's lives. One was a doctor, many were fishermen, and most of them had families. They probably thought they would remain full-time in their original professions for life. However, when Jesus came along, they "left their nets" and followed Him. That doesn't mean that they didn't ever fish or practice medicine again. They had to make a living still. However, they learned how to follow Him wherever He went and began preaching and healing people through the power of Jesus. Their lives took a radical, new path. Just like Jeremiah's life took a different route, our lives should take an altered course when we meet Jesus and His Holy Spirit is poured out on us.

Let's go back to verse one in the first chapter of Jeremiah. Where does it say that Jeremiah is from? Where is his home town located — in Israel or Judah?

_____

It's important to delve into a little bit of history. We must understand some of what happened in the preceding 400 years before Jeremiah came on the scene. God's chosen nation, Israel, had changed considerably from the time of King David to Jeremiah's times.

After King David's son, Solomon, reigned as king, the kingdom of Israel divided into 2 kingdoms in 975 B.C. The Northern Kingdom was called Israel and the Southern Kingdom Judah. In 722 B.C., the entire Northern Kingdom, Israel and some of the Southern Kingdom, Judah was swept away by the Assyrians and taken into captivity. However, parts of Judah remained free from captivity. Unfortunately, the rest of Judah only remained free for approximately 100 years longer before they too were taken into captivity. This time captivity was not brought about by the Assyrians, but instead by the Babylonians. This was the timeframe in which Jeremiah lived.

Look at the map. Please take note of where Israel once was and where Judah was in 586 B.C. Also, note Babylon's proximity to Judah.

Jeremiah lived in Anathoth, a town located 3 miles NE of Jerusalem presently called Anata. It was located in the land of Benjamin.[2] If you know your Bible history well; you will remember Benjamin was Rachel and Jacob's youngest son and Jacob had 11 other children with each having a tribe named after them. Land was apportioned to each tribe after the Israelites entered Canaan (many years after Jacob and Rachel's children had died). People in Jeremiah's day, still referred to the lands according to the former tribes.

The first king of the Israelites in the Old Testament was King Saul, a Benjamite (1 Chronicles 12:2). The Benjamites were famous archers and slingers. This is where Jeremiah came from – the little town of Anathoth, located in the land apportioned to the Benjamites. He was a small town guy, near a thriving metropolis (Jerusalem), with a father who served as a priest.

When did Jeremiah receive his calling, according to Jeremiah 1:2?

_____

Many scholars believe Jeremiah was an older teenager when he received his call to be a prophet. He was perhaps 15-18 years old when God placed His call on Jeremiah.[2] No matter how old Jeremiah was when he was called into the ministry, we know he was young. His career lasted over 40 years, spanning over the course of 5 of the last kings in Judah's history. He was used by God for a long time!

You did a great job on your first day of study. Before we close our books, let's go to the Lord in prayer and ask Him to make His Word come alive to us as we study the book of Jeremiah.

*Before I formed
you in the womb,*
I knew you,
*and before
you were born
I appointed you*
a prophet
to the nations.
Jeremiah 1:5

DAY 2

Created for a Purpose

Before we begin, spend some time in prayer. Make sure you are ready to receive all God has for you today.

Read Jeremiah 1:4-10.

Verse 5 is a popular verse. It's a verse used commonly by pro-life Christians against abortion. God points out the importance of each child before even coming out of the womb in this passage. It is clear in this verse, that He has a purpose for each one of us. While this verse is specifically speaking to Jeremiah's call to be a prophet to the nations, it also speaks directly to each of us.

In Jeremiah 1:5, what does the word consecrated mean? Remember we are using the NASB translation.

_____

Being consecrated means set apart. According to the Strongest NASB Exhaustive Concordance, set apart in Hebrew (qadash) from the word qodesh means "to be set apart, holy, sanctified, and wholly dedicated."1 Jeremiah was consecrated, set apart for God's use. We are to be set apart and consecrated to God as well. We are to be different from the world, not in a weird way, but because we belong to God and serve only Him. "But like the Holy One who called you, be holy yourselves also in all your behavior; because it is written 'You shall be holy, for I am holy.'" (1 Peter 1:15-16).

Read Galatians 1:15-16 and Romans 1:1, to see how Paul was set apart. Does God set apart all believers for a purpose as Jeremiah and Paul were? Explain your answer.

_____

_____

_____

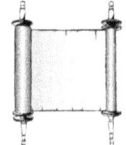

Read Jeremiah 1:6-8 again.

What 2 excuses did Jeremiah give to God as why he shouldn't serve as a prophet?

1. _____

2. _____

Inadequacy as a speaker and being too young are common excuses given by people in the Bible. Have you ever used them before? I have!

In Exodus 4:10-12, you will find another man who didn't feel he could speak well. How did God respond to Moses when Moses said he wasn't a good speaker?

_____

_____

Even though Moses wasn't a good speaker, God said He would give the words to Moses when he spoke, if Moses would speak for God. Unfortunately, Moses gave up his chance to be the "keynote speaker" when he begged God to let someone else do the talking! What a grand job he lost!

How did God react when Moses refused to speak for Him (Exodus 4:13-14a)?

_____

It is hard to believe Moses missed out on this job. However, Moses was given other talents and allowed to be a leader to the Israelites. Still, he missed out on being a God-ordained speaker! How many times have we missed out on God's best for us because we made an excuse we couldn't do it and/or that somebody else was better qualified? Lack of faith causes us to not fulfill God's purpose in our lives.

We may not be "gifted" or "eloquent" in a certain talent, but in God's kingdom, if He calls us to do something He will give us the ability to do it through Him. That is what He's all about. When we're weak, He's strong. He doesn't want us to feel adequate in our own strength, that way we'll rely on Him, instead of ourselves. In Jeremiah 1:9 you'll see how God touched Jeremiah's mouth, and said He'd give Jeremiah the words to speak. He'll do the same for us, if we'll let Him.

Open your Bible to 1 Corinthians 2:1-5. Was Paul an eloquent speaker? Why do you think God didn't want Paul to be a "persuasive" speaker?

_____

_____

We may have varying responses to the last question. As I asked myself the same question, I thought God is not dependent upon the ability of man in any way. If the gospel relied on man's ability to persuade or convince, it would be insufficient in itself. It is rather the Spirit of God and His power that draw people to Christ. People come to Him because of Him and no one or nothing else is required. This is the sufficiency of the gospel.

You may never stand at a podium and speak, but you will be called to share

Christ with your family, neighbors, and friends, and many others with whom you come in contact. God wants your complete heart, mind, and soul. When He requires you to speak, He will give you the words by the leading of His Spirit, if you'll listen to Him.

How does God view the excuse that we can't do what He has called us to do because we're too young (1 Timothy 4:11-12)?

_____

_____

What does God tell us to do in verses 13-16 of the same chapter (1 Timothy 4:13-16)?

_____

_____

Stand Strong in God's Strength.

We need a healthy reminder: Stop making excuses! We have been called by God, set apart for specific works for Him. Even before we were born God appointed us and called us to serve Him in a way no one else can. Repent if you can think of any excuses you have made. Let Him reveal to you areas that He wants to use you in. Through His strength you can accomplish His purposes!

Jeremiah was not given an easy task either. He had to warn the people of impending judgment if they did not turn away from their sins. God may call you to share an unpopular message at times to those who are not faithful to Christ. When He does, do not back down in fear, but instead stand strong in God's strength.

Tomorrow we will study the vision God gave Jeremiah concerning Judah. This vision helped to sustain Jeremiah when he grew weary. For now though we are going to skip over this vision and go to the words God gave to Jeremiah concerning his preaching.

Read Jeremiah 1:17-19. How do these verses encourage you to move forward and obey the job God has given you to do?

_____

_____

My Personal Journey

When I began teaching adult Sunday School, I was scared and nervous to teach and felt like Jeremiah — completely inadequate. However, God revealed to me that I must hold my head high and speak His message. Jeremiah 1:17-19 encouraged me to move forward and teach. The

Lord reminded me in these verses that the enemy would fight against me, but he would not overcome me. Satan attempted to prevent me from teaching the night before I was to first teach. Rachel got a fever out of the blue, which kept us up most of the night with her. The T.V. turned on by itself in the middle of the night while I was studying the Bible next to it (and I was nowhere near the remote or any other device that would trigger it to come on). And last but not least, when I went to dry my hair after my shower that morning, the electricity went out completely and I couldn't dry my hair (there was no storm). I went to church with my hair soaking wet! Talk about trying to keep someone from preaching! Most women would have quit right there! It revealed to me how important this message and me teaching must be. Despite Satan's attempts to prevent me from speaking, God was on my side and delivered me. Interestingly, no electrical problems existed after I got home from church and Rachel's fever was completely gone and she never got sick.

Look at what the word "dismayed" means in the Strongest NASB Concordance. The word dismayed means "to break down, either (lit.) by violence or (fig.) by confusion and fear: abolish, affright, make afraid, amaze, beat down, discourage, go down, scare, terrify."

Satan will try to break us down, discourage us, and terrify us so that we will not obey God. We recognize this tactic by the enemy and refuse to fall prey to it. This is why God gave such clear instructions to Jeremiah because he would be tempted to not speak God's message to others, out of fear of what they might do back to him. On several occasions he was persecuted severely. Christ warns us that we will face opposition as we bear His name. Look at what He said concerning Paul. "Go, for he (Paul) is a chosen instrument of mine, to bear my name before the Gentiles and kings and sons of Israel; for I will show him how much he must suffer for my name's sake" (Acts 9:15-16).

Have you ever had a time in your life when God told you to do something, but you were absolutely petrified to do it or maybe just discouraged? Did you obey? How did your response impact your relationship with the Lord? If you disobeyed, did you experience guilt and shame? How did you deal with that?

_____

_____

_____

In Jeremiah 1:17, God instructed Jeremiah to speak all of what God commanded him and to not fear the people. Jeremiah would have to grow accustomed to the angry, cold stares from those who didn't want to hear his message. God promised to deliver Jeremiah from the enemy, but Jeremiah had to obey Him completely to be delivered and overcome. If Jeremiah was afraid, God would make Jeremiah look foolish in front of the people.

It is the Spirit of God and His power that draws people to Christ.

Please write out Hebrews 13:6.

_____

_____

_____

> *When God is on our side* we have **NO reason** to fear man.

When God is on our side, we have no reason to fear man. We must gird up our loins according to God in Jeremiah 1:17. The phrase "gird up your loins" today could be translated to mean "Get ready for action."[2] "In order to be able to run or work easily, men in that day had to tie their loose robes together with a belt (or in other words, gird their loins)."[3] If not, their loosely hanging garments would hinder their steps.

Read 1 Peter 1:13 in the King James Version (KJV) of the Bible. What does the phrase "gird up the loins of your mind" in this passage refer to?

_____

Peter is not referring to a piece of cloth here, but to our minds. We are to gird up our minds for action. We are to correct those parts of our thinking we know are wrong, deal with the loose ends that exist in our minds and emotions, not permitting things to exist in our lives that will hinder our steps.

If we're to be successful in our walk with Christ, we must deal with the garbage in our mind. If we don't, we're like the person who allows his robe to hang down and get caught in his legs, hindering his steps.

Jeremiah was an amazing man. He, as you'll find out, had many obstacles to face, but he faced them head on with courage. With God on his side, he conquered the enemy repeatedly, even though on the surface you'd think nothing really was going on, Jeremiah made a difference wherever he went. He consistently followed God's lead. He chose to gird up the loins of his mind.

The book opens with the call on Jeremiah's life; as believers we too are set apart for God for His plans and purposes. There is no middle ground in Jeremiah's life, as there should be none in ours. We are either hot or cold; there is no lukewarm. I hope as we enter this study, you too will choose to live a radical, sold-out life for Christ, just as Jeremiah did. End today by spending quiet time with the Lord. Let Him speak to you.

_____

_____

_____

_____

Reflection

How have you been Set Apart?

Week 1

DAY 3

The Almond Rod & the Boiling Pot

Before beginning today, open with prayer. May God speak clearly to you. God, we ask you to help us let go of what displeases you; things we're holding onto which are stumbling blocks. Have your way with us today!

After God appointed Jeremiah to speak to the nation of Judah, God went on to speak of the judgment that was coming on Judah. A vision of an almond tree and a boiling pot was shown to Jeremiah.

The almond tree is one of the first trees to blossom in the spring. It is also called a "wake tree". In the Hebrew, almond branch meant "watching". Basically, God was saying, through the vision, He was awake and watching for His word to be fulfilled.1 And Jeremiah was to speak God's word to His people. Also, in Jeremiah 1:11-12 there is an allusion to another of the meanings of the Hebrew root, which is to hasten. In the first of the two verses the almond tree is mentioned by its name "shaqed" and in the second it is said "for I am watching My word," "watching" being from the same root as almond. The almond was chosen to symbolize God's haste in fulfilling His promises.

The second vision in Jeremiah 1:13 spoke of a boiling pot. What do you think the boiling pot represented after reading Jeremiah 1:13-15?

_____

_____

_____

The boiling pot was a display of God's wrath towards Judah's disobedience. Judgment would come upon God's people if they didn't turn from their sin. The pot was tipped from the north which represented the destruction of Jerusalem would come from enemies from the north. Notice in Jeremiah 1:15 it states, "all the families of the kingdoms of the north" meaning it would be many different kingdoms allying together to defeat Judah. Also, each kingdom would set their throne at the entrance of the gates of Jerusalem, which essentially meant the enemy would have complete control over the entire nation.

These visions gave Jeremiah direction from God and visual confirmation that what God said he was going to accomplish would happen. The visions must have been a constant reminder to Jeremiah as he began his call to spread God's word. As you will find out, eventually, Jeremiah would not be well accepted among his people. In fact, you'll see that he will become outright mocked and persecuted for speaking truth. So the visions must have been a steady and uplifting reminder to him of what his purpose was.

Has God given you a vision before of what He was going to accomplish in the future? How did this encourage you?

_____

_____

Many times God gives us a vision. Visions are meant to inspire us. They are to encourage us to persevere, even when the road to accomplishing that vision may not be easy. Cleave to the vision God has given you. Don't let it fade away, even when circumstances may tell you that it can not be accomplished! He can do it, if you will just believe!

"Now faith is the assurance of things hoped for, the conviction of things not seen" (Hebrews 12:1). Jeremiah didn't know where he was going or how things would turn out once he began preaching for the Lord. However, he moved forward in faith, believing God was going to do what He said. Like Abraham, Jeremiah stepped out in faith.

Read Hebrews 11:8, and 24-27. How does Jeremiah's faith parallel the faith of Abraham's and Moses?

_____

_____

Has God called you to take a step of faith in your life that seems enormous? If so, explain.

_____

_____

How does Hebrews 11:6 speak to you concerning this step of faith you've been called to take?

_____

_____

Cleave to the **vision God** *has given you.*

Many times our steps of faith feel more like leaps of faith, don't they? I am thankful God is always there to accomplish His Word. Many of the great saints of the Bible died before seeing the promises God gave them completely fulfilled. However, the promises were still fulfilled even though they occurred many years later. And some promises still remain to be fulfilled.

What does Hebrews 11:13 say? Write it out.

_____

Will you, like Jeremiah, believe God will fulfill His promises even if you do not see them all fulfilled in your lifetime? Can you think of a Christian relative, maybe a parent, grandparent, or another sweet soul in your family that was given a promise by God that didn't come to fruition before they went to be with the Lord? Has that promise now been fulfilled?

_____

_____

_____

_____

Reflection

What promises await fulfillment in your family?

If you can recall at least one promise fulfilled in your family that is great! If not, you could be the first one in your family to allow God's promises to be accomplished. Write down in a journal any visions or promises God gives you concerning yourself or other family member's futures. Even if some of the promises are unanswered now, they will be accomplished eventually, if the Lord gave you them. Those promises may encourage and uplift future generations and how wonderful for the person who will see them fulfilled!

Of course, in our story of Jeremiah, his vision may not seem as uplifting to you. However, to Jeremiah it brought hope. The promise of God's judgment was ultimately a promise that God would restore His people to Himself because He loved them.

DAY 4

King Josiah — A Reformer

Before we begin, humble yourself in God's presence and ask Him to reveal Himself to you today.

Start by reading Jeremiah 1:2.

Who was the king reigning in Judah when Jeremiah was first called to preach?

_____

_____

Today we are going to learn about King Josiah. He was the first king reigning during the time of Jeremiah. In the thirteenth year of Josiah's reign, Jeremiah was called by God to be a prophet to the nations. Josiah was a good king. He brought many reforms to Judah during his reign from 640-609 B.C. Jeremiah was called to be a prophet in 626 B.C. and Josiah began his reforms in 628 B.C.

Turn to 2 Chronicles 34. Go ahead and read verses 1-7. This chapter is going to tell us a lot about King Josiah – his character and what kind of changes he made in his society.

How old was King Josiah when he became king and how long did he reign?

_____

_____

King Josiah reigned a relatively long time for a king back in those days. Look at how young he was when he started – only 8 years old! He must have had some good counselors to help him out. His father and his grandfather were both dead when he became king. Josiah became king after his father Amon was killed (2 Chronicles 33:24-25). His father Amon "did evil in the sight of the Lord" and his grandfather Manasseh was no better. Josiah was not raised in a home where God was put first. In fact, Josiah's grandfather Manasseh, erected altars to other gods, worshiped carved images, and placed those altars and idols in the house of God. Besides that, Manasseh practiced witchcraft. Eventually, Manasseh did humble himself before God, but it was too late for undoing the lessons he had taught his son Amon. Every idol Manasseh took down after turning back to God, Amon put back up once he was on the throne. It reminds me what we teach our children now, has a huge impact on them later!

The good news emerging from this idol-worshipping family was Josiah, surprisingly, did what was right in the eyes of the Lord. While he was young, he began seeking God. Maybe Josiah's father died before he had much influence on Josiah. Or maybe Josiah realized things did not fare well for his former family members because of their lack of obedience to God. Thankfully, Josiah came to realize there was a better way to live and because of that he saw the goodness of the Lord.

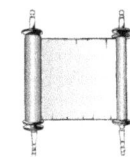

Did you come from a family who did not put God first? How did that affect how you chose to live your life?

_____

_____

Look back at 2 Chronicles 34:1-7. What did King Josiah do in his eighth year of his reign?

_____

How old was King Josiah when he began seeking God (2 Chronicles 34:3a)?

_____

How old was Josiah when he began purging Judah and Jerusalem of the high places and the idols (2 Chronicles 34:3b)?

_____

Notice Josiah couldn't remove the idols in his country until he had first sought God. In fact, he probably didn't recognize how evil those idols were in God's sight until he began seeking God. He was like most of us, wasn't he? We don't realize the idols in our own lives until we really spend some time with God. In fact, most of the idols in our lives seem quite harmless and accepted by others around us because they are worshipping the same or similar idols we are worshipping.

I think of my friend Samantha (I provide fictitious names in my examples throughout the study, so as to not infringe on their privacy), who went to church a long time before she had a personal relationship with God. She had gone to church all her life, but lived completely like the world. Many of her common everyday practices included what her culture had told her was okay. In fact, what she was encouraged to do. She was a good person. She just had a lot of things in her life that didn't glorify God. For instance, her fascination with the dark side was not what God wanted her to be involved in. She read books and watched movies revolving around dark issues. When God took a hold of her and told her this was not what He wanted her participating in, she quickly realized this was an idol she had placed in her life and stopped indulging herself with it.

This friend's experience was not unlike Josiah's. As Josiah sought God more in-depth, God revealed to him things that needed to be removed from not only his life, but his nation's way of life as well. This principle holds true: The closer we get to God, the more we are able to see sin for what it is.

The closer we get to God, the more we are able to see SIN for what it is.

It is also interesting to note that King Josiah changed his ways when he began having children. Cross reference over to 2 Kings 23:31. How old was Jehohahaz (King Josiah's son) when King Josiah began reigning?

_____

Now subtract 23 (the age of his son Jehohahaz) from 31 years (the length of Josiah's reign) and you will get the year of King Josiah's reign when he had his son. What is 31 minus 23? (You didn't know you were going to be tested on your math skills, did you?!)

_____

The answer is 8. So, in King Josiah's 8th year of reigning, he had his son Jehohahaz. Since Josiah began serving on the throne when he was 8 years old (2 Chronicles 34:1) that would make him 16 years old when he had Jehohahaz.

Now, how old was King Josiah when he began following the Lord? Hint: Look at 2 Chronicles 34:3 again.

_____

Isn't it interesting King Josiah began making reforms in Judah when he was 16 years old, the very year his son Jehoahaz was born? Having children will shake up your world! As a parent, it makes you analyze if how you are living is really that healthy because you want the best for your child. Anything in your life that could be harmful to your child(ren) you want to remove. If you are a good parent, you will do everything in your power to make your home and lifestyle as sin-free, as possible. When we had our kids, my husband and I, sure changed our ways! Some of the TV shows we once thought were funny were no longer funny. The way we spoke to one another changed too. We made certain nothing unholy or unbiblical entered our precious, innocent children's lives. Sinful ways once overlooked were seen for what they really were – idolatry and hypocrisy in our lives. This was how King Josiah was affected too.

Now let's look at what types of idols King Josiah removed from Judah. Read 2 Chronicles 34:3-7. What does Josiah first do to reform Judah? List the pagan religious vestiges he removed from Judah and Jerusalem.

_____

_____

2 Kings 23:4-20 gives a more detailed account of Josiah removing these pagan idols from Judah. Take the time to read this chapter too. The idols mentioned in both of these accounts are not objects we typically hear about today. The Asherim, mentioned in verse 3, is the plural for Asherah. Asherah

was made in the form of a wooden pole that represented the Canaanite goddess Asherah and placed near the altar of Baal.1 In fact, many of these poles were placed around the altar, hence the plural form Asherim. According to Vines, "Canaanites believed Asherah ruled the sea, was the mother of all the gods, including Baal, and sometimes was his deadly enemy."2 In Exodus 34:13, God told the Israelites to cut down the Asherim when they entered the land of Canaan. Worshipping Asherah was a serious offense to God. Another item destroyed by King Josiah was the high places. "High places" are geographically elevated spots on earth where pagan worship occurs. In Leviticus 26:30 it is described as a place that brings the Lord grief and must be destroyed. Even now, New Age cults identify high points in the land that have energy attached to them and dedicate them to their cultic practices.

Besides getting rid of the Asherim and high places, King Josiah also destroyed carved and molten images. This refers to any statues or similar representations made of those they worshipped. In Psalms 106:19-22, it talks about God's people forgetting God and exchanging His glory for the image of an ox. If you've ever been to a museum, you've seen countless artifacts dug up of statues of various animals and gods that ancient people worshipped.

> Most of the **idols** in our lives seem **quite HARMLESS** and **accepted** by OTHERS *around us* **because they are worshipping** the SAME or SIMILAR **IDOLS.**

How many of us have or know of someone who has a carved or molten image in their home or vehicle? The carved image or statue is thought to bring a blessing or protection upon their family or themselves. I've seen some idols. What about you? We're not as different as we think from the ancient civilizations. Hopefully, we'll learn from this study how it brought about the destruction of the Judeans and refuse to accept anything in our lives that takes our focus away from God.

Other idols brought down by King Josiah were the altars of Baal. Baal was the god of fertility in Canaan. He was worshipped because he was thought to bring rain that caused their crops to grow. If you've ever been in Sunday school as a child you'll remember Baal in the 1 Kings 18 account where Elijah challenged the Baal followers to have their god bring down fire onto their sacrifice. Of course, Baal never pulled through and the one true God, Elijah's God, did send fire down on the pile of wood. You would think what happened in Elijah's day would have been proof enough for God's people. Perhaps some had not heard about that event.

Baal worship was a form of nature worship. Many times sexual acts occurred while worshipping Baal. People believed they could control the outcome of their crops by pleasing Baal with their sacrifices. Male and female temple prostitutes were thought to arouse Baal by their sexual acts. Baal then brought rain to "fertilize" Mother Earth. The people's survival was thought to depend upon his provision.

Syncretism, the combining of different beliefs and religious practices, is an example of the Israelites combining the worship of God and Baal. It was unacceptable to God and proved disastrous to their nation.

What does Joshua 24:14-15 say?

_____

_____

Do we, like the Israelites, tolerate other religious practices in our lives?

_____

_____

These practices will cause us to fall away from God and be brought into captivity, just like what happened to the Judeans.

Lastly, let's review 2 Chronicles 34:5, before we move on. King Josiah burned the bones of the priests on their altars. A previous king, Jeroboam, was the founder of these false altars.

Look at 1 Kings 13:1-2. Here a man is warning Jeroboam of how the priests during King Josiah's time will be burned. This is a prophecy given way before Josiah was born. Then read 2 Kings 23:16-18. Which man's bones did Josiah not burn in verse 17?

_____

Even in Zephaniah 1:4-5 a prophecy is given for the destruction of the idols by King Josiah. Zephaniah prophesied this message during Josiah's reign before he made his reforms. It is thought that the prophet Zephaniah may have been from royal lineage of King Hezekiah. If that is so, he would have been a possible major influence on Josiah. Maybe helping to reverse some of Josiah's father's and grandfather's mistakes.

What does God say about idol worship? Read Exodus 20:3-6.

_____

_____

> **Idolatry** is often _exposed_ in the subtlety of how we spend our _free time._

The first of the Ten Commandments forbids idol worship. God abhors idolatry. Idolatry can come in various forms and fashions, but it is all the same to God. An idol may be a statue of a person or god, or it could be a person or activity you worship. Idolatry is often exposed in the subtlety of how we spend our free time. Our priorities speak loudly of what takes first place in our life. If anything is placed higher than God in our lives, it is considered an idol.

Read Jeremiah 7:18-20. Who was the idol they worshipped here?

_____

_____

These verses are describing another form of idol worship that God's people were performing during Jeremiah's time. While we may think that outright idol worship, in the form of statues or images is no longer around, look around! It is still rampant in the world today. All you have to do is travel to foreign countries or many times even in your own backyard, to find out that idol worship is still alive and well.

List a place or time when you've seen statues, images, or idols worshipped.

_____

_____

An idolater is "a slave to the depraved ideas his idols represent."3 We all have fallen at one time or another into being slaves to ungodly ideas. We need to recognize forms of idol worship and realize when we're attracted to worship them. Many have been kept from a relationship with Jesus Christ because they were raised to worship idols and not Christ.

Look at Isaiah 43:11. What does it state?

_____

We can only be saved by one true God – Yahweh!

Read Isaiah 42:8 and then write it out below.

_____

_____

_____

God will not give His glory to any other than Himself. How foolish idolatry is. Take some time and think about if there are any idols in your life. Also, consider if there are any idols in your family, community, or nation that you need to repent of. Write them down.

_____

_____

_____

We have the power in Jesus Christ to defeat the enemy. Like King Josiah, refuse to allow idols to tear apart your family, community, or nation. Take them down and destroy them with Christ's authority!

DAY 5

Lost Treasures

We are going to be doing a lot of reading today, so grab a warm cup of tea or coffee and snuggle into your favorite chair! First though, take a moment to pray before you get started.

In the twelfth year of Josiah's reign (622 B.C.), he began purging Judah of idols. After he had destroyed all of the idols, he focused on repairing the Lord's house.

Begin by reading 2 Chronicles 34:8. What year of Josiah's reign did he start to repair the temple?

___

Repairing-it's kind of like this: Before King Josiah could restore the temple to its original purpose; he had to first remove all the junk in it. You can't make repairs on something until you get rid of the old materials first. Right now, my husband, Rob is repairing our walkway in the backyard. The aged walkway fell into disrepair. The old blocks and wood needed to be taken out before the new bricks could be laid. If Rob hadn't removed the aging bricks before laying the new bricks, it would have caused the path to be unstable. However, once the old brick was removed, the new brick could be laid down on the firm foundation below giving us a solid path. Like Josiah's plan, the "old" idols had to be removed, before the temple could be repaired and function as fully intended.

Read 2 Chronicles 34:9-21. (Note: Hilkiah the high priest mentioned in this passage is not Jeremiah's father. It is a different Hilkiah.)

In the process of repairing the temple, the lost book of the Law was found. This was the first part of our Bible. Their lives were supposed to be dependent upon following its commands. However, it had been lost in the midst of them while they followed the world around them. It reminds me of times in our lives when we have lost our way and followed after everything else, but the Bible. Then God draws us back and as sin is removed from our lives, He reveals "lost treasures" just like He did for the Judeans.

Can you think of a lost treasure God allowed you to find when He made repairs in your life?

___

What occurs in 2 Chronicles 34:19-21 that is surprising to you?

___

Week 1

What does Romans 3:20b say? Write it out.

_____

_____

Sometimes we don't know we are sinning until we hear God's commands or His laws. Like Romans 3:20b says, "...through the Law comes the knowledge of sin." Or we may justify a sin. Other people around us may be doing it so it seems okay. Or we may have been involved in a sin for so long it no longer pricks our conscience.

Can you think of a time you didn't know you were sinning, but God's commands opened your eyes to see how He viewed your sin?

_____

_____

_____

> *Through the* **Law** *comes the* **KNOWLEDGE** *OF SIN.*
> Romans 3:20b
>

This has happened to me many times. The Holy Spirit convicts me while praying, reading His word, or listening to one of my pastor's sermons. All of my justifications for my sin go tumbling to the ground. No matter how hard I try to argue my viewpoint!

It was like this for King Josiah too. It mortified Josiah to see his sins and his people's sins once the book of the Law was read. There was no way that he could justify the sin he saw around him.

Next read 2 Chronicles 34:22-33. What is the name of the prophetess in this passage? What did she proclaim to Judah and to King Josiah? After Josiah heard her reply what did he do?

_____

_____

_____

Now let's move on to the next passage. Read 2 Chronicles 35:1 & 17. What other important events did King Josiah restore to his people?

_____

_____

I would like to digress for a moment here to glean the significance of Passover, both historically and spiritually. We will then look at how the celebration of the Passover Feast during the time of Jeremiah relates to our Bible study.

Exodus 12 recounts the original Passover at the Exodus of Israel from the Egyptian nation under Moses. Read Exodus 12:1-13 and Exodus 12:23-27. What did the Passover and the Feast of the Unleavened Bread represent?

_____

_____

_____

As you read the account of the first Passover in Exodus, you can readily understand how God delivered and saved the Israelite nation from the hand of Pharaoh. The Gospel was preached through Moses for all God's people to accept or reject.

The word Passover comes from the Hebrew words "pesach" and means "a passing over" or "to pass or hover over." The Greek word is "pascha" and is derived from the Hebrew. This is a clear view of the Lord's two-edged sword. The Israelites experienced the mercy of God following an act of obedience as they slaughtered the lamb and placed the blood upon the lintel and two side posts of their front door. The Lord not only "passed over" the homes of the Israelites but He "hovered" over them in divine protection. The Egyptians, however, experienced God's judgment – plagues and killing of all their firstborn. Each household responded to the gospel (Passover Feast) through faith and obedience or unbelief and disobedience.

> The **Passover** *is the day the Jews were told to continue to **observe** as a **reminder** to them that **God** had spared their lives and brought them **OUT** of **Egypt**, where they had been for **400 years**.*

The Israelites were instructed by God to recount the story of deliverance yearly in the celebration of the Passover Feast. In recounting the story to their children, they proclaimed the gospel to their children and celebrated His mighty hand to deliver and save.

The Passover is the day the Jews were told to continue to observe as a reminder to them that God had spared their lives and brought them out of Egypt, where they had been slaves for 400 years! This is still an important day the Jews celebrate. There are seven other major references to the Passover in Scripture, the last being the true Passover, Jesus Christ. Read these accounts of the Passover to understand the progressive message taught through this feast.

- Numbers 9:1-5 records the second Passover as Israelites leave Egypt and set up the "Tabernacle of the Lord.

- Joshua 5:10-11 records the Passover at the end of the wilderness journey as Joshua leads the new generation into the Promised Land.

- 2 Chronicles 30 recounts the Passover in the second month held under King Hezekiah.

- 2 Kings 23:21-23 and 2 Chronicles 35:1-19 records the great Passover kept under King Josiah.

- Ezra 6:19 records the restoration of the Passover celebration kept under Ezra at the end of the Babylonian captivity.

- Ezekiel 45:21 tells of the Passover seen in Ezekiel's vision.

Week 1

Matthew 26:26-27; Mark 14-15; Luke 22-23; John 18-19; and 1 Corinthians 5:6-8 all reveal Jesus as our Passover lamb.

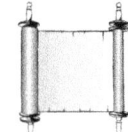

Read 1 Corinthians 5:6-8. As Christians, who is our Passover Lamb and how did Paul command the Corinthians to celebrate this feast?

_____

_____

For Christians, the Lamb of God, Jesus, has become our Passover Lamb. After His death on the cross, we no longer have to kill an unblemished male lamb every year to remember this day.

According to Mark 14:12-15, when did Jesus celebrate his last Passover meal? Read further into the chapter if the first few verses didn't give you enough clues. Read verses 16-25.

_____

_____

The last Passover observed by Christ was the very night He was betrayed and arrested in Gethsemane. Jesus closes out the old ceremony and institutes the Lord's Supper with His twelve disciples. Here is a clear example of how we often times carry out traditions and never embrace what God intended for our understanding. The Jews missed the true Passover in Christ.

The importance of observing the Passover for the Judeans was a significant observance that King Josiah restored. It signified the eventual sacrifice Christ would make for the whole world. It was not an observance that the Lord's people were to disregard or forget about. In fact, they had been quite disobedient by not observing it for many years. The last time they had observed the Passover was during King Hezekiah's reign (at least that was the last time it was mentioned in the Bible). King Hezekiah was Josiah's great-great grandfather.

The reading of God's law and the observance of Passover must have been a glorious day for Josiah and those who attended in Jerusalem. King Josiah was a great leader. He made dramatic changes during his reign. The people seemed to like him.

How is King Josiah described in 2 Kings 23:25?

_____

_____

Josiah pleased the Lord. Not only had he made many reforms, but he did it despite the poor choices of his forefathers! He didn't make excuses for himself. He chose to not follow in his father and grandfather's steps. Instead, he humbled himself and did what was right in God's eyes.

29

While Josiah's reign was incredible, it came to an unfortunate end in 609 B.C. in a battle. Read 2 Chronicles 35:20-22. Who did King Josiah come to fight?

_____

The Egyptian king, Pharoah Neco, went to Megiddo to meet the king of Assyria (2 Kings 23:29). The Egyptians and Assyrians were now allies. After the death of Ashurbanipal, the great Assyrian king that reigned from 668-627 B.C., the nation of Assyria had been weakening. However, Babylon's power had been increasing. Pharoah Necho II was coming to help the Assyrians fight against the Babylonians. Babylon was trying to expel Assyria from their capitol city, Haran, and takeover.

It is unknown why King Josiah wanted to attack Pharoah Neco, but some scholars surmise that he was afraid Egypt would take over Judah and Israel because the Assyrian's power was decreasing (the Assyrians previously had power over Israel and Judah). Either way, Pharoah Neco warned King Josiah to not attack him. The words Neco spoke were said to even be from the mouth of God, but King Josiah didn't listen. Josiah probably couldn't believe that this "heathen" Neco could be speaking the words of the Lord. God is funny like that though, He has no restraints on who He can speak through. Only we limit God into a box of how we think He should operate. It seems that's what Josiah did.

Has God ever used a non-Christian to warn you of something you should avoid? Did you or did you not listen? Why or why not?

_____

_____

_____

I bet Josiah wished he had listened! And I'm sure the rest of the nation felt the same way.

Read 2 Chronicles 35:25 to see how the people felt about King Josiah's death. Record their reaction.

_____

_____

_____

Josiah was a much admired king. Jeremiah and the people lamented his death. While it has been beneficial to hear about the radical reforms that took place during King Josiah's reign, we have much more to learn about Judah. But for now, let's end this lesson by bowing our heads and bending our knees to our Almighty Savior and King Jesus. Choose today and everyday to worship Him with all your heart, mind, and soul. Give Him the praise and honor He deserves.

NOTES

VIDEO QUESTIONS WEEK 1

1. What was the nation of Judah like during Jeremiah's times?
2. Name the five kings of Judah during Jeremiah's day.
3. Why did the Judeans reject Jeremiah's message?
4. What does the word consecrated mean?
5. What would happen if we lived like Jeremiah, knowing our commission by God and living it out?

Video sessions are available for download at www.grassandflowers.org

WEEK TWO
TAKING CAPTIVITY CAPTIVE

DAY ONE
Guard Against Sin

DAY TWO
The Temple Sermon

DAY THREE
The Temple Sermon
(Continued)

DAY FOUR
You Must Die

DAY FIVE
The Babylonians

DAY 1

Guard Against Sin

Today we're going to examine what brought about the decline of the nation of Judah in 600 B.C. It boiled down to one common denominator — sin. You can say it was this or that which brought about their demise, but the bottom-line is they didn't listen to God and they broke their covenant with Him. They chased after idols other nations worshipped. They wanted to be just like the other nations that didn't fear God. They decided to leave God out of their decision making.

Turn to Jeremiah 3:12-14. How does God respond to the Judeans' faithlessness?

_____

What does 2 Timothy 2:13 say about God's faithfulness?

_____

God's message early on to those in Judah is one of graciousness and love. He longs for His people to repent and return to Him. In Jeremiah 3:14, God describes himself as a Master to them.

When you think of the word master, what comes to mind? List all good and bad attributes of a master that come to mind.

_____

_____

_____

Master in Hebrew means "to marry, rule over."[1] In other words, we are in a covenant (like a marriage) with our Lord and He is to rule over us. Another translation of the word master is "owner" or "to have dominion over." Our God owns us! He is to be our Master.

After thinking through all of the good and bad attributes concerning the word master, what kind of a Master do you think God is? What kind of a Master was He to the Israelites?

_____

_____

_____

Getting more personal...do you allow God to be Master over you?

_____

33

The word master reminds me of authority. When God is our master, we are to live under His authority. If He tells us to do something, we are to do it. If He tells us to avoid something, we are to veer far away from it. Pretty simple concept, but not easy to follow! The more we sin, the further we get away from God and the easier it is to continue to disobey Him. Sin distorts our ability to distinguish between right and wrong. We find we are more uncomfortable being in God's presence when we sin, so we replace Him and His ways with things that fit our new lifestyle. We associate with those who don't follow God closely. We replace our love for God with love for idols in our life. Materialism, addictions, money, careers, etc., become our new gods. This is exactly what the people of Jeremiah's day did.

Listed below are some of their sins. Read each passage and match it up with the sin.

_____	1. Idolatry	A. Jeremiah 9:4
_____	2. Deceit	B. Jeremiah 8:10
_____	3. Not Helping Poor/Orphans	C. Jeremiah 7:10
_____	4. Adultry	D. Jeremiah 5:31
_____	5. Greed	E. Jeremiah 9:3
_____	6. No fear of God	F. Jeremiah 5:28b
_____	7. Fat & Rich	G. Jeremiah 5: 22-24
_____	8. Lying	H. Jeremiah 2:35
_____	9. Slandering	I. Jeremiah 5:8
_____	10. Arrogance	J. Jeremiah 16:11
_____	11. Hypocrisy	K. Jeremiah 5:27, 28a
_____	12. Sacrificed Sons/Daughters	L. Jeremiah 7:31

The Judeans were hypocrites in every sense of the word. We would do well to learn from them and not fall into the same trap of sin as they did. Let's take a moment and examine our own ways and repent of any sin in our life. if we truly repent, we turn away from our sin and don't go back to doing it again.

Read Jeremiah 7:3-10.

This is the message Jeremiah gave at the temple gate in Jerusalem. He describes the people's sins and how they come into His temple and say God delivered them from their sins, then go right back to sinning. No change of heart on their part. It doesn't sound much different than our churches today.

It's so easy to go through the motions at church, but not really change our lifestyles at home.

In Jeremiah 7:3 & 7, what does God promise the people if they will repent?

_____

_____

Write out 2 Chronicles 7:14.

_____

_____

_____

If we will humble ourselves and confess our sin, God will forgive us and heal our land. What are some sins we need to repent of in our nation?

_____

_____

_____

Do your speech, behavior, and lifestyle match what God wants? Do you stand out for Christ or are you like the Judeans blending in with their culture, no different from non-believers?

_____

_____

Self-centered and self-serving behavior runs rampant in our world today. Adultery hurts many. Lust lurks around every corner. A healthy fear of God has been replaced by idolizing self and making ourselves our own god. Many trust in their riches and lay up treasures here on earth, instead of in heaven. People pour more money into their material possessions rather than giving to the poor and needy. We are in a sad state of affairs. Many people think they can continue to sin and never have any repercussions from it. They don't even consider that their deeds will someday be judged by an Almighty God.

Summarize what each verse below says about our future judgment:

Romans 14:10, 12

_____

_____

Hebrews 4:13

_____

_____

1 Corinthians 3:13

_____

_____

Matthew 12:36

_____

_____

2 Corinthians 5:10

_____

_____

If we as a people, individually and as a nation, do not confess our sin and repent, we will invite judgment on ourselves. As you continue in this study, you will see exactly what happened to the Judeans as they stubbornly continued to rebel despite many warnings from God through the prophet Jeremiah. May we not be like those Judeans so stubborn and hard hearted in our ways. Instead may we consider how to strive to be more like Christ and less like the culture around us!

DAY 2

The Temple Sermon

After the death of Josiah, the country of Judah never regained another godly leader. The next leader to reign over Judah was Jehoahaz (also called Joahaz). He reigned for only a brief time of 3 months. He was a son of Josiah and 23 years old when he began to reign.

Read 2 Kings 23:33-34. What happened to King Jehoahaz in this passage? Who did Pharaoh Neco put on the throne after Jehoahaz?

_____

_____

After killing King Josiah, Pharoah Neco wanted to exert his authority over Judah. Pharoah Neco made Eliakim king and changed his name to Jehoiakim. He also placed a fine on the land. It was the custom of a nation to change the name of a king, so people understood that the new reigning nation was over them and took on the new nation's identity. If you've been in Sunday school as a child, you'll probably remember another name change that occurred because of a conquering nation. The nation was Babylon and the king was Nebuchadnezzar. He changed the names of Daniel and his 3 friends (Shadrach, Meshach, and Abendego).

See **Addendum 1** on page 246, which shows the last five Kings of Judah and what happened during each King's reign.

By Pharaoh Neco defeating Judah, it ended Judah's independence as a nation and Jehoiakim became a vassal king to Egypt.

When Eliakim (Jehoiakim) came to reign what kind of ruler was he (2 Kings 23:35-37)?

_____

_____

Jehoiakim reigned 11 years. Despite being a son of King Josiah, he was nothing like his father. It was during Jehoiakim's reign that Jeremiah began to preach and take on more of an active role as a prophet.

During Jehoiakim's first year of being king, Jeremiah preached what is now called the Temple Sermon. There are 2 versions of the Temple Sermon. One is in Jeremiah 26:1-6 (the short version) and the long version is in Jeremiah 7:1-8:3. The short version obviously does not give as many details, so we are going to focus our search on Jeremiah 7.

Begin by reading Jeremiah 7:1-11.

Imagine the scene. The temple sermon occurred during the Feast of Tabernacles, when all the men from the cities of Judah were required to appear at Jerusalem (Deuteronomy 15:16).[1] Therefore, there was a large crowd of people. Priests were probably meandering around the temple gate inquiring about the general spiritual conditions of the people coming to the temple. And here walks up Jeremiah, already known as a prophet, ready to give his message. He first had to get people's attention. He had to speak loudly and probably stand up on a platform of some sort to get their attention. When Jeremiah spoke, the people probably listened even if they didn't like what he said. There were no televisions or any other forms of media capturing people's attention back then, so the news of what Jeremiah said at the temple spread by word of mouth. There were most likely many criticisms spoken about Jeremiah as his sermon traveled from one family to the next.

Jeremiah's sermon begins by referring to a phrase the Judeans used to reassure themselves that everything was going to be okay. What phrase did the people use in Jeremiah 7:4 that God told them to not trust in?

_____

_____

You cannot SEPARATE your behavior from your WORSHIP of GOD!

The phrase "This is the temple of the Lord" claimed the Lord's presence was in the temple. The Judeans felt if this was true, that God was in His temple, then it did not matter how they acted because no matter what they did, they were protected by God.

The Judeans conduct reminds me of an attitude which is pervasive in the church today. Bear with me for a moment. How many times have you seen this façade played out before your eyes? On Sunday morning, member of the congregation goes up to the altar to repent (insincerely), and that same person Sunday afternoon returns to a lifestyle of sin with no remorse! It's actually quite characteristic of our "Christianized" culture. This is a self-serving form of religion where a person believes the church is there to serve their personal needs. The altar call made them feel good, but they didn't change their lives. Christ meant for repentance to change us into new creatures, not just give us good vibes on Sunday morning. These souls have not surrendered to the Lordship of Jesus Christ.

The Judean's worship in the Jewish temple was as insincere as that person on Sunday morning that "repents" and goes right back to sinning immediately after they walk away from the altar, completely unchanged. The Jewish people deluded themselves into thinking His temple would compensate for their behavior. In the Hebrew, the word deception ("deceptive words" used in Jeremiah 7:4) is sheqer. Sheqer means false, false hope, lie, lying vision, perjury, slander, useless, and vain.[2] The people vainly believed God would save them from their surrounding enemies, nations like Egypt and Babylon, even if they didn't live like He asked them to. Hmmm...sound familiar?

Have you ever known of a nation that stated they trusted in God, but had little regard for His commands on a daily basis? Name them.

In the Old Testament, there are 113 times when the word sheqer is used and 37 of those times are in the book of Jeremiah.[3] Deception abounded in Jeremiah's times! It was as if the people viewed God's presence in the temple as a lucky rabbit's foot. The people believed in an illusion!

Jeremiah warns them in the Temple Sermon, "You cannot separate your behavior from your worship of God!" This type of worship was meaningless.

Let's read on in Jeremiah 7:12-15.

This passage speaks of a city named Shiloh. God disciplined Shiloh in the same way He intended to discipline the Israelites if they didn't change their ways. The house of God was in Shiloh at one point in Israel's history. Shiloh was 9 miles north of Bethel. "Just when the event occurred to which Jeremiah refers in Jeremiah 7:12-15 we do not know. It is mentioned in Psalms 78:60 and evidently was well known among the people or Jeremiah would not have used it as a warning in his day," according to K. Owen White.[4]

Discover a few passages that mention Shiloh in the Old Testament. Match the verse with what occurred at Shiloh:

_____ Joshua 18:1	a. Shiloh was the location of God's temple when Micah made his molten image and defeat came upon the land.
_____ Judges 18:31	b. The ark of the covenant was taken from Shiloh to protect the Israelites from the Philistines. But in the end the Philistines won the battle and the ark was captured.
_____ 1 Samuel 4:3-11	c. Shiloh was considered cursed in this passage.
_____ Psalm 78:58-61	d. A description of God abandoning His dwelling place in Shiloh.
_____ Jeremiah 26:6	e. The tent of meeting was set up in Shiloh.

Jeremiah 7:16 reads, "As for you, do not pray for this people and do not lift up a cry or prayer for them, and do not intercede with Me, for I do not hear you." God specifically told Jeremiah to not pray for this people. As an intercessor and prophet, this must have been difficult for Jeremiah to not pray for someone. He longed for the people to repent. How strange this must have been to hear from God. It is unusual in Scripture to hear God stating to not pray for others. God also told Jeremiah not to pray for the welfare of His people in Jeremiah 14:11.

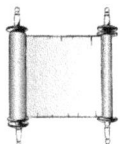

Have you ever had a time when God asked you to not pray for a person or a people group? Give an example without writing down anyone's name. Please honor the person/people by not bringing up their names in your group discussion. Why do you think God told you to not pray for them?

_____

_____

_____

One commentator suggests, "The prohibition (of Jeremiah praying) is an argument for the effectiveness of prayer, since God, now determined to act, guards against himself being dissuaded."5 God's decision had already been made and He would not change his mind. It was too late.

What a terrible situation to be in. It was too late for even God to offer mercy. The sad part was that the Judeans didn't even recognize that it was too late. They were so steeped in sin and idol worship that they had all but forgotten their God.

I fear our own nation at times has almost come to this point. Thankfully, there remain some who still take a stand against the decaying morals of our society. May we take a lesson from the Judeans and not fall into this same trap.

Tomorrow we'll continue on with the Temple Sermon lesson. Before leaving though, spend a moment with God adoring and praising Him. You will be better off for it. Maintain a spirit of thanksgiving all day long. You and all of those around you will benefit.

DAY 3

Temple Sermon (Part 2)

I am using the New Living Translation for the next Scripture passage because it is more readily understood in this version. I've included it below.

"This is what the LORD of Heaven's Armies, the God of Israel, says: 'Take your burnt offerings and your other sacrifices and eat them yourselves! When I led your ancestors out of Egypt, it was not burnt offerings and your other sacrifices I wanted from them.' This is what I told them: 'Obey me, and I will be your God, and you will be my people. Do everything as I say, and all will be well!' But my people would not listen to me. They kept doing whatever they wanted, following the stubborn desires of their evil hearts. They went backward instead of forward" (Jeremiah 7:21-24).

God longs for obedience from His children. Obedience is better than sacrifice. Write in your own words what God says about obedience and sacrifices in the Scripture verses below:

1 Samuel 15:22

_____

_____

Isaiah 1:11-13

_____

_____

Matthew 23:23

_____

_____

Amos 5:21-22

_____

_____

Obedience is better than *sacrifice*.

"The Jews didn't actually abandon the temple ministry; they simply brought their idolatry into the temple courts and made Jehovah one of the many gods they worshiped. If you had watched their worship, you would have thought the people were sincerely honoring the Lord; but their hearts belonged to Baal, Ashtoreth, Chemosh, and the other gods and goddesses of the heathen

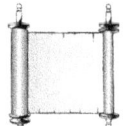

nations around them. Judah paid lip service to Jehovah, but gave heart service to idols."¹

Why do you think people are drawn to make sacrifices to God rather than obeying Him?

_____

_____

God does want sacrifices, but He wants them given with the right heart. He commanded sacrifices to be given to Him in the Old Testament. And in the New Testament, He instructs us to sacrifice our very lives for Him, not by physical death, but by laying down our rights and following Him. God was not denouncing the sacrifice system He'd put in place, but He was not going to accept sacrifices given without integrity of character. It was as if God's people were bribing Him with sacrifices so they could continue to sin.

Read Micah 6:6-8. What does the Lord require of us?

_____

_____

Read Jeremiah 7:30 -31. What was one of the detestable things the Judeans did?

_____

_____

Our Maker KNOWS what's best for us!

The Judeans were way off track. They adopted the practices of the cultures around them. One of those unhealthy practices was sacrificing their children. This was definitely not a part of God's design. They developed a perverted theology in serving God and idols.

How do we worship Christ? Is there anything flawed in how we worship Him? Are we giving Him sacrifices He doesn't want? Name a sacrifice you've given God that was only a guilt offering and had no true worship of Him attached to it. Maybe it's an activity you are involved in at church. It might be something good, just not something God wants.

Read Jeremiah 7:25-28.

Despite God's children obstinacy, He sent His word to them daily through the prophets. Yet, the people were unreachable. They didn't accept correction. Their stubborn disposition was going to ruin them. It's like when your child refuses to listen to you despite you know what is best for them.

Their obstinacy lands them in a heap of trouble. Thankfully, when my children don't take my husband's or my advice and they fail, they usually learn from it. However, the Judeans were not as wise. Just like a good parent knows what is best for their child, our Maker knows what is best for us. He laid out the commandments so we'd prosper. He didn't lay out the rules to make our lives miserable.

Read Joshua 1:7-8. What are we to do in order to prosper?

_____

_____

God's recipe for success is to follow Him wholeheartedly. We can't pick and choose what parts we like or don't like. We can't mix our own ways with His ways. He does not tolerate that.

Think about an idol in your life God wants you to give up. It might be your time. Whatever it is confess it and turn away from it. In its place do what God is calling you to do. Worship Him instead of that idol. Spend time with Him in His Word. Spend some time in prayer right now.

God's recipe **FOR SUCCESS** is to *follow Him* **WHOLEHEARTEDLY.**

DAY 4

You Must Die!

The Temple Sermon caused quite an uproar among the priests, prophets, and people in attendance. They wanted Jeremiah killed. They did not like what he had to say about their lifestyle and wanted him silenced.

I wonder if you have ever experienced this to a lesser degree before? You have spoken the truth and those around you did not want to hear it? Well, this was the same kind of situation Jeremiah found himself in. Thankfully, someone came to his rescue and he was not killed.

The temple sermon is thought to be discussed not only in Chapter 7 of Jeremiah, but also in Jeremiah 26.

Read Jeremiah 26:7-24. Notice in Jeremiah 26:14 what Jeremiah says. Write this verse down:

_____

_____

It reminds me of Christ's sacrificial submission to His Father to die on the cross. Even though, in this instance God did not ordain for Jeremiah to die. What impresses me is Jeremiah was willing to die for God even though he pointed out this would have been wrong for the people to have killed him.

Reread Jeremiah 26:16. Notice in Jeremiah 26:16, the Judeans changed their tune. Instead of yelling a death sentence, they began telling the priests and prophets that Jeremiah was speaking as sent from God. All of a sudden they realized they might be guilty of shedding innocent blood if they killed Jeremiah. Notice in Jeremiah 26:10, the princes of Judah, meaning the king's sons, also joined the crowd with the other officials. Then, the elders spoke up concerning past prophets (Jeremiah 26:17).

Reread Jeremiah 26:17-19. What was the point of the elders bringing up Micah, the prophet in Hezekiah's time?

_____

Who was another prophet who prophesied to Jerusalem during Jeremiah's times (Jeremiah 26:20-23)? Who killed him?

_____

Read Jeremiah 26:24.

Ahikam saved Jeremiah's life. Unlike the prophet Urijah, Jeremiah didn't run away, he stood his ground and God protected him.

Week 2

Who was Ahikam's father (Jeremiah 26:24)? Look up Jeremiah 39:14. In what context is Ahikam mentioned here?

_____

_____

Ahikam, son of Shaphan, is referred to again later in Jeremiah's life. This time referring to the son of Ahikam, Gedaliah, who took Jeremiah home to care for him after Babylon was captured and Nebuchadnezzar, the king of Babylon, entrusted Gedaliah with him.

Read Jeremiah 11:19. How does Jeremiah describe himself as people plot against him?

_____

_____

Read Isaiah 53:7. Who is this verse describing?

_____

The way Jeremiah was treated was a lot like how Jesus Christ was treated. Jeremiah was unfairly accused, despite trying to help the people. Many times Judah's inhabitants attempted to put Jeremiah's life to an end. Even the people of his own hometown, Anathoth, wanted to kill him.

Read Jeremiah 11:21 to see how the people from Jeremiah's hometown, Anathoth, felt about him. What did the men of Anathoth want to do to Jeremiah? What did they tell Jeremiah to stop doing?

_____

_____

If you think about it, Jesus was not respected in his own hometown, so why would Jeremiah be?

Write out Mark 6:4 here:

_____

_____

In Luke 4:24, Jesus says, "Truly I say to you, no prophet is welcome in his hometown." Read Luke 4:24-27. Which other prophets were not welcome in their hometown?

_____

But I was like a gentle lamb led to the slaughter...

Jeremiah 11:19

Let's look at how Jeremiah reacted to men threatening his life. His reflection on this event is thought to be in Jeremiah 12, where scholars call this Jeremiah's 1st confession (or lament) after he had faced the crowds at the temple gate. The men of Anathoth, his hometown, wanted to take his life. Can you imagine how Jeremiah had felt? He had just obeyed God and spoke the words of the Lord to God's people and they wanted nothing to do with him. Instead of receiving the message, they threatened Jeremiah.

How would you feel towards God if He had clearly told you to give a message to people and then you saw instead of them receiving it, they wanted to behead you? Write down what your feelings would have been.

_____

_____

I'm sure some of your reactions were the same as Jeremiah's. Read Jeremiah 12:1-4 and see what Jeremiah said to God about what happened at the temple gate. Record Jeremiah's general feelings.

_____

_____

Aren't you glad God allows us to come before His presence and present our case and plead our cause? I sure am! Many a time I have come before Him and begged an answer to the injustice I have seen in my own life or other's lives. I'm glad He listens and graciously answers. I find, His Word gently comforts me or sometimes gently rebukes me, whatever is needed.

In this case, Jeremiah was asking God why the wicked were prospering. Many of us have asked the same question. Jeremiah described the wicked as prosperous and at ease. The wicked were happy, doing well, and not even feeling any shame about their sin. The wicked were enjoying and abusing what God had given them. Living the good life, but not thanking the Creator who had given the good life to them. They spoke of God, but only gave Him lip service. "Thou (God) art near to their lips" ... but "(God) is far from their mind" (Jeremiah 12:2).

Look at Jeremiah 12:3 again. What did Jeremiah explicitly say here?

_____

_____

Have you ever appealed to God in this manner? Saying, "Look God, you know my heart, it is good. I've had the right attitude. I'm a person of integrity. Now please do what is right in this situation. Give those people what they deserve!"

Read Jeremiah 12:4 again.

Small trials are God's training ground for the days ahead.

Jeremiah went on to say that even the land and animals were suffering because of the wickedness of the people. Our environment and animals suffer because of the wickedness of men. Basically, Jeremiah was saying why should we all suffer here in this land (they were going through a drought) because of a few wicked men?

What does the end of verse 4, in Jeremiah 12:4, mean ("...because men have said, 'He will not see our latter ending.'")?

_____

_____

It may have been difficult to figure out that last verse. Maybe you had to use another translation or a commentary to understand its meaning. I did both! When I read a quote in Scripture, I try to figure out the tone of the person speaking and grab the background of the passage to acquire a richer understanding of what the person says. In Jeremiah 12:4, the men stated Jeremiah would not see what was going to happen in the end. Jeremiah didn't have that knowledge, so why should they put up with listening to him? Rather than changing their minds when hearing a Word from God, they justified the hardness of their hearts. They believed they were invincible, untouchable, and that their prosperity would never end.

Jeremiah 12:5-6 records God's response to Jeremiah. What do you think God was trying to say to Jeremiah?

_____

_____

God empathized with Jeremiah concerning how he had been treated (Jeremiah 12:6), yet He also encouraged him to not stay worn down and depressed about the situation. He pointed out to Jeremiah if he is getting wearied by these small trials ("running with the footmen" or "falling down in a land of peace") how will he handle bigger trials? Eventually, Jeremiah would experience far greater persecution. Little trials prepared him for the days ahead.

What about you? Are you facing trials God expects you to walk through valiantly, but you're having a hard time facing triumphantly? Explain.

_____

_____

The good news is God sees far beyond your present circumstances. He sees the injustice. He knows our pain and acknowledges our complaints. However, He also wants us to know we must not give up. We are to keep running the race and winning the fight. Don't give up and give in! Do what He has called you to do. And know that this trial is preparing you for what is next.

Read Hebrews 12:1-3.

Don't Give Up & Don't Give IN!

Wow! Jeremiah didn't have the privilege of having New Testament scriptures like this one to encourage him. He didn't know the horrendous hostility Jesus would face someday. However, Jeremiah chose to walk by faith and run the good race for God. Jeremiah listened to God and obeyed even when it was not easy. He was incredibly courageous! Jeremiah lived this Scripture well, even though it had not been recorded yet. "I can do all things through Him who strengthens me" (Philippians 4:13).

Lord, may we run in such a way as to be worthy of the calling you've laid before us. Meditate on these Scriptures below before you leave today's lesson. Take them in and apply them. If you are "driven" (like me), you push yourself to be the best whether it's at home, work, or play. Do we do this for Christ as well? Do we incorporate Him in all of the above? Or do we just leave Him on the shelf for prayer time in the morning and nighttime? We're called to be like Jeremiah and give Him our very best every day, all day.

Think about these verses:

"But seek first His kingdom and righteousness, and all these things will be added to you."
Matthew 6:33

"And whatever you do in word or deed, do all in the name of the Lord Jesus, giving thanks through Him to God the Father." Colossians 3:17

"Do you not know that those who run in a race all run, but only one receives the prize? Run in such a way that you may win...Therefore, I run in such a way, as not without aim; I box in such a way, as not beating the air; but I buffet my body and make it my slave, lest possibly, after I have preached to others, I myself should be disqualified."
1 Corinthians 9:24, 26, 27

Reflection

Record your thoughts as you meditate on these Scripture passages.

_____
_____
_____
_____
_____
_____

Week 2

DAY 5

The Babylonians

In 605 BC, King Nabopolassar, the king of Babylon, died. King Nabopolassar's son, Nebuchadnezzar, was in battle at Carchemish, when he heard word of his father's death. He immediately returned to Babylon. However, before Nebuchadnezzar's dad died, Nebuchadnezzar had defeated Egypt's pharaoh, Necho. Egypt was one of the world's super powers at that time. Carchemish, where the battle took place, was located 120 miles inland from the Mediterranean Sea, on the Euphrates River. It was a key site where Assyrians, Egyptians and Babylonians warred.[1] Who knows, if Nebuchadnezzar's father hadn't died at this point maybe the Babylonians would have taken over Jerusalem at this time. However, now that the Egyptians weren't in control, Judah had to pay tribute to Nebuchadnezzar, instead of Egypt. The Judeans had hoped Egypt would protect them from Babylon, but the Babylonians were more powerful. And once Nebuchadnezzar was made king, he became even more of a contender for world power.

I have prepared a **TIMELINE** which traces Jeremiah's call amidst the three deportations and rulers.

See **Addendum 2** on page 247.

Let's refresh our memory. Who was reigning in Jerusalem when Nebuchadnezzar conquered Egypt and how many years had this king been reigning? Look at Jeremiah 46:2.

_____

Throughout your readings you may see the word Chaldeans in place of Babylonians. The Chaldeans are another name for a specific people group of Babylonians. The Chaldeans originally inhabited southern Babylon and they occupied the throne at different times throughout Babylon's history.

Name the man in Ezra 5:12 who was a Chaldean.

_____

"Babylon's greatest period of prosperity and power came under the Neo-Babylonian dynasty founded by Nabopolasser. The city (Babylon) became the capital of an imperial state that spanned much of the Near East under the rule of his son, Nebuchadnezzar II (605-562 B.C.). The Neo-Babylonian kings undertook massive building projects and Nebuchadnezzar...sought to make Babylon the economic and administrative center of the world, a project in which he achieved some measure of success."[2]

The history of Mesopotamia fascinated me as a child. Do you remember learning about Mesopotamia in Social Studies class in elementary school? This is the same land we're talking about now! Babylon situated on the Euphrates River, located in lower Mesopotamia, was known as the land between the two rivers – the Tigris and Euphrates Rivers. The Babylonians used irrigation methods to feed their crops due to only once a year flooding that occurred from the Tigris and Euphrates Rivers. Does any of this ring a bell? Can you visualize the water canals flowing out across the dry land and the workers planting their seeds and praying to their gods for the crops to flourish?

If Babylon were around today it would be located in southern Iraq, southwest of Iraq's capital city, Baghdad.

King Nebuchadnezzar made Marduk, "king of the gods," a supreme god to be worshiped in the city of Babylon. In fact, Nebuchanezzar's name means "O Nabu, watch over my heir." Nabu was a Babylonian deity of wisdom and son of Marduk.[2] Babylon had many temples to a variety of gods. The most important temple was the Esagil, Marduk's temple complex.[3] The ziggurat of Marduk, Etemenanki, is located just north of Marduk's temple. Some scholars speculated the Tower of Babel, discussed in Genesis 11:1-9, was located either where Etemenanki or Esagil were placed. The book A History of the Ancient Near East, states that the massive structure of the ziggurat of Marduk was originally thought to be the Tower of Babel.[4] This structure was removed by Alexander of Macedon in 331 B.C. However, according to Eerdmans Bible Dictionary, some think 'a tower with its top in the heavens' (Genesis 11:4) better reflects the ceremonial name of the Esagil temple, but note that Nebuchadnezzar claimed to raise the head of Etemenanki to rival the heavens.[5] Whether it was the Esagil temple or the Etemananki, where the Tower of Babel lies makes really no difference. It's the thought that either one of them could have been the site for the Tower of Babel that makes the sites worth mentioning and of historical interest.

The gods dwelled in a ziggurat. A ziggurat was a structure built with receding tiers and a temple on top of the formation. Made of sun-baked bricks, ziggurats were massive, tall structures because the people felt the closer they were to the heavens the easier to commune with their gods. "The size and splendor of a ziggurat would show the city and king's devotion to the particular city god being worshipped. They might have temples to other gods but they would only have a ziggurat to the city god." and "The temple situated on the very top of the Ziggurat was 300 ft. high."[6]

Let's look at another reference to the land of Babylon before Jeremiah's time. Look up Genesis 11:1-9. The land of Shinar was at the center of the kingdom of Nimrod and was where future Babylon would be located. What occurred in the land of Shinar in Genesis 11?

_____

_____

During Nebuchadnezzar's 43 year reign, he built fortification walls around the city of Babylon and made several palaces where he resided. His most notable building project, or at least the building project most talked about was the Hanging Gardens. Remember that from your history lessons? The "Greek writers regarded the Hanging Gardens as one of the seven wonders of the ancient world."[7] According to The Seventy Wonders of the Ancient World: The Great Monuments and How They Were Built, "He

(Nebuchadnezzar) built the so-called hanging paradise because his wife, who had been brought up in the area of Media, wanted mountain scenery" (phrase from Josephus, 1st century AD).[8]

The Hanging Gardens were built for Nebuchanezzar's homesick wife. Nebuchadnezzar's wife, Amyitis, was an Iranian princess. Supposedly, the Hanging Gardens were built in 15 days according to the historian Berossus, and were known for their beautiful fountains, waterfalls, groves, and terraces. However, you should know that there are contradictory descriptions of the Hanging Gardens given by historians and it has even been questioned if they existed. Since the palaces of Babylon have been mostly devastated, we will have to wait to see if this paradise really did exist after more excavations have been done.[9]

Archeology confirms that the Neo-Babylonian Empire, during the reign of Nabopolassar and Nebuchadnezzar, built an incredible city of wealth and majesty. Babylon was beautiful. At the end of the nineteenth century, excavations began in the area of Babylon that have confirmed that a great city was once there. The Ishtar gate, the entrance to the city, was found. Also, thousands of bricks and stone tiles inscribed by Nebuchadnezzar have been found.[10] I have read as well that the recent leader of Iraq, now dead, Saddam Hussein tried to rebuild Babylon and put his name on bricks like Nebuchadezzar.[11]

Now that we've learned a little bit of Babylon's history from scholars and archeologists, let's switch gears and discuss Babylon's possible future role in history. We are going to take a look at the book of Revelation. Not only did Babylon have a significant place in the Old Testament's history, but we'll see that it is discussed at great length in Revelation as well, playing a key role in biblical end times.

Let's read Revelation 17:1-5, 18. Pick out the verse in Revelation that matches the description of Babylon:

_____	Revelation 17:1	a. Describes Babylon as a harlot and sits near water.
_____	Revelation 17:2	b. Babylon – a city that persecuted saints.
_____	Revelation 18:9-19	c. Babylon is the center of world commerce.
_____	Revelation 18:21	d. Babylon is immoral.
_____	Revelation 18:24	e. Babylon will be destroyed.

According to Mark Hitchcock in The Complete Book of Bible Prophecy, Revelation reveals that, "...Babylon will be the great religious economic capital of the Antichrist's kingdom in the last days. But what city does Babylon represent? This great harlot of the last days has been identified with the Roman Catholic Church and the Vatican, apostate Christendom, New York City, Jerusalem, and Rome. The most likely view, however, is that Babylon, the literal city on the Euphrates in modern-day Iraq, will be rebuilt in the last days."[12]

Have you noticed Iraq has politically and economically become a more well known country in the last few years? From Saddam Hussein's tyrannical leadership in the 1990's to the War in Iraq to increased terrorism coming from Iraq and its surrounding countries, Iraq has been in the international spotlight. It would make sense that Iraq (once ancient Babylon) could become the Babylon discussed in the book of Revelation.

What do you think? List your thoughts concerning who Babylon will be in the last days?

_____

_____

_____

NOTES

_____
_____
_____
_____
_____
_____
_____
_____
_____
_____

VIDEO QUESTIONS WEEK 2

1. Are your ears wide open to hear God and do what He instructs as in Jeremiah 18:1-2?
2. What lessons do you draw from the analogy of God being the Potter and people being the clay? How does this illustration make you view God differently? Do you view yourself differently?
3. Read Jeremiah 18:17 again. Discuss the concept of God's back being towards you versus His face looking upon you. Have you ever experienced God turning His back to you? If so, describe how it felt.
4. Jeremiah was rejected when he spoke the truth to God's people. What do you think about how Jeremiah reacted to his persecutors? Have you been persecuted recently? How could you apply Jeremiah 18:19-23 to yourself?
5. By placing Jeremiah's lament (Jeremiah 18:19-23) in the Bible, what does this say about God's character (even though God did not respond to Jeremiah)?

Video sessions are available for download at www.grassandflowers.org

WEEK THREE
TAKING CAPTIVITY CAPTIVE

DAY ONE
The Linen Sash

DAY TWO
The Scroll

DAY THREE
The Drought & Jeremiah's Ministry Crisis

DAY FOUR
The Rechabites
Lives of Integrity

DAY FIVE
Jeremiah's Lifestyle & The Sabbath Day

DAY 1

The Linen Sash

You'll notice throughout the book of Jeremiah God likes to speak through Jeremiah with visual images. God used common everyday items to speak to His people. It reminds me of how Christ related to the people in his day.

After reading Jeremiah 13:1-11, write down what common object God used to describe the similarity between the object and the Judeans?

_____

Ezowr in Hebrew means belt. It was not a slender belt, but large enough to be considered part of the outer garment.[1] Sashes or belts served as not only a useful or purposeful article of clothing, but also as adornment. Like the Judeans were supposed to be to God–useful and bringing glory and honor to Him.

In Jeremiah 13:7, how does Jeremiah describe the waistband after it had been hidden?

_____

I love how the NASB Bible describes the belt – it was totally worthless! Just like the people of Judah had become. This waistband was of no use at all. The Hebrew word ruined is shachath. Shachath means to go to ruin, act corruptly, depravity, polluted, ravaged, spoiled, and wreaked destruction.[2] Judah's pride was their downfall. They chose to go after other gods, not content with serving God alone. God had commanded His people to cling to Him and Him alone. The Judeans were to be an example to the other nations of God's glory by how they lived. Unfortunately, they didn't follow God's lead.

Do you bring God glory? Yes, no, or maybe so? Give an example.

_____

_____

God will not allow **His** *Glory to be given to another.*

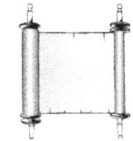

God will not allow His glory to be given to another—whether it is to a person, a nation, or another god. Read Isaiah 48:10-11.

Eventually in this study, we will see Judah taken captive by Babylon then released from captivity 70 years later. From Isaiah 40-66, much of the book speaks of Judah's return from the Babylonian exile, over a hundred years after Isaiah had written it. Isaiah 43:21, "The people (Judah/Israel) whom I formed for Myself, will declare my praise." Often affliction is required before we give God the praise He deserves. It is through our trials we see how He loves and cares for us. I spoke to a friend recently and she commented how differently she sings praise music in church when going through troubled times versus when everything seems to be going well in her life. Many times the only place we'll listen to Him is when things have been stripped from us. In this case, the Judeans were going to have their pride stripped from them if they did not heed God's warnings. Judah's pride was in their nation, their abilities, their connections, and their glorious temple in Jerusalem. Their pride was their downfall. Pride comes before a fall (Proverbs 16:18).

What are common sources of pride for you?

_____

The word cling in Jeremiah 13:11, reminds me of the verse in Genesis 2:24, "For this cause a man shall leave his father and his mother and shall cleave to his wife and they shall become one flesh." The word cleave in Genesis is similar in meaning to the word cling. Essentially, they are both describing how the relationship, whether it be God and his people or a man and his wife, are to stay together. Marriage relationships are to emulate the bride of Christ (the church) and the bridegroom (Christ). However, the Judeans were not doing a good job. They were unfaithful, like a spouse who is adulterous. The Judeans had an adulterous affair with idols of their own making.

Read 2 Corinthians 11:2. How does this verse speak to you concerning how our relationship with Christ should look?

_____

_____

Moving right along, let's look at other places in the Bible the word "cling" was used. Look each verse up and match the verse on the left with the correct verse listed on the right:

____	Deuteronomy 10:20	A.	"I cleave to Thy testimonies; O Lord, do not put me to shame!"
____	Deuteronomy 13:4	B.	"You shall fear the Lord your God; you shall serve Him and cling to Him..."
____	Joshua 23:8	C.	"My soul clings to Thee; Thy right hand upholds me."
____	Psalm 63:8	D.	"But you are to cling to the Lord your God, as you have done to this day."
____	Psalm 119:31	E.	"You shall follow the Lord your God and fear Him; and you shall keep His commandments, listen to His voice, serve Him, and cling to Him."

In the Hebrew, the word for cling is dabaq.[3] It means to cleave, to keep close, deeply attracted, fasten its grip, held fast, joined together, remained steadfast, pursued him closely, stayed close, and stuck together.

How many marriages exemplify cleaving/clinging to one another? Just yesterday, I was speaking to a friend who told me she doesn't know what to say to her friends who are choosing to divorce. About half of her friends are divorcing, for no other reason than they don't love each other anymore. How common this has become even among Christians. I've been married 20 years and let me say this – while I've never fallen out of love with my husband, marriage has not always been a walk in the park! We have to work at our marriage and choose to cling to each other. It doesn't come naturally at times! It's like our relationship with God. We have to choose to spend time with God and get to know Him.

If you are falling out of love with your husband, make a point to call on God and others for help with the matter. There are many other couples struggling with their marriages in the church. Join together and be accountable to one another. Don't walk away because of lack of feelings for your spouse. Ask God to renew those feelings. When we lose the fire for God, He rekindles it for Him if we ask. Why couldn't He do that for your marriage? Remember what God says — He hates divorce.

Do you cling to Christ? If you are married, do you cleave to your husband?

_____

_____

Spend some time in prayer contemplating your relationship with your husband, if you are married. Also, consider your relationship with God. Are you clinging to Him? Enjoy your day!

DAY 2

The Scroll

As we come to our study today, let's bow down before our Savior and humbly acknowledge our desperate need for Him. While He doesn't need us to accomplish His work, He could find someone else, He still chooses us and guides us to do His work if we'll let Him.

Begin by reading Jeremiah 36:1-3.

What was the approximate time frame of Jeremiah's writings?

_____

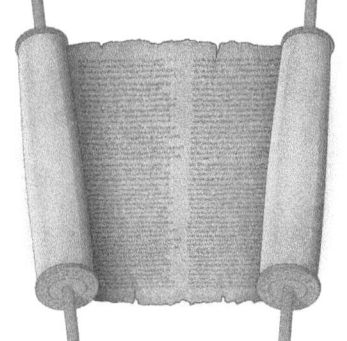

Alexandra Gl/Shutterstock

Jeremiah was commanded by the Lord to write everything God had said to him since the beginning of his ministry. At this point, Jeremiah had been serving God for more than 20 years in the prophetic role.

Now read Jeremiah 36:4-7.

Then look at verse 4. "Then Jeremiah called Baruch..." (Jeremiah 36:4). Jeremiah didn't call Baruch on the phone! What does "called" him in this passage mean? Let's look at what the Hebrew definition of "called" means. Strong's Concordance states that called (qara) is a primary root; to call, proclaim, become famous, cried, dictated, gave, grasps, invited, made a proclamation, read, screamed, shouted, and summoned.[1]

How do you imagine Jeremiah spoke when he announced to Baruch that he was the chosen one to write down what God had said? How do you think Baruch felt?

_____

_____

_____

Jeremiah cried out for Baruch, proclaimed to him that he was the one. Baruch was the privileged one to write down the words of the Lord. I imagine Baruch was ecstatic to serve God in this manner. However, I bet he was a little scared too, since he knew some considered Jeremiah a traitor. He knew if he served Jeremiah, he would not be popular. People might want to harm him because of his associations with Jeremiah.

Baruch was a man of rank and learning. His name meant "blessed."[2]

Read Jeremiah 51:59. It may seem like this verse has nothing to do with Baruch, but who is Seriah's father?

_____

Now reread Jeremiah 36:4. Who is Baruch's father?

_____

Baruch and Seriah are brothers. Baruch came from a prominent and well-liked family. Seriah, Baruch's brother, worked for King Zedekiah, the last king in Judah's history before captivity in Babylon. According to the NKJV Chronological Study Bible, a seal impression of Baruch's has been found in a royal archive. The seal identifies Baruch as a scribe, but not just any old scribe, but probably a royal scribe coming from a prominent scribal family.[3] Seals were only given to those with wealth and influence. A seal gave legal status to a document. Baruch could have worked for anyone he'd wanted because of his family's stature. Yet, Baruch chose to work for Jeremiah – quite a noble path, although I'm sure it was an underpaid and underappreciated path, costing him his community status. Baruch, however, had an eternal perspective and refused to compromise his godly purposes for momentary position or pleasures. He became a dear friend to Jeremiah. He took a stand for truth, along with Jeremiah, despite that it cost him his reputation while on earth. Then again, it boosted his reputation in God's eyes, placing him a spot in the Bible for the whole world to someday know and admire.

Consider Baruch's sacrifice. Like Baruch, we should be about advancing God's kingdom, and not our own personal agenda. We are to reveal the Lord. His image is to shine through us, so others will be drawn to Him, not us! But that's hard to do isn't it? We really want to look good for others. This has always been one of my prayers— to be like Jesus as he was described in Luke 2:52, "And Jesus kept increasing in wisdom and stature and in favor with God and men." It wasn't that Jesus tried to impress people by compromising His beliefs to be cool, but He impressed people by His wisdom and character given to Him by staying in communication with His Father. Showing us an example of how we are to live.

Since Jeremiah was not free to speak in the temple, he sent Baruch to share the message he'd dictated to Baruch. Baruch spoke the words of Jeremiah in the Lord's house.

Read Jeremiah 36:8-9. What did the people from Jerusalem and the surrounding cities in Judah do after Baruch read the words of God?

_____

The Jews held a fast because of the imminent danger that the Babylonians might attack them. They were pleading for God to protect them. Not necessarily because they wanted to change their ways, but because they didn't want to look bad by being attacked. They wanted to hold onto their reputations! The Judeans weren't concerned about glorifying God it seems because nothing in their lives changed. They were just hoping the act of fasting would fix things like it had in the past.

I'm as guilty of it as you are. Think about how many times you've prayed a selfish prayer for your well-being not because you wanted to glorify God when

> _Like Baruch,
> we should be about_
> **advancing
> God's
> Kingdom,**
> _and not our own
> personal agenda._

it was answered, but because you wanted to receive the blessing so that YOU would look good. Not Him. We've come to the point where we use God to serve us, instead of us serving Him.

Read Jeremiah 36:10-13.

There was one man, Micaiah, who heard the message from Baruch and considered it extremely important and relayed it to those in authority above him.

Who was Micaiah's father (Jeremiah 36:11)?

___

What were Micaiah's father's two jobs (Jeremiah 36:10, 12)?

___

Micaiah's father, Gemariah, had a prominent position working for King Jehoiakim. It is assumed Gemariah was a trusted advisor to the king since he was allowed in the royal cabinet (Jeremiah 36:12). Gemariah, along with his colleagues, shared Micaiah's perspective; they recognized the importance of Jeremiah's message. Note some of the other notable men named in attendance in the royal cabinet.

Many of Gemariah's family members protected Jeremiah. God placed Gemariah's family in authority to protect and defend Jeremiah time and time again. While the kings held the power to make change happen, God made sure the kings all had godly counsel, even if they chose to disobey it. The kings had no excuse. They couldn't say they hadn't been warned.

It is believed parts of Jeremiah 1-25 were a part of the scroll written by Jeremiah. In Jeremiah 25:1-3, you can read about how Jeremiah had already spoken to the people for 23 years before he had the scroll written in the 4th year of King Jehoiakim, and the 1st year of King Nebuchadnezzar's reign. Jeremiah was half way through his career when he had the scroll written. He had faced some hardships already, but the next 20 years of his prophetic ministry would prove to be even more difficult.

Read Jeremiah 36:14-19.

While King Jehoiakim's officials were terrified by the words of Jeremiah and felt they must tell King Jehoiakim about God's warnings, they also realized they would not likely be received kindly by King Jehoiakim. The officials knew how King Jehoiakim felt about Jeremiah. In fact, about 3 years earlier, in the first year of Jehoiakim's reign, when Jeremiah preached in the temple, King Jehoiakim sought to kill him. So, wisely the officials instructed Baruch and Jeremiah to hide themselves before they went to share the contents of the scroll with the king (Jeremiah 36:19).

"King Jehoiakim's antipathy to Jeremiah is understandable. Early in the king's reign Jeremiah had dressed him down for thinking he was a king just because he spent money like a king ("So, that makes you a king living in a palace?" Jeremiah 22:15). He compared him unfavorably with his father, Josiah, who had administered justice in the land and honored God, whereas the son was rapacious and plundering. He predicted a donkey's death for him on the city's garbage dump: "They'll give him a donkey's funeral, drag him out of the city and dump him" (Jeremiah 22:11-19). With such rebukes ringing in his ears it is no wonder the king had forbidden Jeremiah to speak in public."[4]

Read Jeremiah 36:20.

Even the actual physical scroll might irritate King Jehoiakim, so the officials left it in a safe spot–"So they went to the king in the court, but they deposited the scroll in the chamber of Elishama the scribe and they reported all the words to the king" (Jeremiah 36:20). However, Jehoiakim wouldn't have it that way. He wanted the scroll and obviously not because he wanted to follow God's message, but because he wanted to silence God's Word.

Read Jeremiah 36:21-26.

Jehoiakim had no fear of the Lord. His arrogance made him feel he answered to no one, not even the living God. Jehoiakim refused to listen. It might surprise you how Jehoiakim reacted to God's word, but if you think about it, it's not much different than how we sometimes react to God today.

According to Eugene Peterson, when Jehoiakim destroyed the scroll, he displayed "...defenses against an awareness that requires a change of life. He was trying desperately to keep the truth of Jeremiah's words and the reality of God's truth at bay...Jehoiakim knew that he was hearing the word of God, but if he gave any indication he knew, he would be accountable for responding in obedience. So he gave an elaborate charade of nonchalance, casually and indifferently whittling away at the scroll, feeding the fire with the parings until it was gone."[5]

While it seems deplorable what Jehoiakim did to God's Word, have we not done the same thing at times, not physically burning God's Word, but intellectually rejecting God's Words? Name a time you have done this.

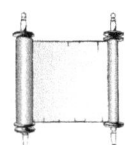

_____

_____

_____

Maybe it's not that you ignore God's message completely, but you follow only the parts that seem good to you. How many times have you made rationalizations for why you didn't give God one hundred percent? You want to be in control and do things your way, not His way. Perhaps, you don't want to see your sin for what it is, choosing to live in denial. Denial is a great coping mechanism people use when they don't want to see their sin. And lastly, maybe you are just uninterested in God's Word. You have other things to do and His plans don't line up with yours.

F.B. Meyer stated, "We are all tempted to use Jehudi's penknife. It is probable that no one is free from the almost unconscious habit of evading or toning down certain passages which conflict with the doctrinal or ecclesiastical position in which we were reared, or which we have assumed. In our private reading of the Scripture, we must be aware of using the penknife. Whole books and tracts of truth are practically cut out of the Bible of some earnest Christians..."[6]

> *Beware of using the penknife on Scripture rather than embracing the truth it reveals.*

The indestructible Word, the scroll, was made to offer God's plan of salvation, to offer a way to avoid destruction. It was meant to help, to give the Judeans one more chance. It declared God's expectations of His people and pronounced judgments if they did not follow it. The scroll was read because as Jeremiah said, "Perhaps their supplication will come before the Lord, and everyone will turn from his evil way..." (Jeremiah 36:7).

Jeremiah still had hope for the rebellious people of Judah. Even though Jeremiah had been shut out of speaking publically, he did not give up. He obeyed God and went from orator to writer. If he could not share the message verbally, he shared through the written word. He persisted. He was not just involved at the lay level, but also involved in addressing the government, having a voice in how his country was run. It's a good reminder to all of us of how important it is to be involved in our government.

What did Jeremiah do after the scroll was burned? Read Jeremiah 36:27-32.

_____

_____

Jeremiah went right back to dictating God's message to Baruch. This time God added on a few more extras in the script, detailing King Jehoiakim and his family's fate.

Can you think of another time in the church's history when the Bible was destroyed? If so, please explain.

_____

_____

I had recently read about William Tyndale when I began studying Jeremiah's scroll being burned. William Tyndale's story reminded me of Jeremiah's story. William Tyndale, in 1526, made the first English translation of the

Bible directly from the Hebrew and Greek texts. He felt that the commoner needed to be able to read and understand Scriptures on their own. It was, however, taken as a direct challenge to the Roman Catholic Church and the English church and state. Cuthbert Tonstal, a bishop of London, bought Tyndale's books and publicly burned all of the ones he bought.[7] Ironically, Tyndale used the money that he earned from Tonstal buying the copies of the Bible to print an even cheaper form of the Bible in even better type![8] He was eventually charged with heresy in 1536 and strangled to death while at the stake, then burned.

The Bible can't be destroyed; every age has tried, but they have failed. No matter how many times men try to destroy God's Word, it hasn't been able to be destroyed. And guess what, it never will be! King Jehoiakim couldn't destroy the Word, Cuthbert Tonstal couldn't prevent it from being passed on, and neither can any other man!

Let's end this study session by seeking Christ's glorious face and praising Him for His indescribably wonderful life-giving Word He's given us and does not allow and cannot allow to be destroyed.

> The **BIBLE** **can't** be **DESTROYED;** every age has tried, but they have failed.

DAY 3

The Drought and Jeremiah's Ministry Crisis

Jeremiah chapters 14 and 15 have become a favorite passage of mine because of the conversation between God and Jeremiah being so direct and unguarded. Jeremiah doesn't hold back his feelings. He lays it all out there with nothing to hide. God seems to appreciate his candor, although He invites Jeremiah to reevaluate things. God responds kindly, but with firmness.

The dialogue illustrates the intimacy of the relationship between Jeremiah and God. And like any good relationship, they are both able to be confrontational when necessary to maintain honesty within the relationship. It is a great example of the character of both parties. God, of course, cannot change His ways. He is just, truthful, and kind. However, as humans we have the ability to respond two different ways to confrontation in a relationship; we can turn our backs on God if we disagree with Him or we can hear what He has to say and follow His ways even if we wish circumstances were different. Jeremiah spoke from his heart. God gave him some direct and challenging responses back. Let's read what these two had to say.

Read Jeremiah 14-15. Yes, it's a lot of reading. Take your time and try to figure out who is talking to whom in these chapters. The conversation goes back and forth between Jeremiah and God and sometimes it's tricky figuring out where one starts speaking and the other leaves off.

It's not known exactly when Jeremiah had this communication session with God, but the droughts upon Judah are believed to have occurred during the latter years of Jehoiakim's reign. It is awful to read how devastating the drought was; even the animals were described as abandoning their young because the drought was so severe.

Jeremiah, watching the devastation and being a part of it, pled with God to have mercy. Jeremiah took on himself the people's sense of estrangement from God, despite he hadn't done anything wrong. To have to stand by his neighbors and watch them suffer and see so many perishing Jeremiah pray hard for his nation. Jeremiah had deep compassion on his countrymen.

Reread Jeremiah 14:8-9. (Jeremiah's plea to God) and then read Jeremiah 14:10-12. How does God respond to Jeremiah's cry for help?

_____

_____

_____

God identifies the real stranger as the people of Judah, not Him. The people wandered from God, not the other way around. God did not leave them. Verse 10 points out they loved every minute of wandering from God.[1] They treated their relationship with God casually before the drought, not paying heed to the warnings the prophet Jeremiah gave them. They lived however they wanted. Now, they expected God to come and rescue them.

Read Exodus 34:6-7. What does God do to those who are guilty of sin and do not seek His forgiveness?

_____

_____

God's covenant with His people was well known. During King Josiah's reign the people of Judah had access to the Word of God. The covenantal relationship of God with His people was not hidden from them or a mystery. If you'll read further in Exodus 34, verses 12-17 you'll see how God explicitly told the Israelites to not worship any other gods. Yet, the people of Judah followed the other nations and chose to worship other gods, ensnaring themselves. Their sin led to their destruction.

It is important to note that just because this particular drought and famine was brought about because of sin it doesn't mean that all famines and droughts are a punishment from God. We must be careful in judging other's circumstances. If someone's circumstances are rough it doesn't necessarily mean they are going through those tough times because of sin. God does allow trials to happen to righteous people as well.

In Jeremiah 14:13, Jeremiah approaches God with another appeal for why God should end this drought. Jeremiah tells God how the prophets are prophesying falsely and misleading the people. However, God doesn't allow this to be an excuse for His people's disobedience. In God's eyes, people are held responsible for discerning the messages given to them. The People's Commentary reminds us of the importance of guarding our hearts and minds from incorrect teaching, "Those who have listened to the false prophets are victims, but they are not innocent. We (and they) bear a responsibility for the kind of teaching we (they) decide to listen to..."[2]

What does it say in the New Testament about those who prophesy in God's name falsely (Matthew 7: 21-23)?

_____

We must be cautious when it comes to who we're listening to. We need to know the Word of God backwards and forwards because as humans it is easy to fall into the trap of believing whatever our ears hear, especially if the words "tickle" our ears.

Write out 1 John 4:1.

_____

_____

Moving on again, let's reread Jeremiah 14:19-22.

Jeremiah continues his plea. Basically, Jeremiah says, "For your own sake God, please don't abandon us. If you desert us, it will reflect poorly on you. Your name will be disgraced." It reminds me of a friend of mine who is in a managerial position at a large corporation. She has to make hard decisions at times. If employees consistently break the rules, they are given a warning and sometimes fired if the offences are repetitive. She hates this part of her job because often employees blame her for the disciplinary action she enforces. She doesn't deserve their hatred. The employees disciplined know the rules in advance. The leadership executives established the rules for managers to enforce for the overall benefit and safety of all employees. Those who choose to break the rules must take responsibility for what they have done, not blame the manager. The same goes with us. If we don't obey God's rules, we shouldn't blame Him for the consequences of our actions. God shouldn't be hated for our wrongdoing.

God wanted to show love and compassion to his "employees," but they kept disregarding His instruction. Eventually when He brought punishment upon them His name was despised, though He had done nothing wrong. So, here Jeremiah says to God that He should consider how others are going to view Him if He brings destruction on his people. God, on the other hand, while still caring deeply for His people, will not compromise His standards. God is more concerned with His people being holy than He is with their immediate gratification. His people will not obey Him and receive His blessings, then there is no other way. Just like the friend of mine, who as a boss had to be more concerned about employees doing their job right than about how her name might be smeared if she disciplined them appropriately.

Reread Jeremiah 15:1, then answer this true/false question:

Even if Moses and Samuel stood in God's presence pleading, God still wouldn't change his mind. (True or False) _____

Psalms 99:6 states, "Moses and Aaron were among his priests, and Samuel was among those who called on His name; they called upon the Lord, and He answered them." Remember in Exodus 32:11-14, God was about to kill the Israelites because they bowed down to a golden calf, but Moses pleaded to God to spare them. God changed His mind and spared the Israelites because of Moses request. However, in Jeremiah's case, God was not going to change His mind.

> *God is* more concerned with **His people** being **H O L Y** than **He** is with their *immediate gratification.*
>
>

Reread Jeremiah 15:10. Circle the appropriate descriptors listed below that describe Jeremiah in this verse:

Cursed by others	Loved by everyone
Wishes he'd never been born	Carefree
A man of controversy	Never borrowed money from anyone

Jeremiah is feeling pretty pitiful here. About as low as you can go, even wishing he'd never been born. It reminds me of the ditty my mom used to sing to my brother and I whenever we acted like we were in the pits of despair, "Nobody likes me, everybody hates me, going in the garden and eat worms..." It always brought a smile to our face and we stopped pitying ourselves for the mess we'd usually brought on ourselves! In Jeremiah's case, he hadn't made a mess for himself, he had just followed God's leading and it caused people to hate him because they did not want to be convicted of their own sin. Sounds a lot like the manager friend I described earlier, doesn't it?

Let's read on. In Jeremiah 15:15b, Jeremiah states "...Know that for Thy sake I endure reproach." Read on in verse 16-18. Describe how Jeremiah is feeling here.

_____

_____

Jeremiah's saying, "God, I did everything you asked me to. I've endured hatred from others for Your sake. I've kept Your words in my heart. I didn't carouse around partying all night like the others around me. Instead, I was alone. I've felt like I've suffered for doing what is right. The heartache I feel never ends. And I just want to know God, where are you in all of this?"

Have you ever felt like you obeyed God, suffered for doing His will, and then felt abandoned by Him? Share an incident in your life when you felt like this. In hindsight, do you feel you reacted appropriately towards God?

_____

_____

_____

How does God respond to Jeremiah's cry? Reread Jeremiah 15:19-21. What is God saying to Jeremiah in verse 19?

_____

_____

If Jeremiah doesn't return to God, he can't be used by God. Jeremiah could either "sit in the garden and eat worms" or he could rejoin God's purposes and be a spokesman for God again. It's like God is saying, "I hear your complaints Jeremiah, but it isn't going to do any good to chat all day about how you feel…you have to make a decision…to follow me or not. As for the false prophets and Israelites, they may come around or not, but I'm warning you do not turn to them and follow their false ways." Jeremiah had to make a choice.

Notice in Jeremiah 15:19-21 there is a conditional clause God placed. He said, *"**If** you do this (verse 19)…**then, and only then,** will I protect you, Jeremiah (verse 20-21)."*

Do you remember back when God first called Jeremiah? God gave Jeremiah words of encouragement. The words He gave then are similar to the words He's giving Jeremiah now.

Go back to Jeremiah 1:17-19 and read the passage. List the ways in which these verses are similar to Jeremiah 15:19-21.

_____

_____

_____

_____

It must have been awfully nice to hear those words of reassurance again. Especially when he was having one of those "Wish I hadn't been born" moments!

Has there been a time in your life when you felt like quitting the ministry God called you to? Describe your experience and how God spoke to you concerning your feelings.

_____

_____

_____

_____

God offers protection when we obey him. However, the opposite is true as well. If we don't obey Him, His hand of protection is lifted from us.

Don't compromise when you preach the Word of God. Don't water down the gospel. You may not be well liked because of it, but choose to be courageous and not a coward. Listen to what Paul says about the matter.

Many of God's promises come with a conditional clause:

IF…

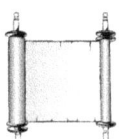

I solemnly charge you in the presence of God and of Christ Jesus, who is to judge the living and the dead, and by His appearing and His kingdom: preach the word; be ready in season and out of season; reprove, rebuke, exhort, with great patience and instruction. For the time will come when they will not endure sound doctrine; but wanting to have their ears tickled, they will accumulate for themselves teachers in accordance to their own desires; and will turn away their ears from the truth, and will turn aside to myths. But you, be sober in all things, endure hardship, do the work of an evangelist, fulfill your ministry.
2 Timothy 4:1-5

We're **CALLED** to *tell others* about the **Word of God.**

Paul voices encouragement to believers. Not unlike Jeremiah's times, we too face those who don't want to listen to God's Word. Paul wasn't speaking to just people who have the title "preacher," he was speaking to all of us. We're called to tell others about the Word of God. Don't hesitate to fulfill the ministry to which God has called us. We are to endure hardship, just like the saints who have gone before us. God will be pleased if we do this and at the end of the day that is all that matters!

DAY 4

The Rechabites — *Lives of Integrity*

Hello dear friends! What a glorious day it has been here in East Tennessee. We've had more than 3 inches of snow falling, with more coming down. Additionally, the snow is actually sticking and staying on the ground – very unlike Tennessee where the snow usually melts as fast as it comes down. It's a perfect winter wonderland, like a picture of Currier & Ives! Snow blankets the tree boughs and the hills are dotted with kids sledding down them.

What an amazing display of God's glory! I just love when God shows off. Today, in our lesson, God is also showing off a group of people who came to live in Jerusalem for awhile around 601 BC. These people defied the culture they were in and stood out like the snow in my yard. They were pure, distinct, and pleasantly reflecting the beauty of obedience, completely opposite the Judeans surrounding them in Jerusalem. The Judeans, in comparison to the Rechabites, look like snow after it's been on the streets for days and cars have traveled over it and made it into a black and brown slushy mess! Tarnished and dirty, the Judeans had become all muddied up from their unrepentant sin.

If you're like me, you've had just about enough of hearing how foolish the Judeans were and are ready for some good news instead! You'd probably like to hear that some human beings can actually live the right way and lead disciplined lives. It's kind of like watching the news on TV; you can only watch so many reports of corruptness before you'd like to hear some positive, uplifting news instead!

The Rechabites would have been the positive news report you were yearning to hear about in Jerusalem if you had lived in their day and they had TV. And Jeremiah would have been the anchor covering the story.

Before we begin, however, let's open our hearts and minds up to Jesus. Close your eyes and picture God before you, with a smile on His face and lovingly reaching His arms and hands out to you, inviting you into His presence. What a sight for sore eyes! Take a few moments to linger in His presence. Be still and listen. Rejoice. He is overwhelmingly delighted to spend time with you. Don't rush the moment. Enjoy His presence. Bask in His embrace. Burst out into song for Him. He is a gift to you.

Okay, if you've spent some one-on-one time with your Lord and Savior, then you are ready to get started! On the other hand, if you haven't made a choice to allow Him into your heart and life, why not now ask Him to come into your heart and reside? Ask Him to forgive your sins. He would love to make His home with you. Listen to what He says, "Behold, I stand at the door and knock; if anyone hears My voice and opens the door, I will come in to him, and will dine with him, and he with me (Revelation 3:20)."

Week 3

Open your Bible up to Jeremiah 35. Read the whole chapter. What does God tell Jeremiah to do (Jeremiah 35:1-2)?

_____

How did the Rechabites react to Jeremiah's offer to drink wine (Jeremiah 35:6)?

_____

To begin with let's learn a little about the Rechabites. We can trace their ancestry way back in the Old Testament. It is possible, but not for certain that the Rechabites came from a people group called the Kenites.[1] There is a brief mention of Rechab (thought to be the leader of the Rechabites) in 1 Chronicles 2:55 as a descendant of the Kenites.[2] The Kenites are mentioned several times throughout the Old Testament. So, let's look up some verses concerning them.

First, read Judges 1:16 and 4:11. Which relative of Moses was a Kenite?

_____

The Kenites became united with Israel through the marriage of Moses and his wife. Moses father-in-law was a Kenite.

Look up some other verses concerning the Kenites and choose which verse to the left matches the description to the right:

_____ Genesis 15:18-19	A. Jael, a Kenite, the most blessed woman of the Kenites.
_____ Numbers 24:15, 21	B. God mentioned the Kenites on the day He made a covenant with Abram.
_____ Judges 5:24	C. The story of how Jehu and Jehonadab, the son of Rechab destroyed Baal worshipers.
_____ 1 Samuel 15:6	D. Kenites showed kindness to Israelites when they came out of Egypt.
_____ 2 Kings 10:15-31 (skim)	E. Balaam's prophecy concerning the Kenites – that they would have a lasting heritage.

Whether or not the Rechabites were descendants of the Kenites, we do know for sure that they were in Jeremiah's times an example to the Judeans of exactly how the Judeans were to live in relationship to their heavenly Father. God's point was, if the Rechabites could obey their earthly forefather and still put into practice his man-made rules made 250 years ago, certainly the Judeans could obey their Heavenly Father's laws which were holy and inspired by God.

The object lesson Jeremiah tried to give the people was not about abstinence from alcohol. The Judeans were allowed to drink wine; they were just not allowed to get drunk. Wine was customarily drunk in this culture on a regular basis. Instead, the Rechabites were an example of discipline and obedience to their clan's traditions. The Rechabites displayed it was possible to be a distinct people group and not conform to the pressures around them. The Rechabites didn't adapt their customs to fit in better. It was a no-brainer to the Rechabites when Jeremiah asked them if they'd drink wine. They automatically said no! If you think about it though, it would have been easy for the Rechabites to justify gulping down a glass of wine; they were in stressful circumstances!

Read Jeremiah 35:11 again. Why were the Rechabites in Jerusalem?

_____

> THE RECHABITES DISPLAYED IT **WAS POSSIBLE** TO BE A DISTINCT PEOPLE GROUP AND NOT **CONFORM** TO THE PRESSURES AROUND THEM.

The Rechabites were in Jerusalem for protection. Typically the Rechabites were a nomadic people group, living in tents. However, they were concerned when King Nebuchadnezzar sent soldiers into Judah to scare the people into submission in the countryside. The Rechabites felt vulnerable. Therefore, they moved to Jerusalem.

Read 2 Kings 24:1-2. Why did King Nebuchadnezzar feel he had to send Chaldeans, Arameans, Moabites, and Ammonites against Judah?

_____

In 601 BC, Nebuchadnezzar's army weakened in a battle against Egypt and suffered heavy casualities. It is thought because of King Nebuchadnezzar's army being weakened and Egypt regaining strength that Jehoiakim unwisely chose to not pay tribute to King Nebuchadnezzar any longer. Obviously, King Nebuchadnezzar was not pleased by Jehoiakim's choice and while he couldn't send his own army at the time due to great losses, he could send neighboring people groups who served him.[3] Nebuchadnezzar's rationale for attacking Judah was to disrupt Judah from forming a resistance against him and to keep Judah under his control.

These were the circumstances the Rechabites found themselves in. It would have been dangerous for the Rechabites to remain in the countryside under these circumstances. However, despite the stress the Rechabites were under, they didn't give in to drinking the wine laid before them.

Can you recall where the Rechabites were when wine was offered to them? Look back at Jeremiah 35:4-5.

_____

The Lord had asked Jeremiah to bring them into the temple where both the general populous and the religious officials in the temple could see the Rechabites display of obedience and faithfulness.[4] Obviously, the Lord gave

Jeremiah favor with this man of God named Hanan who allowed Jeremiah to enter the temple.[5]

Some of you may ask, "Why would God tempt the Rechabites in this manner?" However, in James 1:13 it states God doesn't tempt anyone. The verse says, "Let no one say when he is tempted, 'I am being tempted by God'; for God cannot be tempted by evil, and He Himself does not tempt anyone." So, by the definition of God's nature, we have to assume He was not tempting them, but testing them instead.

In your opinion, what is the difference between a test and a temptation?

_____

_____

_____

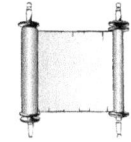

Sometimes, it seems like testing and temptation go hand in hand. However, there is a difference between them. Temptation is what the devil offers. He tries to tempt us to do something against God's commands. Testing, however, occurs in a Christian's life to see if we'll follow through the test with integrity. We may be tempted to not do the right thing during a test, but the actual test itself is not a temptation. Being tested lets us know what our character is made of. God allows us to go through tests. If our character is not developed enough in some area, tests can reveal our weaknesses and refine us.

Think about taking a test at school. It reveals what we do or we don't know. If we want to grow and learn, after missing questions on a test, we'll attempt to find the correct answers. While testing is a good thing, we don't always view it that way! Tests are often stressful, especially if we like to do well on a test. Our lives are tested at times by God, not because He wants to torture us, but because He wants to better us, or in the case of the Rechabites He wanted to show the Israelites what the Rechabites were made of–integrity!

What does God say about integrity? Write out Proverbs 20:7.

_____

_____

_____

HE is a
SHIELD
to those who
WALK
in
INTEGRITY.
Proverbs 2:7b

How I love promises given for our offspring. I pray and yearn I will walk in integrity so my children and grandchildren will be blessed. A righteous woman or man's offspring are blessed when they walk in integrity. The Rechabites descendants were going to be blessed because of their forefather's integrity.

God also says that, "He who walks in integrity walks securely..." Proverbs 10:9a and in Proverbs 2:7b, "...He is a shield to those who walk in integrity."

"Integrity is the glue that holds our way of life together. We must constantly strive to keep our integrity intact. When wealth is lost, nothing is lost; when health is lost, something is lost; when character is lost, all is lost."[6] Maintaining integrity is a constant battle for all of us. It requires turning away from temptation when it beckons. Going the extra mile and not taking the easy way out.

The God of the universe was trying to show the Judeans this through the Rechabites. Eugene Peterson said it well:

"If you think that (it) is too rigorous a life for mortal human beings (meaning the life God was asking the people of Judah to live – holy and upright lives/ obedient lives), think again. The Recabites are ordinary, mortal human beings, and they have been doing it for 250 years. Don't just look at them. Don't just talk about them. Pay attention to what is distinctive about them. They are not entertainment, they are example. Let them show you how badly and boringly you live — and how well you can live. There is not a single person in Jerusalem who is not up to living consciously and deliberately as a child of God, and then practicing the distinctive disciplines that support and preserve a life of faith. But you have let the crowd turn you into spectators and consumers. You have let your lives get flabby and indulgent. You have ignored the best things that have ever been said to you – God's word!—and let the chatter and gossip of the crowd fill your ears. You have abandoned the simple actions that people of faith have used for centuries to keep in touch with the truth of God ..."[7]

The Rechabites were an excellent example not only to the Judeans, but to us as well. Hold to the high standard God has called you to. "And do not be conformed to this world, but be transformed by the renewing of your mind, that you may prove what the will of God is, that which is good and acceptable and perfect" (Romans 12:2).

Have you known someone who, like the Rechabites, was so self-disciplined that nothing distracted them? Share with your study group an example of someone you know who holds to a higher standard of integrity than you usually encounter.

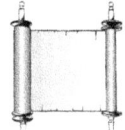

Reflection

What character traits need development or improvement in your life to become more like who you admire?

As you think about that person of integrity, remind yourself, with God's help, you are able to live a life of integrity as well. Have a wonderful day choosing to live an upright and honorable life! See you tomorrow!

DAY 5

Jeremiah's Lifestyle & The Sabbath Day

Begin this day with prayer. Tell Jesus your thoughts and lay down your burdens at His feet. Get ready to listen to what Christ has to say to you in His Word! Today is about two different subjects–Jeremiah's lifestyle and how God has called all of us to keep the Sabbath day holy.

Begin by reading Jeremiah 16:1-9. What kind of lifestyle did God call Jeremiah to?

_____

_____

Jeremiah was called to a life of celibacy. In Jeremiah's society, a life without marriage was not considered a blessing. According to Thompson, "In the ancient Near East, and therefore in Israel, a large family betokened divine blessing (Genesis 22:17; Psalm 127:3-4). Sterility and barrenness, on the other hand, were regarded as a curse (Genesis 30:1; 1 Samuel 1:6-8), and virginity was regarded as a cause for mourning (Judges 11:37)."[1] It was obviously a lonely road at times for Jeremiah to not have the privilege of a wife and children.

Why do you think God called Jeremiah to remain separate?

_____

_____

Some scholars claim that because marriage is mentioned Jeremiah may have wanted to marry. Likely, he did want to marry as this was the custom. Have you ever watched the movie Jeremiah by Patrick Dempsey made in 1998? It portrays Jeremiah as being in love with a beautiful young lady in his youth he had grown up with and how he had to choose to obey what God asked of him or go after the woman he loved and marry her. The movie showed the heartbreak they both went through as Jeremiah chose to serve God. While a similar relationship may or may not have really happened, we can clearly assume it was a hard choice for Jeremiah to remain celibate. It would have been quite a lonely life at times to not have little ones running around at your side or a wife to keep you warm at night. Thankfully, God does not call all of His servants to live this kind of lifestyle. I'm afraid some of us would never make it! I know I'm one of them! However, I do believe God wanted Jeremiah to live this way for a special reason. This was no ordinary call on a man's life. God was desperately trying to awaken the people to the horrific impending destruction that was going to take place if they didn't change their ways. By having Jeremiah lead a life of extreme deprivation, God was trying to awaken the Judeans. He was a sign to the Judeans. Jeremiah was to live in such a way, fully expecting the prophecies he was giving the people to come true very shortly, thus denying himself the typical pleasures of life.[2]

By the description of what was going to happen to Jerusalem, ultimately God was protecting and caring for Jeremiah by not allowing him to have a wife and children. At least then he would not have to see the horror of their starvation and probable deaths. Plus, if he had children it would have distracted him from completing the mission he was sent to accomplish. He would have undoubtedly been tempted to preach less to avoid being punished and stripped away from his family. Also, he would have had to work harder at making money to provide food and shelter for his family; and his family would have required basic relationship nurturing, taking more time away from his ministry.

What does Paul say in 1 Corinthians 7:32-35 concerning the difference between being unmarried and married?

_____

While not many are called to celibacy, some are. However, it is important to remind ourselves of how God made us. He made man and woman for one another. That's not hard to figure out! We fit together right, both physically and emotionally (each being completely polar opposite, but meant for one another!) Now, that is not to say if you're single you aren't complete. I don't mean that at all. In fact, we are all made complete in our salvation through Jesus Christ, whether married or single. Our marital status has nothing to do with completeness. Marriage is the only time when two single whole people, complete in Him come together to make a new whole, a complete singular picture of Christ even though they are two distinct people. I will say that those who think they need to be married to be complete are entering marriage on false assumptions and are destined for trouble. If God calls you to celibacy then you are complete in Him. However, my point is this, not many are called to live a lifestyle like Jeremiah's.

Read Genesis 2:18 and write it out.

_____

_____

_____

Whether you are single, like Jeremiah, or married, fulfill the responsibilities to which God has called you to. Don't be so wrapped up in the things of this world that you are not effective or useful for His kingdom. Don't waste time on things that don't matter.

In Jeremiah 16:3-4, God describes the destruction coming to the inhabitants of Jerusalem. They'll die of deadly diseases, sword, and famine and they won't even be given a proper burial. In the ancient Near East it was considered a curse not to be buried.³

According to Deuteronomy 28:15, 26, why would the Judeans corpses become food for the birds and the beasts?

_____

_____

Read Jeremiah 16:5-9. Why do you think God didn't allow Jeremiah to join in the normal rituals of mourning and wedding festivities?

_____

_____

Thompson suggests this was done to reveal Jeremiah had withdrawn from the activities of normal living, just like God had withdrawn from His people because they had broken their covenant with God.⁴ "His (Jeremiah's) own separateness, was a powerful testimony to the separateness of Yahweh as his people turned away from him."⁵

Why did Jesus tell one of his disciples to allow the dead to bury their own dead (Matthew 8:21-22)?

_____

_____

Does this mean we can't bury our own loved ones? I don't believe this was what Jesus was trying to say. He wasn't against funerals. Obviously, He himself was buried and Lazarus too. He was assessing the disciple's heart seeing if he would leave it all for Him. Some think this man's father was only old and not likely to live many more years due to his age. Others believe the father may have been sick, dying, or dead. At first glance, it seems to be a reasonable plea from the man. However, Jesus was pointing out that putting our earthly duties above God's call was not giving Him complete Lordship. Following God is not about when we're "ready," but now. There will always be social obligations in our life that we deem necessary and good, but our full allegiance should be to Christ, not to those social obligations. Many are hindered by their over-concern for their families and neglect and postpone serving God fully.⁶

Does this mean we are not supposed to care for our families? Read Ephesians 6:1-3. What do these verses say?

_____

_____

_____

Obviously, we are to honor our parents. God wasn't saying to not honor our parents in Matthew. Jesus, in Matthew 8, was just trying to weed out any weak commitments to Him. He wanted them to know the cost of discipleship up front. He demands that if we be true followers, we place Him and what He is telling us to do above everything else.

In Jeremiah's case, Jeremiah showed his loyalty to God by not participating in normal activities of living such as funerals and weddings. The act of burial was not wrong.

Read Leviticus 19:27-28 and Deuteronomy 14:1. What do these say about these practices?

_____

_____

_____

The word Sabbath in the Hebrew means intermission.

Ezekiel, another prophet who lived during the time of Judah's disobedience, was also used as an example in his personal life of how God's judgment was coming upon the people and that the death toll would be so great when Jerusalem fell that those surviving wouldn't even be able to mourn properly.

Read how Ezekiel's tragedy of losing his beloved wife was an object lesson to the people. Read Ezekiel 24:15-27. What thoughts do you have concerning this passage?

_____

_____

_____

Ezekiel's prophetic career occurred in Babylon after he was deported to Babylon (the 2nd deportation) in 597 B.C. He began his prophetic ministry 4 years after his deportation.[7] He was an interesting man! If you haven't read about him, open and dig into the book of Ezekiel. He made Jeremiah look normal!

One point God is trying to make in this passage is that He calls all of us to live in different ways. Each prophet in the Old Testament lived uniquely. Think about Hosea – he was called to marry a harlot. Ezekiel lost his wife. Jeremiah was not to marry anyone. God uses diverse people and circumstances to accomplish His purposes.

Read Jeremiah 17:19-27. Then look up Exodus 20:8-11. Fill in the blanks (Exodus 20:8-10a) below:

Week 3

"Remember the _____ day, to keep it _____. _____ days you shall labor and do _____ your _____, but the _____ day is a Sabbath of the Lord your God: in it you shall not do any work..."

The word Sabbath in the Hebrew means intermission.[8] In essence, the Sabbath means take an intermission or take a break! It's like when we take an intermission at a football game or during the middle of a theatrical production. It gives us a chance to take a break. We can go to the bathroom, get a snack, or talk over what's gone on in the game/theatre so far. The Sabbath is an intermission from our work week; a time to rest, relax, and contemplate what's gone on and what's coming up. The Sabbath gives us a chance to spend dedicated time with God and other believers. Notice in the text, where this command is given. Keeping the Sabbath Day holy is one of the Ten Commandments. I'll have to admit that before reading this verse, I thought I could list off all the other Ten Commandments by heart, but I had forgotten that this command was one of them!

Read Exodus 31:12-18. What was the Sabbath a sign of?

_____

_____

The word "sign" in Exodus 31:13 means, "banners, omens, pledges, standards, witness, wondrous" in the Hebrew. The word "sanctifies," in the same verse, means "to become set apart or consecrated" become holy, purified, made it holy, transmit holiness, and treat me as holy."[9]

The Sabbath reminds us God has set us apart and made us holy. It reminds us of our covenant relationship with Christ. If we don't rest one day weekly and make God a priority on that day we quickly forget the reason we're here on earth and become fatigued. If I don't rest from work and give Him priority one day a week, I find I get caught up in things that don't satisfy me long-term and that drain my energy so I'm not able to hear God clearly and do His will. Notice in Jeremiah 17:24-25, there is a conditional clause — If you keep the Sabbath...then you will receive a covenantal blessing, but *if* you don't (vs. 27), **then** you'll be cursed.

How does God want us to view the Sabbath — in a sullen or joyful way? Read Isaiah 58:13-14 and write out what the attitude of our hearts should be.

_____

_____

_____

How many times have you seen grumpy Christians coming to church? Perhaps you are one of them! This is not to be our demeanor on the Sabbath! We're to celebrate the opportunity to come to worship and give reverence to our Lord.

The Sabbath day was again compromised by some of the exiles after they returned from Babylon, but look at how quickly Nehemiah put a stop to this. Read Nehemiah 13:15-22. What were the people doing similarly on the Sabbath day before and after their exile in Babylon?

_____

_____

_____

How quickly the Judeans forgot! They were trying to make a profit on everything imaginable, never resting. Greed is what drove them. Just as the power of the almighty dollar ensnares many today and yes even us at times. We have to watch ourselves carefully to keep the Sabbath day a holy day!

End today by writing out one thing you could do in your own family to make the Sabbath day more holy:

_____

_____

_____

Share with your study group what changes you have made the next time you meet. Have a great rest of your day!

NOTES

VIDEO NOTE QUESTIONS WEEK 3

1. Think about some practical ways in your own life that Jesus may be telling you to follow Him. Is there a cost involved? Is it worth it?
2. While truly following Christ costs us some comforts/luxuries on Earth, what are the benefits of following Him?
3. Think of a situation that might cause someone to persecute you for being a follower of Christ. How would you stand up to the ridicule/persecution?
4. How are we to act when persecuted, according to Matthew 10? How did Jeremiah act when persecuted?
5. What does it mean when Jesus says, "Do you think that I came to bring peace on the earth; I did not come to bring peace, but a sword" (Matthew 10:34)?

Video sessions are available for download at www.grassandflowers.org

WEEK FOUR
TAKING CAPTIVITY CAPTIVE

DAY ONE
Garbage!

DAY TWO
The Kings

DAY THREE
A Good Leader

DAY FOUR
The Coming Righteous Branch

DAY FIVE
False Prophets

DAY 1

Garbage!

Good day to you! Hope this day finds you well. Today we are going to study at the site of a garbage dump and the stocks of persecution. Get ready to put on your nose plug to diminish the stench you are about to smell and brace yourself for the harassment and maltreatment our favorite prophet Jeremiah is going to experience.

Would you ever have thought one of God's great object lessons would have taken place at a garbage dump? Imagine the stench that emanated from the rubbish. Sometimes, we too have sin that needs to be discarded and we don't even realize how smelly the sin is. God is willing to remove that stinky garbage called sin from our lives if we'll let Him and God eventually did this for the Judeans when they were taken into captivity. However, in this chapter, He first had to deal with the Judeans' sin. The putrid smell of their disobedience filled His nostrils, just like a waste disposal site would fill our nostrils with objectionable smells. Their sin was abhorrent to God and it was time for them to repent or God's judgment would come down on their sinful deeds.

Begin this lesson by praying, and then read Jeremiah 19.

What repulsive sin occurred in the valley of Ben-hinnom (Jeremiah 19:4-5)?

_____

_____

The valley of Ben-hinnom had been a place where Jerusalem's inhabitants worshipped idols and sacrificed their children to Baal, acts clearly forbidden by God. During the reign of King Josiah, the valley was made into a landfill, after Josiah removed the high places.[1] The valley of Ben-hinnom ended up acquiring several names, none of them very pleasant. One of the valley's names was Topheth. The word Topheth means a "fire pit, a hearth"–named this because the children had been put through the fire there.[2] Eventually, after the Babylonian invasion, the valley took on a different name, the valley of Slaughter, and those killed in Jerusalem during the invasion, were buried there.

According to John Guest in The Preacher's Commentary, the valley of Ben-hinnom was not only a place where garbage was burned, but also where the bodies of criminals were cremated.[3] Obviously, this site was an undesirable place. The fact that Jeremiah convinced the elders and the senior priests to accompany him there was an amazing feat! Jeremiah brought the elders and civic leaders who endorsed the messages of the false prophets, so it makes one wonder if they had other reasons for following Jeremiah out there.[4]

Why do you think the elders and priests were willing to listen to Jeremiah's prophetic words?

_____

_____

_____

It took tremendous courage for Jeremiah to lead those men to the valley of Ben-hinnom and deliver God's message, especially knowing the disdain they held for him. It makes me wonder if they intended to frame him, passing on his words to the leaders of the city.

How is the destruction of Jerusalem and the siege described in Jeremiah 19:7-9?

_____

_____

_____

> Smashing the **pot** SIGNIFIED how *irreparable* the *Judeans* were!

The siege on Jerusalem would be so horrendous that fathers and mothers would resort to eating their own dead children, because there was no food. God was pointing out to the elders and the priests how distressing and demoralizing the destruction in Jerusalem would be if they would not turn back to Him.

How does Jeremiah symbolically display what is going to happen to Jerusalem? Look at Jeremiah 19:10-11.

_____

_____

_____

Smashing the pot signified how irreparable the Judeans were. In the previous chapter of Jeremiah, God used clay to describe how pliable it can be before it hardens. Yet, in this passage, it shoed the opposite. It described what happens to clay after it hardens, clay being God's people, when they don't allow God to make them into a vessel that glorifies Him.[5] It reveals quite a contrast between God's mercy and His judgment.

Read Jeremiah 19:14-15. After prophesying in Topheth, where did Jeremiah next go to prophesy?

_____

Jeremiah went straight from Topheth, the garbage dump, to the temple to give the same message to all of the inhabitants of Jerusalem, so not just the priests and elders heard it. One priest in the temple, however, did not like Jeremiah's message. Read how Pashur, a priest, responded to Jeremiah's prophesy.

Read Jeremiah 20:1-2. What did Pashur do to Jeremiah after he prophesied in the temple?

_____

_____

_____

Pashur resisted Jeremiah's message. I wonder how the crowd at the temple responded to Jeremiah? They probably were not followers of him either. Jeremiah was beaten and then tortured in the stocks. Imagine the shame and pain of being locked up in the stocks overnight. The stocks were at the upper Benjamin Gate, near the temple, a public place where many would have passed by Jeremiah and mocked and ridiculed him. The stocks immobilized victims by placing boards around their legs and/or wrists and sometimes the victim's head was placed through the board as well. While the stocks were physically uncomfortable, they also left the victim at the mercy of the population. Anybody could assault them, throwing stones or rotten food at them. The stocks subjected the victim to whatever weather might be occurring — rain, cold, and extreme heat. One author suggests Jeremiah might have been placed in a twist frame stock which clamps the victim in a position that causes increasing distress.[6] Whether Jeremiah was placed in a typical stock or a twist frame stock, Jeremiah was treated cruelly. According to Matthew Henry, the method used to silence Jeremiah was done illegally—the high priest and the other priests should have consulted and examined Jeremiah's words before putting him in the stocks.[7]

Ermess/Shutterstock

Though Jeremiah was treated inhumanely, Pashur was about to reap what he had sown. While Jeremiah was locked up in the stocks, God was right by Jeremiah's side. God spoke to Jeremiah that night and told him all about what was in store for Pashur.

Read Jeremiah 20:3-6. What was the new name God gave Pashur?

_____

_____

Magor-missabib means "terror on every side." In fact, the phrase "terror on every side" is commonly used throughout the book of Jeremiah.[8]

Let's see how many times this phrase was mentioned in Jeremiah and Lamentations. Match the verses on the left with the correct verse on the right:

____ Jeremiah 6:25	a. "Thou didst call as in the day of an appointed feast my terrors on every side and there was no one who escaped or survived…"
____ Jeremiah 20:10	b. "They will take away their tents and their flocks; they will carry off for themselves their tent curtains, all their goods, and their camels, and they will call out to one another, 'Terror on every side!'"
____ Jeremiah 46:5	c. "…and their mighty men are defeated and have taken refuge in flight, without facing back; terror is on every side!"
____ Jeremiah 49:29	d. "Do not go out into the field, and do not walk on the road, for the enemy has a sword, terror is on every side."
____ Lamentations 2:22	e. "For I have heard the whispering of many, 'Terror on every side'…"

The phrase "terror on every side" was not only a popular phrase in Jeremiah's times, but commonly used in King David's day as well. Read Psalm 31:13 and describe how the phrase was used there.

_____

_____

Pashur being named "Terror on every side" was not a becoming name to be given! Imagine your name being changed to that. How differently people would view you with that kind of a name.

Reread Jeremiah 20:4. What do you think God meant when He said Pashur would be a terror to himself and to all his friends?

_____

_____

Matthew Henry's Commentary describes Jeremiah 20:4 like this, "a terror to himself" meant Pashur would be "subject to continual frights, and thy (his) own fancy and imagination shall (would) create thee (for him) a constant uneasiness." Also, Pashur would be a terror to his friends meant, "thou shalt (he would), upon all occasions, express thyself (himself) with so much horror and amazement that all thy (his) friends shall (would) be afraid of conversing with thee (him) and shall (would) choose to stand aloof from thy (his) torment."⁹ I chose to adapt what Matthew Henry said in the parentheses because his old English style of writing was a challenge to understand otherwise.

Basically, Pashur became emotionally unstable. He was severely distraught at what might happen to him and to others. He was so full of paranoia even his friends didn't want to be around him.

Besides feeling terrorized by his own thoughts, what else was Pashur going to have to face (Jeremiah 20:6)?

_____

_____

Pashur was given a death sentence.¹⁰ No wonder why he felt a little on edge after what Jeremiah told him! Not only was he told about his own death, but he was also told about the location of his death and burial. That was a shameful and scary prospect for him to have to consider. "For a Jew to be buried outside his own land was considered a judgment, for the Gentile lands were considered unclean." ¹¹

Pashur hoped to silence Jeremiah by torturing him, but it didn't work. Instead, he heaped a curse upon himself. Pashur, while a prominent and well respected leader in his city, was also a false prophet (Jeremiah 20:6). He chose to tickle the ears of his hearers, instead of giving them the hard core truth.

Ever known anyone like Pashur? Maybe you can think of someone in a leadership position such as your government, workplace, or a religious institution. Tell us what you've seen.

_____

_____

_____

_____

Unfortunately, today it seems some leaders are not much better than Pashur. In the case of the United States, leaders may not use forms of torment like Pashur did to Jeremiah, but they sometimes mock, lie, and use character assassination to promote their own cause. I feel like we watch this almost every time there is a local or federal election coming up. The smear campaigns are degrading to their opponents. And the promises they make sometimes are only given to tickle our ears, so we'll elect them, not because they plan on necessarily fulfilling them.

Pashur HOPED

to **silence**

J E R E M I A H

by torturing him,

but it **didn't WORK.**

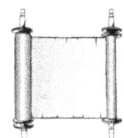

We're going to shift our focus now to Jeremiah 20:7-18. It reveals how Jeremiah responded to being treated harshly. It is generally believed among Biblical commentators that Jeremiah 20:7-18 was Jeremiah's reaction to the persecution he underwent from prophesying in the valley of Ben-himmon and the temple.

Read Jeremiah 20:7-18. Circle how Jeremiah felt in these verses:

Deceived by God	Expectant
Mocked	Betrayed by friends
Joyful	An over comer with God's help
Defeated	Wished he hadn't been born
Sorrowful	Shameful
Proud	Loved

Honesty with *God*  is a requirement *if* **we're going to stay sane** throughout *life's* **trials** and **TRIBULATIONS.**

What a beautiful unedited prayer Jeremiah offers in this passage. It's as if Jeremiah had a spiritual tug of war. He went from feeling taken advantage of by God and bewildered by all the ridicule he received from preaching to breaking out in praise and sharing how protected he felt with God. After his brief encounter with praise, he then plummets back into despair wishing he'd never been born. I just have to say, it's nice to know that we, like Jeremiah, can come to God in total despair and vent our raw feelings to Him. Honesty with God is a requirement if we're going to stay sane throughout life's trials and tribulations. Thankfully, after airing our anguish on God, God isn't thrown off balance by what we say. Instead, He's compassionate and loving, welcoming us back into His loving arms. Jeremiah, because of his close communion with God, felt in a safe place to lay it all out there. Hopefully, you feel the same way with God.

Discuss with your group if you feel safe or unsafe sharing your feelings with God. Why or why not?

_____

_____

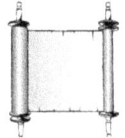

Some of you may have grown up in a home where feelings were not discussed. Therefore, you buried your feelings deep down, losing confidence anyone would even want to hear about them, even God. On the other hand, maybe you had a parent(s) that openly communicated, but didn't share their feelings in a healthy manner. For instance, they took their feelings out on each other and you through anger, making you wonder if you could trust

God and if He was going to get angry with you for expressing your feelings, just like your parents did. And of course, some of you had parents, though not perfect, really did communicate in a healthy fashion. They loved you no matter what you said and gave you the benefit of the doubt. No matter what kind of parenting you experienced, do not let it impact your relationship with the Lord in a negative manner. He is always waiting to dialogue with you. He is not surprised by your emotions. He desires to help you work through your troubles. And though the troubles may not resolve, He will offer you peace in the midst of them.

Look back at Jeremiah 20:10, how did Jeremiah's friends treat him?

_____

Have your friends ever treated you like this for standing up and speaking God's words? Explain what happened. How did it make you feel?

_____

_____

_____

Hopefully, your friends have not treated you like this before. However, if we're following God, we are running the risk of this happening at some point. Especially if God gives us a hard message for others to swallow, which He often does! I can't imagine the way that Jeremiah must have felt at this point in his career. He had been mocked, tortured, felt like all of his preaching was for naught, because none of it had come true yet. Others thought he was committing treason to his own beloved country who he diligently prayed for, and to top it all off, his closest friends deserted him when he needed them most. Yet, despite the torment Jeremiah underwent emotionally, he did not stop prophesying.

His Word burns in my heart like a fire!

Write out what Jeremiah said in Jeremiah 20:9.

_____

_____

_____

Jeremiah had to prophecy! So filled with the Holy Spirit, he could not help but prophesy! It wearied him to withhold God's message from them. He couldn't stop thinking about what God had told him to speak to Judah, even though he would have liked to get away from it all sometimes.

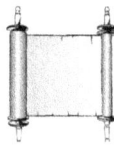

Have you ever felt tormented by not sharing the message God told you to speak to someone? Name an instance.

_____

_____

_____

Maybe, like the story of Jonah and the big fish, you tried to run away from speaking God's words, but no matter where you went or who you avoided, the Spirit of God would not stop telling you to go and obey His command. I think this is what Jeremiah was feeling. He wished he could have run away from it all, but if he had stopped prophesying the message, the Holy Spirit would not have left him alone. This is how the Spirit of God works.

How does Paul in the New Testament describe the same feelings? Read 1 Corinthians 9:16.

_____

_____

We, like Jeremiah, may be tempted to think God has put too much on us. However, if God has called us, which He has, He warns us there will be trials and tribulations. It will be rough at times when we stand up for Him. God warned Jeremiah early on in his ministry, tumultuous times were ahead in his interactions with people. Go back to Jeremiah 1:18-19 and reread it. God told Jeremiah in these verses the people would fight against him, but they would not overcome him because God would deliver him. We too must not lose hope when persecuted for Christ. We may wish we were never born, like Jeremiah. However, God is still in control and willing to help us. Jeremiah could speak candidly with God because he felt safe with God. Jeremiah poured out every thought to God; living in close companionship with Him, finding satisfaction with Him despite the difficulties he went though.[12]

"No one becomes human the way Jeremiah was human by posing in a posture of victory. It was his prayers, hidden but persistent that brought him to the human wholeness and sensitivity that we want. What we do in secret determines the soundness of who we are in public. Prayer is the secret work that develops a life that is thoroughly authentic and deeply human."[13] May our relationship with God be like Jeremiah's connection with God.

We will end on that note. Take your thoughts and struggles to God right now. Let Him converse with you.

Prayer: God, help us to bring our troubles to you with as much candor as Jeremiah did. May we not be afraid to speak the truth even if we are ridiculed for it. And thank you for being by our side and protecting us when we stand up for You. We love you Jesus. Amen.

DAY 2

The Kings

God's message has gone from offering the Judeans forgiveness if they will repent to the lesson of the smashed pot in the garbage dump, signifying they are no longer repairable because of their unwillingness to repent. The only way God could transform them was to take them into captivity.

Read Hebrews 12:11. Write out the verse.

_____

_____

_____

_____

If we're not willing to learn from God the easy way, then we will have to learn things the hard way. For those of you who have kids, I'm sure you can relate to this theory! When my kids like to test the water, and disobey me, they receive discipline. When they obey me willingly, they receive praise and are given more privileges. Now, maybe you've just had easy kids to raise, generally obedient and perfect angels. However, if you've ever raised a strong-willed child, you can relate to God's concept of discipline!

Judah was at a point where there was no turning back. Judah's leadership and the townspeople had made unwise decisions, not taking seriously the warnings God had given through Jeremiah. God's patience had run out and He had to act. King Nebuchadnezzar had had enough of Judah as well. King Jehoiakim, Judah's king, had not given him the tribute due him (a payment Judah was to give regularly to Babylon acknowledging their submission to Babylon). Remember, Judah was a vassal state under Babylon at this time, meaning Babylon was in charge of them and they had to show their submission to them by paying tribute to them on a regular basis or they would be violating the rules placed on them by Babylon and opening up the door to Babylon disciplining them through military force.

Let's open with reading 2 Chronicles 36:5-9. Grasp the significance of the message that God spoke. We are about to say goodbye to Jehoiakim, a disliked and foolish king.

How old was King Jehoiakim when he was taken off of the throne by King Nebuchadnezzar?

_____

At first glance, it seems Nebuchadnezzar bound Jehoiakim in chains and took him to Babylon, but if you'll notice carefully, that is not what the verse says. 2 Chronicles 36:6 states Nebuchadnezzar, "bound him with bronze chains to take him to Babylon." The verse does not say he was taken to Babylon, only that he was prepared to take him there. Maybe you did "get" that the first time you read it, but I sure didn't! Eerdman's Dictionary of the Bible states, "Jehoiakim was 'bound in fetters' by Nebuchadnezzar and threatened with deportation. Whether the Babylonian king actually deported Jehoiakim or simply frightened him into submission is impossible to determine from the text."[1]

What does 2 Kings 24:6 say concerning where Jehoiakim was buried?

_____

_____

2 Kings 24:6 leads one to believe Jehoiakim died in Judah and was never taken to Babylon. Although this passage of Scripture describes Jehoiakim's burial in a peaceful manner, it wasn't anything like that. His burial may have been described diplomatically in 2 Kings because that was the standard way to address a king's death. However, as you will read in other passages, there was no lament for his death and no reverent burial given. The theory that Jehoiakim died in Jerusalem, not Babylon, is also confirmed by what Jeremiah said in the following passages concerning Jehoiakim's death.

Read Jeremiah 22:18-19 and Jeremiah 36:30. Describe Jehoiakim's burial. Why do you think Jehoiakim was buried in such a humiliating fashion?

_____

_____

_____

_____

"According to Josephus (Antiquities, X.vi.3) it was Nebuchadnezzar who had his (Jehoiakim's) body 'thrown before the walls, without any burial'."[2] Jehoiakim was a tyrant. He "gave his mind to trivialities at a time of crisis, and who saw his subjects only as exploitable."[3] Jehoiakim didn't pay those who built and worked on making his palace more elaborate. He was having his house enlarged and enhanced, when he should have been worrying about his people and the imminent danger his country was facing.

Looking back at 2 Chronicles 36:8-9 (make sure you are using the NASB translation), who replaced King Jehoiakim on the throne? How old was this new king? How was he related to King Jehoiakim?

_____

_____

Now look at 2 Kings 24:8. How old was Jehoiachin described here?

_____

Read 2 Kings 24:15. What makes one believe that Jehoiachin must have been 18 years old, instead of 8 years old? (Note: Only 3 months after Jehoiachin was made king, he was deported to Babylon.)

_____

From all of my readings, all authors seem to agree Jehoiachin was 18 years old, instead of 8 years old. This makes sense considering Jehoiachin's wives were to be taken with him to Babylon and it would be hard to find a reason for him to have had wives at the young age of 8!

Jehoiachin had a couple different names. Coniah was an abbreviation for Jehoiachin's name and another form of his name was Jeconiah.4 Jehoiachin, King Jehoiakim's son, reigned for a 3 month period during 598-597 B.C.

Read Jeremiah 22:24-30. This is a message from God to Jehoiachin (also known as Coniah). What is going to come to pass with Jehoiachin and his mother?

_____

_____

The Babylonian Chronicles, clay tablets from ancient Mesopotamia recording historical Babylonian events, report Nebuchadnezzar left Babylon in December 598 B.C. on a campaign against Judah to besiege Jerusalem.5 It was during this siege of March 597 B.C. that most of the people from Jerusalem were taken captive to Babylon. Jehoiachin and his mother were taken along with them. This siege is considered by most scholars to be the first deportation of the inhabitants of Judah, with two more deportations to come. Even after he was exiled to Babylon, many still considered Jehoiachin the rightful king of Judah. Jeremiah did not encourage this line of thought though.6

Addendum 1 on page 246 shows the 4 deportations of the Judeans to Babylon.

In Jeremiah 22:30, God mentions Jehoiachin will be deemed childless. Yet, later in the same verse, God describes Jehoiachin as having descendants. According to Scripture, Jehoiachin did have children. What do you think God meant by saying Jehoiachin would be childless?

_____

_____

_____

Read 1 Chronicles 3:17-18. How many children do we know for sure that Jehoiachin (Jeconiah) had?

_____

At first glance it looks like God missed the mark by saying Jehoiachin would be childless. However, God did not mean Jeconiah wouldn't have any children. What God meant was none of Jehoiachin's descendants would ever be on the throne of David.7 For Jehoiachin that would be like not having any children because of the shame associated with an heir not ascending to the throne.

Despite that Jehoiachin did evil, and never had his own children on the throne, God did bring redemption to Jehoiachin's descendants. While God could not provide a spot for Jehoiachin's children on the throne, Jehoiachin was still placed in the genealogy of Christ!

Read Matthew 1:11-12. Describe how God showed Jehoiachin great mercy.

_____

Of course, remember other people in the genealogy of Christ did some awful things too and they were still mentioned!

In Jeremiah 22:24, God refers to Jehoiachin as a signet ring. Do any of you know what a signet ring represented?

_____

A signet ring was used for several reasons by a king. First, it symbolized political authority. Secondly, it was used as a device to make a seal, an impression on documents to be considered a way of binding any verbal commands he gave.8

Wiersbe points out, "A signet ring was valuable because it was used to prove authority, identify possessions, and 'sign' official documents, but Jehoiachin was useless to the Lord, fit only to be thrown away in Babylon."9

However, there was another man, Jehoiachin's very own grandson, who was also referred to as a signet ring. No coincidence, I'm sure. Read about him in Haggai 2:20-23. How is Zerubbabel described as a signet ring?

_____

_____

Interesting how both Jehoiachin and Zerubbabel were both described as signet rings. The former being described as inadequate and worthless and the latter described as useful, a chosen one and special. In fact, Zerubbabel was one of the leaders who helped bring back the captives from Babylon when they returned to Jerusalem 70 years later. It goes to show God can redeem any family, no matter what the extent of their wickedness! This should give hope to all of us!

God can REDEEM **any** *family!*

Go back to Matthew 1:12-13 and read Zerubbabel's name listed in these verses. Then go to the genealogy of Jesus Luke wrote in Luke 3:23-38. Zerubbabel's name is listed in verse 27; notice Jehoiachin is not mentioned in the genealogy written by Luke. Isn't that interesting? For an explanation of the difference between Matthew and Luke's accounts read below:

"The genealogy in Matthew 1 traces Christ's ancestry through His legal father Joseph. Since Jehoiachin is in that family tree (Matthew 1:11), however, none of his descendants can claim the throne because of the curse pronounced in Jeremiah 22:24-30. Our Lord gets His Davidic throne rights through His mother Mary, whose genealogy is given in Luke 3:21-38. From Abraham to David, the lists are similar, but from David on, they differ. Luke traced the line through David's son Nathan and thus avoided Jehoiachin, a descendant of Solomon."[10]

Kamira/Shutterstock

While Jehoiachin didn't get the privilege of being mentioned in both genealogies, he was later blessed in his life, in the sense of being shown kindness. How many years was it before Jehoiachin was released from prison (2 Kings 25:27-30 and Jeremiah 52:31-34)?

_____

Besides releasing Jehoiachin from prison, what other kinds of favors did Evil-merodach, a king of Babylon after Nebuchadnezzar, do for Jehoiachin (Jeremiah 52:32-34)? What happened to Jehoiachin in Jeremiah 52:32?

_____

_____

Evil-merodach was Nebuchadnezzar II's son. Obviously, Evil-merodach gave Jehoiachin great respect and treated him kindly. "Babylonians respected Jehoiachin as the rightful king of Judah. Cuneiform tablets (documents written on clay tablets, one of the earliest known forms of writing) have been found mentioning the provisions which were supplied to Jehoiachin and his five sons."[11] So, in the end, Jehoichin didn't fair too badly.

In Jeremiah 22, we encountered the consequences of Judah's kings' disobedience. While these kings were poor examples of quality leadership, we will learn tomorrow of a king that is an exemplary leader, one that beats all, the coming Messiah, Judah's future hope.

Prayer: God we've seen over the last few weeks what a powerful difference those in leadership can make for good or for evil. We ask You make us into leaders that do nothing for selfish gain. May our actions glorify You. We pray for those in authority over us that You would make yourself known to them and guide them. If they don't know You, please open their eyes to see You clearly. Help those in our own government to repent of any sin holding them back and to put into action Your just ways. Thank You for hearing our cries and longing to heal our nation. Amen.

DAY 3

A Good Leader

Today, we'll go from evaluating unrighteous kings to examining the One King who is the ultimate righteous king.

Start by reading Jeremiah 23:1-8. Who are the shepherds considered to be in this passage?

_____

Noel Powell/Shutterstock

The shepherds were the kings of Judah. In fact, the last 4 kings of Judah – Jehoiahaz, Jehoiakim, Jehoiachin, and Zedekiah (Zedekiah being a king you haven't heard about yet, but will be hearing about soon). The last 4 kings of Judah were bad shepherds. Besides the kings though, the shepherds also consisted of the civil leaders who had oversight over the kingdom of Judah, those directly under the kings.[1]

What were the bad shepherds accused of (Jeremiah 23:1-2)?

_____

_____

What is a good shepherd supposed to do with his sheep?

_____

_____

> Those in **AUTHORITY** are **CALLED** TO BE **SHEPHERDS!**

The word shepherd (ra'ah in the Hebrew), according to the Strong's lexicon from the Blue Letter Bible online means, "to tend to and feed a flock, to guard, to care for, to rule, to govern; to furnish pasture for food, to look upon with pleasure."[2]

Judah's kings and the direct leadership under them had not tended to or cared for their flock. Instead, they had neglected and used them for their own selfish gain. Instead of cherishing them and making sure they had plenty of food and had their spiritual needs met, they were more concerned about meeting and nourishing their own egos. The rulers viewed their subjects as inferiors, treating them with contempt, which eventually led to the nation's demise. The leaders of Judah failed to realize their shepherd character and fulfill their shepherd function.[3]

Those in authority are called to be shepherds to those under their leadership. If you're an administrator in a business, a Sunday school teacher in your church, or the leader of any organization, whether it be religious or nonreligious, it is a requirement of your job to be a good shepherd to those under your care. Unfortunately, leaders may fall into the trap of using their authority abusively if they don't guard against it. Let the kings of Judah be a warning to you if you are a leader.

Week 4

According to God, what was the job of a king to entail? Read Jeremiah 21:11-12.

_____

While this job description is specifically given to the new incoming King Zedekiah, it is what all of the kings should have been implementing. And it is definitely what the righteous King Jesus brought into effect when He came into the world showing us what a true leader is to look like. Jesus came administering justice and delivering us from the power of the oppressor — Satan.

Look up 1 Peter 5:1-4. Describe how the elders of the church are to shepherd the church.

_____

_____

_____

Do you think this passage (1 Peter 5:1-4) could apply to any leadership position, even outside of the church? Explain your answer.

_____

_____

Let's read some verses about our Chief Shepherd, the keeper of our souls. Match the following verses on the left to their general theme on the right-hand side:

_____ Psalm 23:1-3	a. Jesus – the Shepherd and guardian of our souls.
_____ Isaiah 40:11	b. God will tend to his flock and gather them into His arms, gently leading them.
_____ Micah 5:4	c. He will arise and shepherd His flock.
_____ John 10:14-15	d. The Lord is my Shepherd and takes care of all my needs.
_____ 1 Peter 2:25	e. The Chief Shepherd will lay down his life for the sheep.

Sheep are defenseless animals. A good shepherd considers the needs of the flock above his own personal comfort and needs. The flock counts on the shepherd to take them to green pasture for food and water. Often, shepherds had to travel far from home to find the sheep high quality pasture and water. The shepherd also guarded the sheep against thieves and wild animals, took care of the wounded and sick sheep, and if one was missing or trapped he would rescue it.[4]

Besides elders, kings, and the Chief Shepherd, can you think of any other shepherd figures in the Bible (meaning those called to care for God's family?

_____

Just like an earthly shepherd, our Heavenly Shepherd watches over us, protecting us against the thief of our soul and searching for us fervently if we have strayed from the flock. Thank goodness we have an all-knowing, all-wise Shepherd over us or we'd be lost!

Zerubbabel and Nehemiah were shepherds to God's people after their captivity in Babylon. Many other prophets came along as well, in the Old Testament, serving as shepherds. Later on in the New Testament, others were called to shepherd the flock of God after they witnessed the dynamic leadership of Christ himself. The disciples were some of the first shepherds of the early church. One disciple in particular was given specific instructions to shepherd the flock.

Read John 21:15-17. In the NASB translation, Jesus tells Peter to "Tend my lambs." And "Shepherd my sheep." Do you think, like Peter, that we are to shepherd His sheep too? If so, whom are you shepherding?

_____

_____

God has given each of us some "sheep" to care for and tend. Maybe your "sheep" are your children or perhaps it's your Sunday school class. Or maybe your sheep are your neighbors or coworkers. We've all been given "sheep" to feed and nurture with God's Word. If we love Jesus, we will nurture the sheep He has called us to tend! Jesus is asking you the same as Peter, "Do you love Me?...Do you love Me?...Do you love Me?" And if the answer is yes, then you will demonstrate your love for Him by feeding His sheep.

Read Acts 20:28. Paul is speaking to the elders of the church of Ephesus. What do the elders "shepherding" qualities consist of here?

_____

_____

Do you protect and nurture the "flock" God has given you?

_____

_____

Do you treat the flock under your leadership as inferior to you, using them to enhance your own image and to enrich your assets like the kings of Judah did? Would God call you a good or a bad shepherd?

_____

_____

Take some time to evaluate how you are as a leader. Are those under your leadership fruitful in their endeavors? Do your "sheep" feel free to come to you and feel like you will listen to them? Do you listen to them?

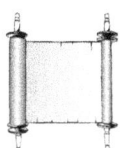

_____

_____

_____

If you are a leader, reading this chapter, please take some extra time to evaluate your leadership. It greatly matters to God and the people under your authority how you lead. You have the potential to make or break a team, an organization, and even a country, if you are in leadership.

Ezekiel, a prophet who came on the scene after the Jews were sent into captivity in Babylon, gave many powerful messages to God's chosen people during their captivity. One of those messages was concerning the shepherds (leaders) of Israel/Judah.

Please read Ezekiel 34:1-16. How are the shepherds (leaders of Judah) described in Ezekial 34:1-10?

_____

_____

How is God described as a shepherd in Ezekial 34:11-16 compared to the shepherds (leaders) in Judah (Ezekial 34:1-10)?

_____

_____

We have spent a lot of time on sheep and shepherds, because it's an integral part of the Old Testament and New Testament teaching. The imagery of God as our Chief Shepherd is a comforting image, if we'll allow Him to shepherd us. We can't lead or "shepherd" anyone else unless we are allowing the Chief Shepherd to lead us. We need our Shepherd to care and tend to us. Continue to spend time in His presence and let His Word and His love minister and lead you in your life.

DAY 4

The Coming Righteous Branch

Yesterday, we talked about bad shepherds; the kings of Judah. Today, we will discuss the future Messiah, the Good Shepherd.

Read over Jeremiah 23:5-6. Who do you think the righteous Branch is?

_____

Jehovah Tsidkenu

The Lord is our Righteousness!

Jeremiah coined the term "Branch." Branch means sprout or shoot.[1] When it was thought no more kings could come from the line of David, one did. Just like when a tree branch is pruned, but then a year later, a shoot will come from the cut branch, the Davidic line continued.

The term "Branch" became the classic term of the expected ideal king, Jesus.[2]

Match the following verses about the "Branch" to their general themes:

_____ Isaiah 11:1-2	a. Jesus grew up as a tender "shoot".
_____ Isaiah 53:2	b. Shoot will spring from Jesse (King David's father). A description of Jesus.
_____ Zechariah 3:8	c. The "Branch" will build the temple.
_____ Zechariah 6:12	d. The "Branch," God's servant, is coming.

What is the name Jesus will be called in Jeremiah 23:6?

_____

Jehovah Tsidkenu is the Hebrew word for "The Lord is our Righteousness." The term "The Lord is our Righteousness" is a play on words here. Zedekiah's name, the last king of Judah, meant "My righteousness is Yahweh."[3] As you will come to find out, Zedekiah did not serve the Lord with a clean heart. Therefore, it's ironic that he was given this name. However, a better king was on His way and this King to come would serve as righteousness to all men.

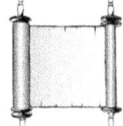

What does "The Lord is our Righteousness" mean to you?

_____

_____

Week 4

Righteousness involves being in a right relationship or right standing with God. However, no matter how hard we try to achieve this righteousness we can't attain it on our own.⁴ Jesus must become our righteousness.

What's does 1 Corinthians 1:30 say?

_____

_____

Read 2 Corinthians 5:21. How do we become righteous in God's eyes?

_____

_____

We must accept Christ's gift for us. There is no other way to become righteous. If we don't accept His gift of righteousness, believing in Him, we cannot be a part of the Kingdom of God and receive eternal life.

Righteousness is portrayed as a garment or a robe in Matthew 22. Open to Matthew 22:1-14 and read the parable about the wedding banquet. What does the wedding banquet stand for?

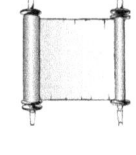

_____

_____

The wedding banquet is an invitation to all people: first the Jew, then the Gentiles, to be a part of God's Kingdom. The Jews foolishly refused both invitations to the feast and some even killed the messengers (the prophets). God, pictured as the King in this parable, was throwing a wedding feast for His son, Jesus, and He became enraged with the Jews for not accepting or being too busy to honor His Son. The invitation to the party was then sent out to the Gentiles. Both good and bad, rich and poor, and anyone that could be found was invited to the feast. The Gentiles filled the wedding hall. Notice, however, one man was singled out.

Read Matthew 22:11-12. What was unique about this man compared to the other wedding guests?

_____

Big banquets in the Eastern world, if the host were rich or of royal descent, would provide each guest with a wedding robe to wear. The guests would wear these robes in honor of the host and bridegroom and the bride. It was a sign of respect for them.⁵

To wear the wedding garment at the king's request in Matthew 22, was also a sign of respect for the king and his son. However, this one man refused

101

to wear it. He defied the king's command. The wedding clothes given to the guests at the wedding banquet represented righteousness.⁶ The wedding garment, in Matthew 22, is a picture of the righteousness God imparts on us when we make Him our Lord and Savior.

Write out Isaiah 61:10.

_____

_____

_____

_____

Notice when we become Christians we are given new garments to wear. We wear the garment of salvation and the robe of righteousness when we are made new creatures in Christ.

Read Isaiah 64:6. How is our self righteousness described compared to God's righteousness?

_____

_____

In order for the Lord to be our Jehovah Tsidkenu, "The Lord our righteousness," we must allow Him to cover our sins with His holiness. Otherwise, none of us would be able to stand before Him.

Who then does the guy in Matthew 22, who wasn't wearing the wedding clothes, represent?

_____

This man represents people who go to church, but don't accept the gift of salvation. The man wouldn't allow the King (God) to cover his "old rags" (representing sin) with God's robe of righteousness.

What do you do with an old outfit if it can't be cleaned up?

_____

My son, Aaron, recently stayed overnight in a cave with his father and 60 other non-claustrophobic fathers and sons from our church. We were warned before they went they should only wear clothing that could be thrown out because their clothes would be covered with red clay from the soil in the cave. When Aaron arrived home, after the trip, every bit of his attire had to be thrown out – shoes, jeans, shirts, and socks. It would have been impossible to get the red clay out of the fabric. Therefore, I didn't try!

> The **wedding garment** is a **picture** of the RIGHTEOUSNESS God imparts WHEN HE becomes our Lord and Savior.

They went straight to the trash! It reminds me of our own righteousness being like filthy rags. No matter how hard we try to clean ourselves up, we can't do it. We are still covered with sin, just like those clothes were stained with red clay and it wasn't going to come out!

Each of us must exchange our self righteousness (old rags) for Christ's true righteousness (wedding clothes). We can't enter the Kingdom of God without this divine exchange taking place!

Have you received Christ's free gift of salvation or are you still trying to get by on your own goodness?

_____

Your own goodness won't get you to heaven. Look at this man in Matthew 22:13. He was sent to hell because he refused to allow Jesus in his heart. He wanted to enjoy the feast and live how he wanted to live, and not do what God required which was to accept Jesus had died for his sin, admit he was a sinner and needed to be cleansed by Christ's sacrifice on the cross, and receive the gift of salvation He offered him. There is only one way to Christ. "For the gate is small, and the way is narrow that leads to life, and few are those who find it (Matthew 7:14)."

My Personal Journey

In 7th grade, I was confronted with the fact I had never really made Jesus my Lord and Savior. Many of my friends came to Christ through our church's youth group. I saw friends' lives change radically and I knew I didn't have what they had. They went from "churchy" kids to Jesus freaks! They spoke about Jesus non-stop, quoting Scriptures frequently, and wearing non-stop smiles on their faces (some went from angry non-smilers to joyful happy kids). The change was dramatic. However, while I wanted what they had, I wasn't sure I wanted to get it the way they did. I searched for a loophole. I did not want to have to say the sinner's prayer. I felt I had led a good life, attended church regularly since I was a youngster, and I would be considered a hypocrite if I told people I had not asked Christ in my heart yet. I had always called myself a Christian. So, what would people think of me? In fact, I called myself a Christian even more as my friends got saved because I didn't want them to think I needed it. I read Scripture for one month every day after school trying to find a loophole in Scripture for my situation. I couldn't find one!

One night at youth group a football player from our hometown's university came and spoke at our church. He shared how he had struggled with the same feelings I had. In fact, his situation seemed identical to mine. He used the same Scripture to justify himself in trying to avoid salvation. As I listened, my conviction became so intense, I left immediately after youth group to avoid breaking down in tears in front of everyone. At home, I told my mom my struggles through my tears. I then prayed and asked Jesus in my heart. I immediately felt cleansed from my sin and a new person. I remember hardly being able to contain my joy for days! In fact, I was so different, my brother even noticed it. Five days later, my brother invited Christ into his heart because he wanted what I had. Pretty cool stuff!

My point of telling you my story is because I know there are still many in the church and some in this Bible study that have not given the reins of their life to Christ. He is waiting for you and He loves you deeply. He wants to remove your sin and cover you with His righteousness and make you whole.

If you haven't already, will you confess your inability to save yourself and accept Jesus as your Lord and Savior? Take an honest look at yourself. Will you stand the inspection of the King at the wedding feast?

If you trust Christ as your Savior, you are made righteous by your faith and you don't have to worry! But if not, won't you take this time to bend your knees to the King and ask Him in your heart? Here's an example of how you can ask Jesus into your heart.

Admit you are a sinner.

Believe that Jesus is God's son and that He paid for your sins on the cross through His death.

Give your life to Christ and ask Him to rule your life.

_____

_____

_____

It may seem peculiar to discuss the message of salvation while doing a Jeremiah Bible study. However, God's salvation message is throughout the entire Bible. God begins telling us about salvation early on in the Old Testament. His very name Jehovah Tsidkenu "The Lord Our Righteousness" describes perfectly what God did for His chosen people. He came to save them from their sins. And He came to save us as well!

DAY 5

False Prophets

Today, we will study the false prophets who led the Jewish people astray. Jeremiah had his fill dealing with them. Pray God will open our eyes to understand the difference between a true and a false prophet. Sometimes it is difficult to distinguish the difference between the two. False prophets can be some of the most charismatic and seemingly sincere and sweet people. Even nowadays, Christians can be deceived by them, just as the Judean people were back then. It's important to understand the difference between them so we are not tempted to follow their maligned ways.

Read Jeremiah 23:9-40. As I read, I noted some general characteristics of the false prophets that jumped off the page. I've listed them below.

Characteristics of a False Prophet:

1. The false prophets allowed false gods to lead them.

Notice in Jeremiah 23:13, the false prophets "prophesied by Baal." The prophets didn't prophesy from words heard by God, but instead obtained their prophetic words from Baal, one of the idols they served. They received their prophetic words from the wrong source!

It reminds me of those who currently seek "enlightenment" from other gods than the one true God. Examples would be those involved in blatant occult practices (like seeking spiritual guidance through ouji boards, tarot cards, palm-readers, spirit guides or fortune tellers), or those who are involved in false religions or cults, seeking a counterfeit god. Those who follow such practices or religions think spiritual "wisdom" gained from these sources will guide them. However, it does the opposite, causing them to be misled and harmed spiritually. Oftentimes, these people are supernatural seekers, but not seekers of the ultimate Supernatural One. They search for spiritual meaning in the wrong places. Places that appease their minds and make them comfortable with the way they live. Not looking for the final truth, but instead with what makes them feel good.

God says we shall not have any other gods before Him. He is against us receiving our spiritual insight from the occult, false religions, or cults. We're not to seek out fortune tellers or other spiritual forms of "hearing" something spiritual. It disrespects God.

Where does your spiritual insight come from? Even more importantly, where do the people who are leading you spiritually receive their direction? Do you seek "spiritual enlightenment" from other sources than God?

*You will **KNOW** a false prophet by **HOW** he LIVES.*

_____

_____

If you are seeking out spiritual guides who look to anyone but Christ for their spiritual insight, you are in a precarious place. Those whom are true prophets obtain their message from God alone and don't speak a vision of their own imaginations, like the false prophets did (Jeremiah 23:16b).

2. The false prophets led corrupt lives.

In verse 14 of Jeremiah 23, the false prophets in Jeremiah's day were committing adultery, walking in falsehood, and strengthening the hands of evildoers. The false prophets were immoral characters. Obviously, they weren't going to tell their followers to lead holy lives, if they themselves weren't leading them. It would have convicted their own lifestyle too much if they had!

Read 2 Peter 2:1-3, 10-21. List some descriptors of how the false prophets in the New Testament led and still lead corrupt lives.

_____

_____

_____

The lifestyles of the false prophets mentioned in the New Testament are identical to the false prophets of old. Notice how false prophets live today: they never cease from sin, have adulterous eyes, despise authority, walk in greed, and are vain. You will know a false prophet by how he lives.

Read Matthew 7:15-20. What does a false prophet look like initially today (Matthew 7:15)?

_____

How will we eventually, over time, know if someone is a false prophet?

_____

_____

We may not recognize a false prophet immediately, but if we spend enough time with one we will observe they are counterfeits by the fruit they bear.

3. The false prophets gave false confidence to others saying everything would be alright, when everything would not be alright.

The false prophets didn't let the Jews know they would have to pay for the consequences of their sins. Instead, they told them what peaceful lives they would live and that no calamity would befall them, despite their continual, unrepentant sinning.

Sounds like the Devil himself speaking! Satan would say, "Do whatever you please and you'll be just fine! And look at how great you'll feel doing whatever you want!" He makes sin appealing, but once you fall into it, it's anything but pleasant. In fact, sin leads to bondage and misery.

In Jeremiah 23:17, it says the prophets kept saying, "...The Lord has said, 'You will have peace'; And as for everyone who walks in the stubbornness of his own heart, They say, 'Calamity will not come upon you'."

It is no different than today. Some despise the Lord and live how they want, encouraged by others to live like this. Similar to the false prophets in Jeremiah's day, our culture says it's all right to live independently, led by selfish desires and by the stubbornness of our own heart. People justify ambitious behavior, allowing them to walk over others and place themselves above others, for personal gain. Another fleshly desire that manifests is sexual immorality. Pornography, reading sleazy romance "novels," watching seedy TV shows, or fantasizing about a person is acceptable nowadays. Some women tell themselves it won't hurt their marriage or the man they're someday going to marry if they lust after another man. However, sin does hurt people; it has destroyed many individuals, marriages, and families.

The world declares "do what feels good," but rarely explains the dire consequences of those actions. Many T.V. shows and movies encourage us to give in to whatever feels right at the moment. Sleep with whomever, dress however you want, and don't worry about how you may tempt a man to lust by what you wear. Instead, dress so you feel good about yourself. Flaunt your stuff. And say whatever you feel, not caring about who you hurt in the process. Assert yourself. Listen to your heart, they tell us, but they don't tell us that our heart is full of deceit and following our hearts can destroy us.

Remember what Jeremiah 17:9 says? Write it out.

_____

_____

What is the outcome if we follow our own heart (or our flesh), instead of the Holy Spirit? Read Romans 8:11-13.

_____

_____

_____

Also, read Romans 8:6. If we set our minds on the Spirit versus on our flesh (our deceitful hearts), what do we receive besides just life?

_____

We have to set our minds on the Spirit. It doesn't just happen. Naturally, if we don't set our minds on the Spirit, we follow our flesh. We all struggle with conflict between our two natures, if we belong to Christ (Romans 7:23, 8:9). The false prophets, on the other hand, didn't follow God's Spirit at all. Instead, they were led and are still led only by their flesh.

4. The false prophets led people to futility.

Read Jeremiah 23:16 and 23:32.

The dreams the prophets gave the Judean people didn't furnish them with the slightest benefit! The words they prophesied led the people to live useless and ineffectual lives.

What does the word futility mean? Find a dictionary or look online for the definition of this word and write it out.

_____

_____

The Judean people were given the opportunity to hear both true and false prophets. The majority of Judah's inhabitants gave more credibility to the false prophets' messages, and followed their corrupt ways. God gives people a free will to choose who they will follow. He lets them know the right way to go, but they choose the path to take!

Like the Judeans, if we choose the path of our flesh it leads to bondage, hence ineffectual, wasted lives. This is not the life God wants for any of us.

Read Romans 8:20-21. How do these verses apply to your own life?

_____

_____

If you're like me, you don't want to live a futile life! In order not to live a useless life we must allow Jesus to deliver us from the bondage of sin and into the freedom in Christ which is our inheritance as children of God!

5. The false prophets didn't listen to God's Word.

Read Jeremiah 23:17-18.

The false prophets did not stand in the council of the Lord. They may have gone to the temple and been in prayer meetings, but they didn't actually listen to Him. Just like today, some are in the church and going through the motions, but not actually listening to Him.

Week 4

When I looked up the word council of the Lord in my concordance, it gave me a fuller picture of what the word meant. Do the same. Look up the word council in your concordance and tell what other meanings of the word you gained from the search.

_____

_____

In the Hebrew, council meant, "circle, company, consultation, fellowship, friendship, gathering, intimate, plans, and secrets."[1] It reminded me that when we seek the Lord's council we gain more than wisdom from the consultation, we also gain friendship and intimacy with the Lord, and God shares His plans and secrets with us. Wow! What's not to like about that?!

What would have happened if the false prophets had stood in the Lord's council? Reread Jeremiah 23:22.

_____

_____

As God's chosen, we are expected to stand in the Lord's council. He wants to speak to us. We can hear, if we'll just quiet down and listen. God has mysteries to share with us. In 1 Corinthians 4:1 it says, "This, then, is how you ought to regard us: as servants of Christ and as those entrusted with the mysteries God has revealed" (NIV). True servants of Christ are entrusted with His mysteries and they are revealed to us so that we can share them with others.

Look up Jeremiah 33:3. Write out the passage.

_____

_____

_____

_____

Do you call on God and hear Him tell you great and mighty things (Jeremiah 33:3)? Or do you rush through your devotion time with God, and not give Him time to speak?

_____

_____

6. The false prophets ran to tell though not sent.

Look at Jeremiah 23:21.

7. The false prophets were eager to tell their thoughts concerning the future, despite that they weren't instructed by God to do so. They went around boasting.

Read Jeremiah 23:25-32.

The false prophets obsessed about dreams and words God had supposedly given them. They said things like, "I had a dream, I had a dream" (Jeremiah 23:25) and "The Lord declares..." (Jeremiah 23:31). They were more focused on the dream than on God. In fact, they used the dreams to intentionally make the Judeans forget about their God.

What does Jeremiah 23:28 mean?

_____

_____

Read what two authors concluded about Jeremiah 23:28, "God often spoke to people in the Bible through the dreams of godly people. In these verses, God compares dreams to straw and His Word to grain. If you feed straw to cattle, they'll die. They will sleep on it, but they won't eat it because it has no nutrients. In the same way, dreams are of some value, but they are never to be made equal to God's Word as the basis for our faith or our walk. Dreams must be checked out against God's Word; it's never the other way around."[2]

The false prophets' dreams had no "nutritional value." It was like straw. However, the prophets continued to boast about their dreams.

What does 2 Corinthians 10:17 say? Write it out.

_____

_____

The false prophets were definitely not "boasting" in the Lord. They loved to give themselves a pat on their own backs. It was the Lord, however, who was supposed to praise them, if they had deserved it, not themselves. 2 Corinthians 10:18 goes on to say, "For not he who commends himself is approved, but whom the Lord commends."

8. The false prophets perverted the words of God. Every man's own word became "God's Word."

Read Jeremiah 23:36.

False prophecy causes every false prophet's words to be construed as God's word, when their words are not God's Word. How repugnant for God to hear people prophesying in His name when the words they shared were far from the truth. Eventually, the Lord had the final word and the false prophets were punished for their phony ways.

What was going to happen to the false prophets because of their wrongdoing? Read Jeremiah 23:39-40.

_____

How will the false prophets in the world today be held accountable for their corrupt ways? Read Matthew 7:21-23.

_____

The false prophets and false teachers we hear about today are not just in church sanctuaries. They are everywhere: in schools, universities, and businesses; they are all around us. A false prophet could be a leader that's telling us it's ok to be led by the stubbornness of our own hearts and teaches philosophies contradictory to God's Word.

Some false prophets today are easy to spot. For example, a leader of a cult comes to mind. I believe the larger group of false prophets is not so easy to identify, however. They are masked by their outward identity and appearance (some, if not most, unknowingly leading others astray). They are wishing their words would be true. They sprinkle their false ideas throughout their teachings and books.

Can you think of another type of false prophet or false teacher that is wearing sheep's clothing?

_____

Can you think of a false prophet/teacher by whom you have been deceived? How did you come to recognize the false teaching? How have you or will you guard against this kind of false teaching in the future?

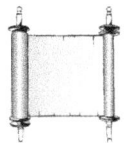

_____

_____

Read 1 John 4:1-3. What is the difference between a true and a false prophet?

_____

_____

Real prophecy still exists today. However, there is still plenty of false prophecy to go along with it. It is imperative we learn to discern the difference.

End your time in prayer asking God to open your eyes to any false prophets that could be influencing you today. If He reveals any false prophetic ways/ or words you've followed, repent and claim the freedom in Christ that is rightfully yours. And remember this... Romans 8:1, "Therefore there is now no condemnation for those who are in Christ Jesus." Don't hold onto any guilt after you've repented of your sin!

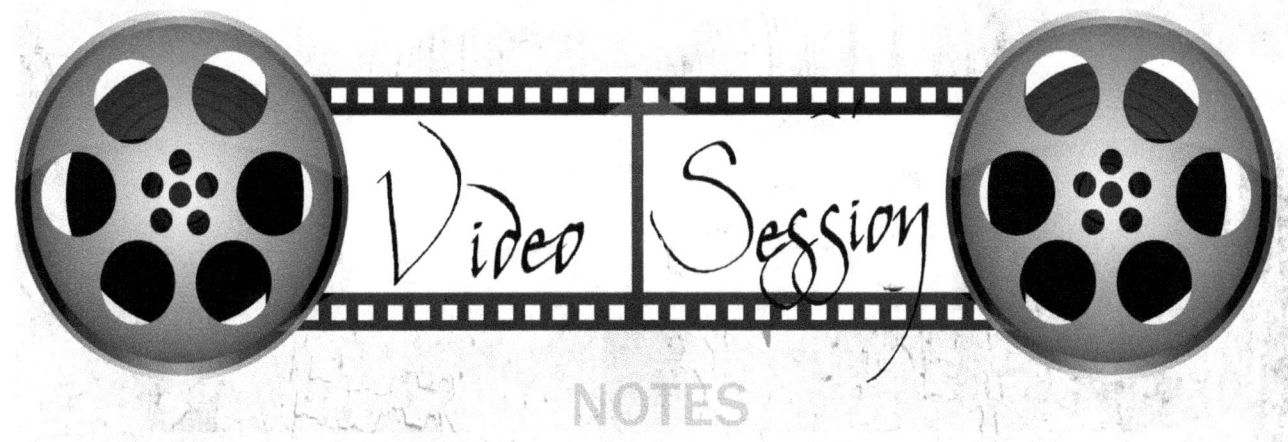

NOTES

VIDEO QUESTIONS WEEK 4

1. What were the four metaphors from Jeremiah 17 that were described in the teaching?
2. What are the differences between a cursed and a blessed heart?
3. Discuss Jeremiah's 3rd lament (Jeremiah 17:14-18).

Video sessions are available for download at www.grassandflowers.org

WEEK FIVE
TAKING CAPTIVITY CAPTIVE

DAY ONE
A Turning Point

DAY TWO
The Yoke of Babylon

DAY THREE
Oracles to the Nations

DAY FOUR
Oracles to the Nations

DAY FIVE
Babylon's Future

DAY 1

A Turning Point

We're approaching a pivotal turning point in the book of Jeremiah. Nebuchadnezzar grew weary of Judah's continued non-compliance to Babylonian rule and determined to assert his authority by moving God's people. In 597 B.C., the largest deportation of the Jews from Judah occurred. Around 10,000 Jews, which included King Jeconiah, were taken to Babylon. The next deportation of Jews occurred between 588-586 B.C., approximately 10 years later, under the leadership of the last of Judah's kings, King Zedekiah, after the Babylonians had laid siege to the city. In 581 B.C., the final deportation of Judeans to Babylon took place. Only 745 persons were deported by Nebuchadnezzar at this time and the only place this deportation is mentioned is in Jeremiah 52:30. One last possible deportation of the Jews should also be mentioned, although this deportation is only mentioned by Daniel. It occurred in 605 B.C. This is the deportation many Biblical scholars believe Daniel and his friends (Shadrach, Meschach, and Abendego) were taken to Babylon. You can read about this in Daniel 1:1.

Let's begin our lesson by reading 2 Kings 24:10-16. Describe who Nebuchadnezzar took into captivity in 597 B.C.

_____

_____

Which people were not taken into captivity?

_____

Who served as a puppet king in Jerusalem? Read 2 Kings 24:17.

_____

How are Zedekiah and King Jehoiachin related?

_____

What is King Zedekiah's real name?

_____

Many believe the 597 B.C. deportation included the prophet Ezekiel. While there are no recorded words of Ezekiel prophesying while he lived in Jerusalem, after he moved to Babylon he began prophesying heavily to the Jewish captives in Babylon. His message lined up with Jeremiah's message.

TAKING CAPTIVITY CAPTIVE

The siege of 597 B.C. took King Jehoichin, his officials, and most of the people from Jerusalem. Only the people of lesser importance were left behind in that siege.

Read Jeremiah 24. Who did the good figs represent (Jeremiah 24:5)?

_____

Pirhal/Shutterstock

Who were the bad figs (Jeremiah 24:8)?

_____

How did God view each of these different people groups – the good figs and the bad figs?

_____

_____

What were His plans for each group?

_____

_____

The good figs were the exiles carried off to Babylon. Notice God had good plans for them, despite they were being punished for their sin and taken to Babylon. On the other hand, the bad figs represented the survivors in Jerusalem. God said He would abandon these people and destroy them.

Read Jeremiah 25:1-12.

This was a prophetic word Jeremiah gave the people during Jehoiakim's reign before Nebuchadnezzar came and deported them. The people had been warned countless times by Jeremiah. However, no one seemed to listen.

How many years did Jeremiah tell them they would be in captivity (Jeremiah 25:11)?

_____

The Judeans would not have had to be taken into captivity if they had just obeyed the Lord. However, they didn't obey God, and He had to get their attention! He knew that if they were taken to a strange land, they would be forced to finally examine themselves. If all they held precious was stripped from them, they would have to contend with God and chose either to follow Him or not. Also, because the Babylonians were not particularly nice to them it was an opportunity for them to realize maybe following God's ways weren't so bad after all. They couldn't dig their way out of the mess they

Week 5

had made, so they were going to have to let God help them now. What their enemies, the Babylonians, meant for evil, God would use for their good.

Have you ever been in circumstances like the Judeans? You did not listen or obey God until He rocked your world to get your attention! Tell us about your story.

_____

_____

_____

_____

I certainly have! My story is long and complicated, like yours, I'm sure. Take a rest and read a bit of my testimony:

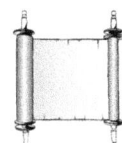

My Personal Journey

Early on in my walk with God, I followed Him faithfully. I was 12 years old when I became a believer and I took God at His Word. I was in a youth group and church that strongly supported my walk with Christ. I remember being sold out for Christ. My Bible was never far from me and I had good friends that I prayed with on a daily basis at school in both junior high and most of high school. I thought living like this was the norm for every true believer. I loved Jesus wholeheartedly and shared His love with others. It was an incredible time of growth spiritually. However, slowly my world began to crumble apart in my last couple years of high school. It began with my mom dying of cancer when I was 15 years old. She struggled with T-cell lymphoma for 9 months and it eventually took her life. My mom was the most remarkable woman I've ever known. Her death devastated our family. However, through it all, the chemotherapy, radiation, bone marrow transplant and then the grief of losing her I still clung to Christ. He gave me strength through the deep grief I experienced.

If you have ever lost a parent at a young age, you know the impact this loss has on your life. I felt a part of me died when I lost my mother. The loss was deep and intense. While the grieving process has become easier with time, it never ends completely. No one can fill the void my mom left, except for God. God has done that for me, but I still miss my mom immensely. The pain, even after 26 years, is still there at times.

Unfortunately, not only did I lose my mom during that time, but I also lost my father, in a sense, for a few years. My mom's death and experiences surrounding it overwhelmed my dad. He went into severe depression a year after her death. Like my mom's death, my dad's struggles with depression impacted my brother and I tremendously. While I can say

TAKING CAPTIVITY CAPTIVE

My Personal Journey

now both my brother and I made it safely to the other side, it was not an easy road. The severe depression left my father almost completely unable to raise us. To this day, my dad regrets his pain and grief had such a tremendous affect on us. If he could go back and change things he would. Needless to say, with my dad enveloped in his own suffering and with us feeling quite alone without any parents (one dead, and the other in emotional anguish) I felt for the first time in my life, completely out-of-control. Up until this point in my life, my life had been wonderful. Great parents, good community, and wonderful friends—I couldn't have asked for a better life.

With my world now turned upside down, I didn't know how to respond. I desired to get life back and not feel so out of control. I didn't know it at the time, but the enemy attacked me heavily and told me that I was fat. I was by no means fat, in fact I was a skinny little thing, but in my mind I really thought I was overweight. And without the support of the church and my distancing myself from anyone that might help me (partially because people didn't know how to deal with my dad's mental illness and him not being a Christian), I slipped into a condition called anorexia nervosa.

Unfortunately, anorexia has become all too common in our society. The media's attention and misguided focus on physical appearance leads many young girls and women in general, to become overly critical of their body shape and size. I fell into the same trap.

I didn't know I struggled with anorexia at first. The core of my deception centered on control. By controlling my food intake and excessive exercising I felt better about myself and my life. However, I didn't realize the anorexia only served to cover up my general unhappiness and depression I tried so hard to forget about. If I could stay happy by controlling my physical body, then I could deal with everything else that was going on around me. I went from a 135 pound to a 106 pound 16 year old, within a matter of a few months. I became skin and bones, but still felt overweight.

Thankfully, my best friend's mom recognized the signs and symptoms of anorexia. She took me to my doctor who was quite frank with me about my condition. These two people caring about me, by taking the time to talk with me, restored my world to right side up once more. Within another couple of months, I regained the majority of my weight back and looked and felt better. However, an inner struggle still remained. I remained at my original weight, but I still at times struggled with thoughts of feeling overweight, when I was not. During my sophomore year in college as I came to understand anorexia, I came to the end of the struggle. Since then, thankfully, anorexic thoughts have not haunted me again.

Week 5

My Personal Journey

During this time in my life, I also began dating my future husband. Rob, is an encourager and as he built my faith, he helped me to recognize the deceptive lies anorexia built in my self-image. Because I felt loved, I became involved in my church again. My faith began to soar once again.

The next several years were a normal progression of a healthy life. I went through the typical passages of life: marriage, a career in nursing, going back to school to obtain my master's degree and then began serving in my new career role as a nurse practitioner. There were essentially no big bumps in the road. I thoroughly enjoyed my life. Life was good again.

At 30 years of age, I faced another major trial which became a life changer. This trial literally brought me to my knees. Probably the only way God could get my full attention was to have me go through this because I had become quite independent, successful, and didn't give God the full attention He deserved anymore. I know that while I stand a free woman now, it took me going into a spiritual and mental bondage to eventually learn how to live freely. I went into my "Babylon" (a place of captivity), just like the Judeans went into a physical Babylon because they were living however they wanted.

This is what happened... four months after my second child was born I went into postpartum depression. It didn't start how I thought depression would begin. In fact, I wasn't depressed at all when it first started. It began with insomnia over the course of a week with only getting 2-3 hours of sleep a night. So, what kept me up at night? My inability to shut my mind off, with all of the many things I needed to do and little anxieties I had as a young mom. Some of you know what I'm talking about, if you're a mom! The kids were sleeping perfectly throughout the night, which I know is disgusting to hear for all of the young moms out there, but both kids when they were infants slept through the night by 8 weeks to 4 months respectively, so that was not the cause of my insomnia. I was just trying to be super mom and with being super mom comes tremendous fatigue. Plus, I'd like to blame some of it on the hormones, which are all over the place after giving birth to a child!

I tried to be perfect and control everything in my life because once again it seemed like everything was spinning out of control in my world. This time however, I didn't fall into the trap of anorexia, but instead I faced depression head on. God couldn't be put on the sidelines this time for me to become healthy. Now don't get me wrong, we are supposed to be good moms and take great care of our kids. However, we need to care for them as we care for ourselves. You just can't keep giving as a parent and never put anything into your own personal development. It isn't healthy! At that point in my life I wasn't taking any

My Personal Journey

time for myself. I wasn't exercising, eating right, spending time with friends, or having any dates with my husband. Plus, going from being in the workforce full-time to being at home 24 hours a day with little adult interaction was a big change for me. By the end of a week of insomnia I knew I needed to see a healthcare provider for help. Being a nurse practitioner, I knew if I didn't start sleeping again and learn to control my anxiety I would go into postpartum depression. Thankfully, the physician assistant who saw me gave me 2 days worth of sleeping pills so I could get back into a regular sleep schedule. Thank God that worked! She also suggested I start on an antidepressant. I was hesitant at first to take medicine, but a couple days later I realized my need. The medicine helped, but what made the biggest difference was that I learned how to live healthy to minimize my risk of being depressed. I wanted to change my pattern of thinking and my lifestyle. I didn't want to be a perfectionist any longer and I wanted to learn how to not worry so much... all things that led me to be depressed and unhealthy habits I had learned over the course of a lifetime. I had to learn how to take my thoughts captive, and live wisely in every area of my life. I began to eat/exercise right, go on dates with my husband, go on girls nights out regularly, and spent much needed time in God's Word, praying, and memorizing Scripture. I posted verses on my fridge, in my car, on my bathroom mirror that helped me with my thought processes. It helped me to fight the enemy back when I would hear his lies. Plus, it helped me to see how God viewed me and my circumstances.

Through some of the darkest hours of my life, not only did I survive, but through Christ I became victorious; He delivered and brought me fully through. I have a few good friends to thank for helping me through this time too. While I wouldn't ever wish to go back through depression again, what I learned was invaluable. That was 10 years ago. I only had to take the antidepressant for a few months, but I struggled much longer with learning how to replace my negative/destructive thoughts with God's life-giving Words. His peace thankfully won out!

My experience with depression reminds me of what the Jews went through when they experienced Babylon. They hit rock bottom, but through that they learned how to praise their God and gave God His rightful place in their lives once more. They learned how to live triumphantly. It is through the most painful hours/weeks/months/years of our lives we learn to really live (if we let God use it for our good). Of course, some are hardened by life's circumstances, but we all have a choice to make concerning the trials we face. We can choose the abundant life Christ offers, or we can opt to follow our own sinful ways.

It's funny; sometimes the things we think are so terrible, in the end save us from ultimate destruction. It reminds me of the story of Joseph who was sold into slavery by his brothers. Later on, he was able to save their lives when he was made second in command

Week 5

My Personal Journey

over Egypt and a famine occurred where his brothers lived. In Genesis 50:20, Joseph says, "You (Joseph's brothers) intended to harm me, but God intended it for good to accomplish what is now being done, the saving of many lives." Satan wants to harm us like Joseph's brothers did to Joseph, but God can use it for our good.

A friend recently said to me, "All I have learned, I've learned through pain." While I can't say everything I've learned has been through pain, I will say there are many lessons learned through painful or uncomfortable circumstances. When I become comfortable, like the Judeans of Jeremiah's times, I certainly don't listen to God much. When I think I can control life on my own, I don't hear from God either. Sometimes, it takes a good whack on the side of my head to hear Him! I can be pretty stubborn and self sufficient, (as my husband will readily agree), so I'm thankful in the end God woke me up, despite it taking awhile to get me out of my mental Babylon.

One of the driving forces behind writing this study is to help those who have fallen into bondage. By spiritual bondage, I mean any area of our lives where we come into agreement with a lie from the enemy that is in direct opposition to God's Word. This gives the demonic legal access, and it's like an open invitation for them to come and torment us.

I was in bondage. My bondage originated from anxiety. My anxiety became so overwhelming, it controlled me. I couldn't function. It led me into depression. It incapacitated me. It became like a prison, I couldn't get out of it on my own. It started with not letting God have control of my life. I was trying to control my own life. This is sin, by the way. I took everything on my own shoulders and tried too hard to do everything just right. Most of us don't think of that as sin, because we've been raised to be independent. It's not willful sin. It's a learned behavior and if it is not changed can destroy you. It can get your mind, body, soul, and spirit out of complete alignment. When you dwell on negative and anxious thoughts all day long, it is not living by faith. I had to retrain my mind. I had to train my mind to think like Christ. I had to open the Word and let it penetrate my inmost being, allowing it to transform my mind.

Perhaps you struggle with something different than I did. Perhaps when things get out of control, you get angry. What have been the consequences of your anger? Has your anger destroyed relationships? Have angry spoken words hurt and harmed those you love dearly? While there is righteous indignation, most forms of anger are sinful and harmful to you and those around you. Maybe your struggle isn't negative/anxious thoughts or anger, but lust. You fantasize. You know it's wrong, but you can't seem to control it. If you don't allow the Spirit to infiltrate every area of your mind and let God's thoughts be yours, you eventually will fall into the trap of adultery or fornication.

TAKING CAPTIVITY CAPTIVE

My Personal Journey

See, the thing is that if you just have a negative thought once in a while, it's no big deal. Or if you are just angry now and then, it may not destroy a relationship. Or if you have a fleeting lustful thought once in a while it may not lead you into the sin of adultery, but if these sins become a pattern, they will take over your life and destroy you and others in your life.

My negative thinking processes nearly destroyed me. Could you imagine if I had allowed the waves of depression to not only crash over me, but to suffocate my life (whether I'd committed suicide or just emotionally become dead to the world and remained in the pit of despair)? It would have destroyed not only me, but left my kids without a mother physically or emotionally and left my husband alone struggling. It would have had a huge and lasting impact on all involved.

It matters how we allow our thoughts to reign over us. Our thoughts are either sinful or full of faith. We are either in the Spirit or in the flesh in our thought life. We have to be trained to live in the Spirit. It is not an easy task.

The Israelites and Judeans were similar. They fell into bondage. They no longer served their God with sincere hearts. They went through the motions, going to the temple, worshipping God and saying they loved God, but they didn't allow God to transform them. They followed the cultural norms of their day. They wanted to be like the other nations around them that weren't serving God. They just wanted to fit in culturally.

Most of us don't realize how often we are seated on the throne of our heart, instead of Jesus. We lose our identity in Christ or we never learned it to begin with when we became a Christian. As an adult, my identity became who I was professionally. Once I no longer was working out of the house, I faced an identity crisis. The person I used to be, a strong, confident leader, independent and career-oriented had slipped from my fingers, as I became a fledgling new mother, unsure of myself. It was not until my anxieties took over that I realized how far off course I had veered from following Jesus.

The same thing occurred with the Judeans. They didn't "get it" until they were carried away from their beloved Jerusalem, stripped of their identity and placed in chains and taken to Babylon. It was there that they were forced to depend on their God and learn their true identity as followers of God. It was there that they comprehended how little they looked to God for direction in their lives. Exile revealed to them that they needed Him. In fact, they found they couldn't survive without Him. They wouldn't have been able to forgive their persecutors without Him after all the agony and torment they endured from the Babylonians. They had no hope for a future without His words of encouragement. Without

Week 5

My Personal Journey

God, they would have given up and been forever destroyed as a people group, never returning to their land or seeing the promises God had in store for them.

Is that your story too? While the enemy tries to destroy us with depression, anxiety, anger, hopelessness, and lack of purpose, the Lord gives us hope. He encourages us with promises in His Word. He gives us Scriptures we can cling to and sustain us in trying times.

He took me out of a pit of despair. It never should have surprised me I fell into that pit because if we're not following God each one of us will fall into a pit of one kind or another eventually. If you're as independent as I was (or the Judeans) I imagine you may have to have the rug pulled out from under you too before you see the light. Instead of rebelling and getting angry though, let Jesus tenderly and gently lead you back home from your Babylon. And what does home look like? A place where you are no longer living your life independently from God and letting Him in only when it's convenient, but instead a place where you are able to trust Him in every area of your life. A place where you are no longer defined by what you do (your career, abilities, talents), but by who Christ says you are.

Let's wrap this up by praying and spending some time thinking about where you are right now. Are you in "Jerusalem," living lives of mediocrity, or are you in "Babylon," learning from your past mistakes and allowing God to meet and mold your mind to His way of thinking? Or have you come out of "Babylon" and learned from your captivity experience? Explain your situation.

_____

_____

_____

_____

I pray no matter where you are that you are attentive to His Spirit. God is speaking, you just have to open up His Word and listen!

One last point… as if I haven't said enough already! I've had one incredibly blessed life. While I've spoken of difficult times in my life the majority of my life has been positive. My first 15 years of life were wonderful. The 20 years I've been married to my husband, Rob, have been great ones (mostly -with a couple bumps in the road)! It has been incredibly rewarding to watch my kids grow and flourish. I have had the opportunity to make many wonderful friends during the years I struggled with depression and since then. I am blessed and thankful Christ has made something beautiful out of my dark days. Plus, I know with certainty, He'll never leave nor forsake me in whatever lies ahead.

DAY 2

The Yoke of Babylon

Welcome back! With your cup of coffee or tea in hand, let's get back to our study. Without hesitation, open your heart up to God, asking Him to lead you into a place where He can speak to you personally.

Shortly after Babylon deported Jerusalem's "cream of the crop" citizens, the political powers of the day decided to convene together to formulate a plan on dealing with the threat of Babylon. It was during this meeting, Jeremiah was sent by God to dissuade the leaders from revolting against Babylon and command them to submit to King Nebuchadnezzar's rule.

Read for yourself what Jeremiah had to say to the nations. Read Jeremiah 27:1-11.

Which nations did Jeremiah address?

_____

Who gave Nebuchadnezzar the power to rule over these lands (Jeremiah 27:5-6)?

_____

What would happen to these nations if they didn't put their neck under the yoke of Babylon (Jeremiah 27:8)?

_____

What would happen to the nation who would submit to King Nebuchadnezzar (Jeremiah 27:11-12)?

_____

See **Addendum 3** on page 248 to see a map of the world in Jeremiah's times.

Jeremiah's prophetic word seemed treasonous to the foreign delegates. How could the nations just sit back and surrender to their enemy? It seemed illogical. God thought differently, however. He commanded the nations' submission to King Nebuchadnezzar, not to harm them, but to protect them. Babylon's rise to power was part of God's plan.1

Jeremiah demonstrated the need for submission to Babylon by wearing a yoke around his neck. In our day and age, we rarely see yokes on oxen in our country because of the development of farm machinery such as tractors and combines. Back in those days, however, yokes were used on oxen. The yoke's purpose literally was to help the farmer direct the two animals bonded together and make them work more efficiently. The yoke figuratively represented submission to authority.2 If Judah didn't surrender and submit to King Nebuchnezzar's authority (yoke), war would be waged.

Week 5

Go ahead and read Jeremiah 27:12-22.

After Jeremiah finished speaking to the foreign ambassadors, he addressed King Zedekiah personally, and then moved on to warning the priests and the people. Jeremiah tailored the speeches he gave to accommodate the 3 audiences' different perspectives. When Jeremiah addressed the priests and the people, he focused on the temple vessels. "...knowing that they (the temple vessels) would incite the people's interest because the temple was their central preoccupation, particularly the priests. Unfortunately, they were not preoccupied with the God of the vessels nor with the truth for which the vessels stood, but they respected only the vessels themselves and the rituals for which they were used."[3]

Again, Jeremiah displayed courage. Despite having been ridiculed before, he addressed the people again, this time in a political arena. He wore a yoke and didn't shy away from speaking the Lord's Word even though it seemed quite unpatriotic. Jeremiah took on a commanding, yet humble posture as he spoke. He was prophetic, yet practical. Jeremiah took a stand on the political issues of his day.

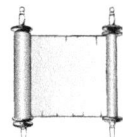

Think of your own life. Have you ever voiced political views that lined up with God's will, but didn't necessarily line up with the views of others around you? Did you have the courage, like Jeremiah, to stand up for what was right? If so, name the circumstances and how you knew this was God's will.

_____

_____

_____

_____

"Prophetic faith does not live in a religious vacuum, but must take sides on the public issues of the day."[4] If you're like me, your political views can sometimes cause friction with others who don't see eye to eye with you. That's okay. As long as you do not speak antagonistically and you speak out of love, you should make a stand for what is right. Political discussion is important. It causes us to run to God for answers to our sometimes difficult questions.

Next, we are going to jump into Jeremiah 28. This passage seems to be a continuation of Chapter 27. Although it is not known exactly when Jeremiah's encounter occurred with Hananiah, it is assumed to have happened shortly after Jeremiah addressed the three audiences because Jeremiah was still wearing the yoke.

This scene involves a prophet named Hananiah challenging Jeremiah's prophetic word. He didn't give any validity to the message Jeremiah gave.

Instead his message "from the Lord," contradicted what God had said to Jeremiah. Hananiah gave words the people wanted to hear. His words offered a quick fix to their dilemma. It made them not have to look at the root of their problem. They could go on living like they were and imagine in a short few years everything would be back to normal.

Judah's reaction reminds me of our own government. U.S. citizens and politicians naturally want a quick fix to our economic crisis. There isn't one though. It's about learning to live within our means and paying off our enormous national debt. God wants people to change their ways, not just bandage things up. How do we get healthy if we cover things up and never get to the root of our problems? It doesn't work, at least not long-term.

Examine Jeremiah 28:1-11.

Hananiah made all sorts of wonderful promises to the people and priests as he spoke to them in the temple. According to Hananiah, instead of a 70 year exile, the people had only a 2 year wait, until all of the exiles, their beloved king Jeconiah, and the treasured temple vessels were brought back. How much easier for the people to gravitate towards Hananiah's message than Jeremiah's.

How did Jeremiah initially respond to Hananiah's message (Jeremiah 28:6)?

_____

_____

When I first read verse 6, I thought Jeremiah was being sarcastic with Hananiah. However, one Biblical commentator, points out Jeremiah sincerely wished what Hananiah was saying would come to pass, as Jeremiah was a patriot of his own country.5 Jeremiah hoped his country would suffer as little as possible.

However, Jeremiah would not bend because by speaking a message that made the people feel good, but was not true. He commented on the tradition of prophecy (Jeremiah 28:8-9). Many times the prophetic message God gives is not what people want to hear. Jeremiah wasn't hateful towards Hananiah. He wanted the audience to reflect on Israel's past in order to help them differentiate between true and false prophecy.

After Jeremiah spoke, what did Hananiah do (Jeremiah 28:10)?

_____

Read Jeremiah 28:11. How did Jeremiah respond to Hananiah breaking the yoke?

_____

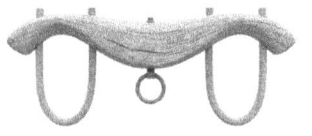
Slavoljub Pantelic
Shutterstock

He walked away. He didn't fight. He didn't make a comment. He simply went away and waited to hear from God. What an example. Most of us, if we had a yoke broken over our heads, would have fought back. Jeremiah did neither. He humbly left. He wasn't going to speak, unless God told him to. A lesson we could all stand to learn!

Ever been in a situation like this where you knew you should walk away, but didn't? What happened? What do you think would have happened if you had just walked away instead of defending yourself?

_____

_____

By walking away, God was able to work and Jeremiah was able to listen. Look at what God had to say to Hananiah.

Study Jeremiah 28:12-17. What were the yokes of wood replaced with? What is the difference between these two materials?

_____

_____

Wood is obviously softer and more pliable than iron. Iron is much heavier and burdensome to wear than wood. If you'll look back in Deuteronomy, this is not the first time God mentions a yoke of iron. When God gave His commands at Gerizim, He also spoke of curses that would come upon the people if they disobeyed His commandments.

Why would an iron yoke come on their necks according to Deuteronomy 28:47-48?

_____

"It's always the case that when we reject the light yokes of God's will we end up wearing a heavier yoke of our own making," states Wiersbe.6

Do you agree with Wiersbe's postulation? If so, do you have an example you can give us of that theory?

_____

_____

_____

In my own life, Wiersbe's statement is true. I saw a sign recently on Facebook that a friend posted, it stated, "Christians, are you humble and grateful or grumbling and hateful?" Have you seen this? What an awesome reminder

A **Yoke** symbolizes *submission*.

as we face challenges in our day. We are supposed to serve God with a joyful, thankful heart and not complain. We can either accept God's light yoke or we can complain, grumble, and rebel and make everything worse.

Read Matthew 11:28-30. Write out verses 29 and 30 below and meditate on these words for a few moments.

_____

_____

_____

_____

A yoke symbolizes submission. We are to be submissive and do the will of our Father in heaven. Yet, this yoke He puts upon us (to direct us and keep us safe) is meant for our good. God is not a hard master. Remember the yoke is easy, light, and gives rest to our souls.

"Farmers used to yoke the young ox with the old experienced ox to train them. The old ox will take the major lead and the young one will be walking along and learning from him."7 What a picture of us being yoked to Christ! He being the old ox, full of experience and strength, leading us (his youngsters) along the path, side by side, and carrying the majority of the load for us.

Going back to Jeremiah and Hananiah, look at how God showed the world who was the true prophet and who was prophesying falsely. Rarely does God kill someone outright for their sin, but here was one incident where God was not going to mess around! Hananiah had caused the people to believe in a lie and God wouldn't tolerate it. God wanted the people to know the truth.

How long did it take for Jeremiah's prophetic words of Hananiah's death to come to fruition? Look back at Jeremiah 28:1 and compare to the month mentioned in Jeremiah 28:17.

_____

The death of Hananiah should have made the people realize the authenticity of Jeremiah as a prophet. Jeremiah prophesied of Hananiah's death and two months later Hananiah keeled over and died. It is not known how he died, but he died and the people still didn't listen to God. I ask myself here, why didn't they listen? Wasn't that a big enough sign for them? What more did God have to do to get their attention? Surely news of Hananiah's death and the prophetic word of his death would have traveled throughout the city like wildfire. It goes to show how skeptical people are in general. People believe what they want to believe. Or perhaps the Judeans didn't take the time to determine if this prophecy was from God. The Judeans didn't make time to seek God's face in other areas of their lives, so why would they in this instance?

Does God send prophets to warn us today? If you believe so, how do you know who to trust? Do you take time with God to determine whether a word given to you is true or false?

_____

_____

What does Deuteronomy 18:20-22 state about how you will know a true versus a false prophet?

_____

Today has been an interesting day. Jeremiah made a political demonstration and he prophesied of Hananiah's death because of Hananiah's false prophecy. The message was clear. God didn't take false prophecy lightly and His iron yoke was coming down upon the people soon, whether they believed it or not.

Take a few minutes to meditate on God and what He is telling you about the direction of your own life. Ask Him for specific instructions on situations you're dealing with right now. Then listen. Open your Bible and pray for a word directly pertaining to your circumstances. He will hear you and reply if you're coming to Him with a sincere and open heart. He may not always answer you how you would like, but He will respond! Have a great day ladies, and "see" you tomorrow!

DAY 3

Oracles to the Nations

Chapters 46-51 of Jeremiah are the oracles given to the nations surrounding Judah. While these chapters are at the end of the book of Jeremiah, I've decided to place these oracles here in our study for three reasons. First, at this point you probably know very little about the nations surrounding Judah. Second, while these predictions are placed at the end of Jeremiah, it is actually not known when these oracles were given to each nation.[1] Since each forewarning contains prophetic words from Jeremiah, we assume these words were given to each nation before judgment and destruction came upon them. Thirdly, it seems an appropriate place to discuss these nations, because we juat finished chapter 27, where Jeremiah commanded some of these same nations to submit to King Nebuchadnezzar.

The message is clear in these chapters: God cares for all people groups. God is over all nations and wants all to follow His statutes. Those nations who trust in their own strength or riches will fall. They are not impenetrable or protected by their own skills, cleverness, or location. God can humble those nations who refuse to obey Him.

If you've seen the movie Prince Caspian, you'll probably remember the scene at the river where the Telmarine army was chasing the people of Narnia. The river piled up, taking on the figure of God, and then came crashing down, killing the arrogant leader, King Miraz, who refused to accept Aslan's people and his ways. Just as this picture of God's fury in Prince Caspian was shown in the river, the same was going to happen to the nations surrounding Judah. God warned the nations. God cared deeply for them. However, He was sovereign and was not going to allow unjust acts to prevail.

On judgment day, God will judge each nation and hold them accountable for their actions. "The Oracles to the Nations" held out hope to the Judeans who were in captivity. These passages proclaimed judgment on their enemies. Their enemies would be defeated for their abhorrent acts.

The purposes of the oracles are numerous:

- They warned of evils God wouldn't tolerate.

- They displayed that God is just and would take revenge against those nations who mistreated Israel and Judah.

- They offered a message of salvation to the Judeans and to some of the countries who were judged (Egypt, Moab, Ammon, and Elam).

- They revealed all nations and people groups are important to God.

- God is sovereign. He directs and controls history.

- Every nation is accountable for their actions.

Begin by reading Jeremiah 46.

In Jeremiah 46:1, to whom were these prophetic words given?

_____

Jeremiah was not only sent to earth to be a prophet to Judah, but also a prophet to the nations.

What does Jeremiah 1:5 say?

_____

According to Eugene Peterson, these oracles reveal Jeremiah's character as well. Read below:

"All of these oracles show an extraordinary knowledge of the geography, the history and the politics of these nations. He (Jeremiah) was not interested in them in general but in particular. He bothered to find out the details of their lives. He spoke God's word in relation to the actual conditions of their existence…they were being addressed with attentive and personal seriousness. The nations were not lumped together as "pagans" or "lost sinners" and then assaulted with stereotyped formulas."[2]

Jeremiah cared for the nations just as God did.

Chapter 46 can be broken up into three categories. The first set of verses 2-12 speak of 605 B.C. when Pharoah Neco was defeated at Carchemish by Nebuchadnezzar. Verses 13-26 speak of the future destruction that was going to occur in Egypt's land by Nebuchadnezzar. It's unknown when this attack occurred. Dates proposed are 601 B.C., 588 B. C., or 568/7 B.C.[3] Lastly, verses 27-28, offer a small respite from the ensuing destruction of Egypt by offering hope to the Judeans of their future salvation from captivity.

Read Jeremiah 46:2-26. What does Jeremiah 46:15 say about the Egyptians?

_____

_____

While the Egyptians had a strong military, even they couldn't prevail. The chapter describes their horses and chariots. It states, "The swiftest warriors can't flee; the mightiest warriors cannot escape" (Jeremiah 46:6 NLT). The Lord made it clear, the days on which the Egyptians were attacked both in 605 B.C. and in the future were days orchestrated by God.

What does Jeremiah 46:10 say about who that day belongs to?

_____

> *Jeremiah cared for the nations just as God Did!*

Who destroys Egypt, according to Jeremiah 46:26?

_____

God wanted to make it clear. Nebuchadnezzar was the instrument used by God, but God was the avenger.

How does Jeremiah 46:17 describe Pharaoh, the king of Egypt?

_____

Pharaoh was a big talker, but he didn't put his talk into action. He was an inept leader.

Despite poor leadership and Egypt's corruptness, they would eventually be restored. At the end of verse 26, it states, "Afterwards (after their punishment), however, it (Egypt) will be inhabited as in the days of old." Eventually, life would begin again in Egypt.

Read the second half of Isaiah 26:9 and write the words of the verse out below. Do you think Egypt learned righteousness from God's judgment?

_____

_____

_____

Whether you believe God causes disasters or not, He obviously does allow them to happen. Have you ever noticed how quickly God gets our attention when a natural disaster or any other tragedy occurs? I think God was trying to get the Egyptians attention in this manner.

If you've ever been in a natural disaster you realize how helpless you are. A couple years ago, an EF-1 tornado (86-110 mph winds) hit parts of the city we live in during the April 25-28, 2011 tornado outbreak which touched the Southern, Midwestern, and Northeastern United States. Compared to many areas affected in other states or in other parts of Tennessee, we were fortunate. The tornado only beat up the siding on our house and left our car with hail damage. However, many others were not as fortunate as us and had their homes completely destroyed. Far more tragic, many lives were lost. My children and I remember vividly clinging to each other on our basement steps with blankets surrounding us as we heard the 100 mph winds and pounding hail overhead. It was scary. There was nothing we could do except hope and pray God would keep us safe. I imagine that was how the Egyptians and all the other nations felt as God's hand of destructive power came upon them. Of course, their fear must have been far greater than ours, as their destruction was more ominous and they did not trust in God.

Week 5

As I've looked back on 2011, many natural disasters occurred that year. In fact, 2011 was one of the worst years of natural disasters for the U.S. in a long time. Tornadoes, droughts, fires, earthquakes, ice storms, hurricanes and floods ransacked our nation, causing tremendous cost to our country.

I read a post on Facebook from a friend about natural disasters. It was something to the affect that it's frowned upon in our nation to believe natural disasters are caused by God. However, as she pointed out, natural disasters are actually one way God wakes us up to our spiritual conditions. Her comment was posted shortly after a presidential candidate got smeared on jesting in public that the earthquake and hurricane hitting the East Coast in August 2011 was God trying to get our politicians' attention in Washington D.C.

What do you think? Is God still an agent of destruction, like He was in the Old Testament? Do you know of a verse that backs up your opinion?

_____

_____

Do you think God is trying to speak to us when tragedies occur? Can you Scripturally support your opinion?

_____

_____

_____

I'm leaving my opinions out. I've placed these questions here to make you think and discuss your thoughts in your Bible study groups. These are not easy questions to answer. We all have a lot of opinions on these matters, but please take time to diligently search out answers in Scripture. God's answer may not be the same as your opinion.

Read Jeremiah 46:27-28. Remember these verses are speaking to the Judeans. What kind of hope does this give you after answering the last two difficult questions above?

_____

_____

Hopefully, these verses give you comfort and diminish any fears you may have. Just like God was trying to comfort the Judeans, He reaches down and comforts us in tragic situations.

Moving right along, read Jeremiah 47.

Surely, you recall the Philistines. The Philistines were the ones who sent Goliath out against David in the battlefield. They had been enemies with the Israelites a long time. The Philistines had lived along the Mediterranean coastal plain since the late 13th and early 12th century B.C.[4]

Matching: Read the passages concerning the Philistines to the left and match them with the correct content of the passage on the right.

_____ Judges 13:1	a. The Philistines killed 4,000 Israelites in battle.
_____ Judges 16:28-30	b. King David obtained battle plans from God concerning war with the Philistines.
_____ 1 Samuel 4:1-2	c. The Philistines oppressed Israel 40 years.
_____ 1 Samuel 4:10-11	d. The Philistines killed 30,000 Israelite foot soldiers and took the arc of God.
_____ 2 Samuel 5:17-25	e. God avenges the Philistines through Sampson.

The Philistines were a continual threat to Israel and Judah. They were vengeful people. The water discussed in Jeremiah 47:2, was symbolic of the enemy (Babylon) coming from the North to annihilate the Philistines.[5] Notice how the Philistines were so helpless while the Babylonians attacked, that they didn't even turn back to rescue their kids. The Philistines were "attacked by Nebuchadnezzar in 604 B.C. for resisting him (according to the Babylonian Chronicle)."[6] There was no promise of restoration for Philistia. The Philistines were wiped off the map.

Read Jeremiah 48. The oracle to Moab is the longest oracle to a nation besides Babylon. Moab was located east of the Dead Sea, southeast of Judah.

Circle all of the correct descriptions of Moab in Jeremiah 48:

Shattered	Shameful	Haughty
High Achievers	Complacent	Wealthy
Mighty	Life of ease	Poor
Weak	Proud	Boastful
Glorious	Humble	Insignificant

In whom did the Moabites trust (Jeremiah 48:7)?

_____

The Moabites were a proud people. In fact, they were well known for their pride.

Read Isaiah 16:6. What does Isaiah say concerning the Moabites?

_____

Before reading on, read Genesis 19:30-38. Who was the father of the Moabites and who was their mother? Also, while we're here, who was the father of the Ammonites and who was their mother?

_____

_____

*The Moabites were a **PROUD** people.*

Pretty creepy, huh? And you thought you had problems in your family?! Wow! Lot had two really messed up daughters. I can't imagine how Lot felt once he found out how his daughters had deceived him.

Obviously, the Moabite and Ammonite lineage didn't exactly start off on the right foot. In fact, it began in outright evil. The Moabites and Ammonites continued to lead corrupt lives throughout the rest of Biblical history. They were longstanding foes of Israel and Judah. When the Israelites tried to enter Canaan, Moab tried to prevent them from entering because the Israelites frightened the Moabites due to their large number. The Moabites even tried to place a curse on them. Read Numbers 22-24 to find out about that curse. It includes the story of the donkey who talked!

Draw a line between the verse on the left and the correct description of each verse on the right. These verses reveal how Moab was a thorn in Israel's side for many years:

1 Samuel 14:47	David defeated Moab.
2 Samuel 8:1-2	The Moabites helped destroy Judah.
1 Kings 11:7	King Saul fought against Moab.
2 Kings 24:1-2	Solomon built a high place for a Moabite idol.

God
can transform
ANYONE

Despite all the corruptness of the Moabites, one Biblical heroine emerged from the land of Moab who was not evil. Ruth, the woman who had a whole book of the Bible dedicated to her, not only was a Moabite, but she ended up marrying Boaz and converted to his religion, Judaism. If you'll also remember, Boaz, was the son of Rahab, a former prostitute in Jericho who was transformed by God's grace. Ruth and Boaz eventually had a son named Obed, who became the father of Jesse, who was the father of King David (Matthew 1:5 – read it for yourself). So, the point is God can make good out of something originally quite screwed up. God can transform anyone...a Moabite, a prostitute, you name it!

One of the great things in this chapter about the Moabites is that God's heart is revealed about them. Even though God can't stand Moab's pride and is going to have to discipline them for it, He mourns that they must go through this tragedy.

How many times does God mention His grief over Moab's destruction? Read over Jeremiah 48:30-32; 35-36.

_____

God took no pleasure in Moab's pain. He grieved for them. However, He knew something much bigger was at stake.

Read Ezekiel 18:23 & 32. What does God think about death and destruction of the wicked?

_____

How does 2 Peter 3:9 describe God's character?

_____

While God has a heart of compassion and patience, if individuals will not repent from their sin, they will eventually face judgment. Moab's complacency, arrogance, power, and prestige had got the best of them. Moab was told to "come down from your glory and sit on the parched ground..." (Jeremiah 48:18). They could no longer boast of their strengths. Instead, "The horn of Moab has been cut off, and his arm broken, declares the Lord" (Jeremiah 48:25).

How would you describe God's character during tragedies that you've gone through?

_____

_____

Write out a prayer of thanksgiving to God below. Pour out your heart to Him if you have a burden on your mind. Once you've written your prayer to Him, then listen and write down what He says back to you.

Week 5

Dear God,

_____

_____

_____

_____

_____

_____

What I heard God speak back to me:

_____

_____

_____

_____

_____

DAY 4

Oracles to the Nations

(Continued)

Today, we'll continue our study of the nations Jeremiah prophesied to in Jeremiah 46-50. We left off with the Moabites. We'll wrap up learning about them and then study the other nations.

If you remember from yesterday's readings, the Moabites were a proud people. Go back to Jeremiah 48:25, and reread it. How did God deal with the Moabite's arrogance?

_____

_____

Have you ever broken your arm? If so, explain how it disabled you in your activities of daily living.

_____

_____

_____

Both the words horn and arm are metaphors for strength in the Old Testament.[1] If you've ever had a broken arm you know it leaves you powerless, with no strength in that arm. This is exactly what happened to the Moabites. They were weakened and defenseless.

My Personal Journey

My daughter, a couple years ago, not only broke her arm, but also dislocated her elbow at the same time, causing a severe ligament tear as well. It was a serious injury and required emergency surgery with two pins placed in the right elbow. She went from being a strong competitive cheerleader to being out for the season within a matter of a few seconds after a flip off our backyard trapeze bar. If it had not been for a terrific surgeon, her arm would have been crippled for life.

Rachel's fractured and dislocated arm caused all of us to slow down. It literally flipped our world around (no pun intended!). While, Rachel didn't have any arrogance or disdain towards the Lord like the Moabites, she did have to stop and look to her Maker through this experience. It gave us an opportunity to reexamine ourselves individually and as a family.

Three days after the injury, while we were eating lunch together, Rachel looked up at me and said, "Mom, I know God has a purpose in all of this." And I said, quite interested in her response, "Oh yeah Rach (our nickname for her), what do you think God's purpose is in this?" She sweetly responded, "He wants to use this so I'll spend more time with Him." She didn't feel sorry for herself. Instead, she had a great attitude and it amazed all of us.

Week 5

My Personal Journey

I hadn't told her, but in the hospital while she was in surgery I reached for a Gideon's Bible lying next to me on an end table in the surgery waiting room. I begged God to speak to me and show me His purpose in all of this and to comfort us in our distress. I asked Him to give me answers to my questions.

When I opened up the Bible, my eyes landed on Psalms 90. At first glance, what stood out on the page were the words "children" and "teach me to number my days". I had just been pondering the phrase "teach me to number my days" the week before as I celebrated my 40th birthday. A popular Christian song on the radio at that time, called "Blink" by the group Revive, also played every day that week, talking about doing just that — teaching us to number our days.

Here is what I read during Rachel's surgery: "Teach us to number our days aright, that we may gain a heart of wisdom...Relent O Lord! How long will it be? (I was thinking how long will the surgery be? How long will her healing be?) Have compassion on your servants. Satisfy us in the morning with your unfailing love that we may sing for joy and be glad all our days. Make us glad for as many days as you have afflicted us, for as many years as we have seen trouble. May your deeds be shown to your servants, and your splendor (glory) to their children. May the favor of the Lord our God rest upon us; establish the work of our hands for us — yes, establish the work of our hands" (Psalms 90:12-17).

After reading this, I went back and read the rest of the Psalm and was impressed with its description of how fleeting our days are, just like Rachel's...and what is really important in life...not competitive cheer, although He can use that...but our relationship with God and people. In any tragedy, things you once thought important are usually found to not be quite as important as you originally believed and instead what really matters becomes crystal clear. It made me rethink about what we were doing or not doing for the Lord. I pondered how God might want to use Rachel if her arm didn't completely heal (the doctor had said there was a possibility that she would only get 80% function back in her arm), making it risky to cheer. I wanted Rachel to understand God's purpose in all this, as well as ourselves.

How wonderful it was to hear Rachel say so innocently day at lunch that she did know the purpose in all this. There was not an ounce of resentment in her for what had happened. She was fearless of what lay ahead. Total peace was written all over the child. Of course, we had a lot of prayer warriors praying, but part of it was just the resilient, upbeat personality and beautiful character of Rachel I was witnessing. It was a privilege to see her reaction to the injury and to spend time with her that summer. Despite I would not wish a broken arm on anyone, it ended up being a blessing. I would never have thought I'd have felt that way when it first occurred.

I didn't realize until Rachel broke her arm how overbooked we really were. We had been rushing from one activity to another and I started to feel I was losing intimate and

My Personal Journey

much needed family time with my kiddos, especially Rachel who was involved in activities that required a lot of her time. I sure wish it hadn't taken an injury for God to get our attention and slow down our pace, but it offered precious time with our daughter that we would not have had otherwise. She became dependent again on us for many normal daily activities that we take for granted. It was also beautiful to see how her brother reached out and helped Rachel and was patient with her, as she needed assistance with many things around the house (such as pouring her milk, opening food/drink containers, carrying stuff for her, etc.) Aaron readily and happily helped his sister. I was proud of him.

Another beautiful piece of the story was what happened at the hospital in a conversation with a nursing assistant. We felt like God was saying Rachels arm would be completely restored to full function again from the nursing assistant's story. Just like the Moabites were promised restoration after their tragedy, Rachel was promised restoration too. How much hope it gave us. I have revisited what God said through that nursing assistant at the hospital many times as to not lose hope during Rachels recovery.

Here is the story:

When we were about to leave the hospital (she had already been discharged), Rachel became dizzy and nauseated as I was getting her into the wheelchair to leave. I decided we weren't going to leave on a bad note, so I laid her back down and got a nurse to give her some medicine to help her. After she was given some medicine, a nursing assistant we had never seen before came in to take her vitals. The nursing assistant began asking Rachel how she had injured her arm. Rachel gave a one to two sentence answer and then the nursing assistant began to tell us her own story. The nursing assistant stated at the age of 10 (Rachel was 9 ½ years old when she injured her arm), she had the exact same injury occur to her. She fractured her right elbow and had an anterior elbow dislocation as well, causing severe ligament damage. The nursing assistant had no idea on the specifics of Rachels injury, but her injury was almost identical to Rachels. Then she stated that just before her injury, she had made a competitive cheer team and couldn't cheer that year on the team because of the injury. Low and behold, Rachel had made the exact same competitive cheer team as this nursing assistant had, just a week before. For both of them it was the first time on the team and exactly the same time of the year — right when school ended and summer was to begin! At this point, I could hardly believe what I was hearing. I then asked her when she was able to get back into cheer, if at all. She stated in December of that year, she began taking tumbling classes again. She was able to try out the next spring for the same competitive cheer team and made it, cheering with this organization until her 8th grade year. I was struck by how crazy that was that her story was so similar to Rachels.

At this point in our conversation, Rachel was feeling much better so, I left her with the nursing assistant while I went to get the car. The nursing assistant took Rachel down in a wheelchair to meet me. As I got out of the car to help Rachel into it, the nursing assistant said to me, they had found something else they shared in common. They both had the same middle name – Lynette. Now Lynette is not a common name and it also was my mom's name, so it is a very dear name to me. I was flabbergasted! Not only did the girls have the same exact injury, same cheer team they made, same month of their injury, and the same age the injury occurred, they also had the same unusual middle name. It was obvious God was trying to say something! If Rachel hadn't felt nauseated we would never have met this gal and seen God's glory! It was incredible! When we got into the car and drove off, I felt like heaven had just opened up and God's hand had reached down and touched us. It felt surreal. Have you ever had one of those moments? When I called Rob and told him, he said it sounded like she was an angel. Whether or not she was an angel, didn't matter, what did matter was God had heard our cries and He was going to restore Rachel to full health again.

It's been two years now since her arm was broken and dislocated. She has gained almost complete range of motion back with her elbow. It is only missing less than 5% of its ability to flex, which is amazing, considering the orthopedist's first predictions. Rachel became more reliant on God through that trial. She now calls the doctor her hero, as it was amazing the work he did on her arm to restore it back into place. The physical therapists deserve a round of applause as well, as the road became difficult at times, and we all sometimes wondered if she'd even get 80% of her function back. They tirelessly pushed her through the pain and frustration she faced. We even thought cheerleading might be a thing of the past, but five months after the injury, she was able to reenter the world of tumbling and one year later she was back on the same cheer team! She is still going strong! This injury brought us back to putting God in the center of our lives. I hope we'll never forget the lessons we learned through that trial. God granted physical healing. He spiritually healed us as well. We have much to be thankful for!

Read Jeremiah 48:47. What will God do for Moab?

_____

_____

God will do whatever it takes to get our attention. His ultimate desire is that we'd know Him. He longs to bless us. We have to trust Him.

The Moabites were thought to be defeated in 582. "If Josephus (Antiquities X.ix.7) is to be believed, Nebuchadnezzar...marched against Moab and Ammon in 582 – and apparently against Judah too, for this was the year of the 3rd deportation... (he) defeated and subdued them. Soon thereafter Moab, like Edom, fell victim to... (an) Arab tribe...and ceased to exist..."[3] However, God did remember them and restore their fortunes.

Read Jeremiah 49:1-6. As you will remember, the Ammonites were descendants of the incestuous union between Lot and his second daughter.

Week 5

My Personal Journey

God will do **whatever IT TAKES** to get our *attention.*

The capital of Ammon, Rabbath-Ammon, back in those days, now is known as Amman and is the capitol of modern-day Jordan.[4] Ammon was also an enemy of Israel.

Draw a line between the correct verse and what the Ammonites did:

Judges 10:6-10	Saul and Israel defeat the Ammonites.
1 Samuel 11:1-11	The Ammonites were cruel to the pregnant women of Gilead.
2 Samuel 10:1-6	The Ammonites humiliated King David's servants.
Amos 1:13-15	The Ammonites and Philistines oppressed Israel.

This exercise gives you a little history on the Ammonites. They weren't a real congenial group of people. It sounds like they deserved what was coming to them.

The first accusation (Jeremiah 49:1) Jeremiah holds over the Ammonites is that they confiscated Israel's land when Assyria took Israel captive in 722 B.C.[5] Not only were the Ammonites presumptuous, they also worshipped a god that required child sacrifices. Malcom, their god, was also known as Milcom or Molech.[6] Their worship of false gods provoked God's wrath. One other wrong the Ammonites got in trouble for was murdering Gedaliah, a leader of Judah.[7] You'll learn about him in a couple more chapters.

Thankfully, there was a promise of restoration for Ammon, surprising as that may seem. The country addressed next, however, didn't fare as well as the Ammonites.

Read Jeremiah 49:7-27. The Edomites were descendants of Esau, Jacob's twin brother (Genesis 25:29-34), who sold his birthright to Jacob for bread and stew because he was famished.

THE EDOMITES

were descendants

of **ESAU**,

Jacob's *twin brother*.

Draw a line between the correct verse and what the Edomites did:

Numbers 20:14-21	Edom was King Saul's enemy.
Deuteronomy 23:7-8	Edomites were Israel's brothers. Their sons, of the third generation, could enter the assembly of the Lord.
1 Samuel 14:47	Edom refused to allow Israel to pass through their territory when Moses made a request.
1 Kings 11:14-17	Hadad, the Edomite, was an adversary of Solomon.

The Edomites encouraged the Babylonians in the destruction of Jerusalem and gloated over its capture.[8]

Read Ezekial 25:12-14, Psalms 137:7, Lamentations 4:21-23, and Obadiah verses 1-4 and 10-13. How does Obadiah describe the Edomites?

_____

_____

Obadiah verse 3 and Jeremiah 49:16 tell about how the Edomites lived in the clefts of the rock. Edom seemed to think because of their mountain fortresses they were safe and invincible to enemies. The mountain fortress they are famous for is Ummel Biyara, lying behind the later Petra, a difficult place to access.[9] One of my son's favorite movies, Indiana Jones and the Last Crusade, had a scene in Petra. When Sean Connery, Indiana Jones father, was trying to find the Holy Grail, they entered through a narrow passageway into Petra, a city with walls and pillars carved directly into the face of the rocks.[10] Do you remember this scene?

Petra's beautiful and unique architecture draws many visitors to the area still. It is located 50 miles south of the Dead Sea in Jordan. Archeologists are still working there to uncover hidden remnants of earlier civilizations. Petra's location was very difficult to access both in Edom's time and now. There are many ways to get into Petra, but no easy ways.[11] Edom felt overly secure and did not expect to be brought down because their location was difficult to access.

Between 550 B.C.-400 B.C., Nabatean Arabs ransacked Edom. It was inhabited until the Crusades and then forgotten about until the 1800's when archeologists rediscovered it.[12]

Edom's city Teman (Jeremiah 49:7) was known for its sages.[13] God commented how it seemed wisdom had disappeared in Teman.

Edom was destroyed completely. Their fall was so great that it was heard all over the world – "the earth has quaked of the noise of their downfall..." (Jeremiah 49:21). The only mercy shown to this nation was to their widows and orphans (Jeremiah 49:11).

How does God describe pure religion in James 1:27?

_____

_____

God obviously cared for the widows and orphans of Edom, just like He commands us to do today. The next four people groups we'll breeze through a little quicker.

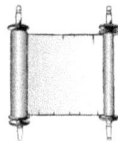 **Briefly skim Jeremiah 49:23-39. Name the four places or people groups addressed.**

_____

Damascus was a famous city. It is mentioned several times in the Old Testament during the times of Abraham, King David and King Solomon. However, Damascus is probably most well-known in the Bible for being the location of Saul's conversion. You may remember hearing the phrase, "Saul on the road to Damascus" (Acts 9:1-25). Damascus is now the capital of modern-day Syria. It was in the news frequently a couple years ago, because of the uprisings that occurred against President Bashar Assad's rule.

Kedar, another people group mentioned in Jeremiah 49, was an "Arab tribe of the Syrian desert east of Palestine".[14] Hazor, is not to be confused with a well known city in Palestine. Hazor is thought to be either a specific place or a group of people in unwalled villages.[15] Their origin is really unknown. Both the peoples of Kedar and Hazor lived in tents securely with the ability to be mobile (Jeremiah 49:29-31). Elam was located in present day southwest Iran, east of Babylon and known for their expertise in archery.[16] Notice God made a reference to breaking the bow of Elam in Jeremiah 49:35. While no mention is made of Damascus, Kedar, or Hazor being restored, God does say He will restore the fortunes of Elam.

In Acts 2:1-13, what event were the Elamites at?

_____

To hear the defeat of Judah's enemies was an important component of God's reign and their future salvation.[17] The Judeans had been mistreated by most of these nations for hundreds of years. However, their judgment day was coming.

The message of God was for both the Judeans and the other nations. The warnings to these countries are a warning to our own nation as well. We must guard against relying on our military prowess, wealth, intelligence, pride, and self-sufficiency, like these nations did. These attributes we generally consider strengths for a nation will not save us in the end. It is our faith in God that will.

Spend time in prayer today for our nation. Meditate on 2 Chronicles 7:14, "If my people, which are called by my name, shall humble themselves, and pray, and seek my face, and turn from their wicked ways; then will I hear from heaven, and will forgive their sin, and will heal their land" (KJV).

DAY 5

Babylon's Future

Open with prayer. Remember God has created this day and wants to walk with you through it every step of the way!

I had a hard time knowing where to place this lesson. It can fit here because it was given to the Babylonians during the fourth year of King Zedekiah's reign. However, it describes Babylon's future destruction, making it tempting to place it closer towards the end of the study after you have read all of the horrible things Babylon did to Jerusalem.

Chapters 50 and 51 include the oracle given to Babylon. It is the longest oracle given to any of the nations. Babylon, while used as a tool by God to awaken the Judeans to their rebellious ways, also overstepped their bounds. Their hunger for power got to their heads, and they ended up oppressing the Judeans. God eventually had to punish their cruel regime.

Read Jeremiah 51:59-64.

How was Seraiah related to Baruch, Jeremiah's scribe? Compare Jeremiah 51:59 to Jeremiah 32:12.

_____

Seraiah is Baruch's brother! Seraiah served as an officer in Zedekiah's cabinet.[1] Jeremiah trusted Seraiah to read these words of doom to Babylon and then throw them into the Euphrates river with a stone tied to it. A curse was placed on Babylon. The scroll sunk to the bottom of the river symbolizing Babylon's future demise.

Antonio Abrignawi/Shutterstock

We are going to skim through chapters 50 and 51 due to the enormous length of the oracle. However, feel free to read the chapters entirety if you feel so inclined.

Begin in Jeremiah 50:1-2. Who is Marduk? Make sure you are using the NASB translation.

_____

Remember we learned about Marduk earlier in our lessons? Marduk was the chief deity that Babylon worshipped. This god, as well as all of the other idols, would be destroyed. God was not going to tolerate their idol worship.

Read Jeremiah 50:29-33. Using one word, how does God describe Babylon?

_____

The Babylonians are full of pride, an imperial power. What Babylon has done to others, will be done to them. What goes around comes around. They oppressed Judah, refusing to let her go. Because of this, Babylon would be oppressed next. They would have to reckon with Yahweh.

How does God say He'll deal with the Judeans who are not being released from captivity in Babylon? Read Jeremiah 50:33-34.

_____

_____

Like Satan, our archenemy, Babylon, Judah's archenemy, refused to let go of her. However, we have a strong Redeemer and His name is Jesus. He stands up for us and pleads our case, just like Judah's strong redeemer, Yahweh, stood up for them.

Write out Romans 8:33-34.

_____

_____

_____

_____

_____

Read Jeremiah 51:5-10.

Jeremiah 51:5-10 is referring to 70 years after the Judeans had been in exile. God was telling both Israel and Judah He had not forsaken them and they needed to get out of Babylon while they were able. Babylon was not able to be healed even though the Judeans had tried to bring healing to the Babylonians. While some of the Judeans may have become comfortable in Babylon, God didn't want them hanging out there any longer. Their work in Babylon was done. God had melted and molded them in Babylon, but now it was time to return home.

In 539 B.C., the Medes and Persians captured Babylon. One year later, King Cyrus issued a decree stating the Judeans could return to their land. Approximately 50,000 Judeans did return to Judah.[2]

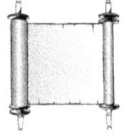

Read Jeremiah 51:13-18. God describes His work versus mankind's workmanship. What is the difference?

_____

_____

Read Jeremiah 51:34-35. Who is speaking in this passage and how do they describe Nebuchadnezzar, the King of Babylon?

_____

_____

It's not a pretty picture of King Nebby! He was viewed by the Judeans as a monster. The Judeans were reminding God of what Nebuchadnezzar had done to them.

What does God say in response to their comments? Read Jeremiah 51:36.

_____

Once again, God stated He'd plead their case and destroy Babylon.

Read Psalm 140:12. Who will God stick up for?

_____

Read Jeremiah 51:45-50.

God reminded them to get out again (Jeremiah 51:50)! While Babylon served its purpose, it was over and it was no longer a safe place for the Jews to remain in. God wanted them to return to Jerusalem and accomplish all that God had for them there.

It's much like us after we've gone through our season of discipline. Once He's trained us it's time to get on with things and accomplish what's next. We can't just stay put, never applying what we've learned. No further growth will occur in our spiritual "Babylon" when it's time to go to our "Jerusalem". Sure, it is fine to serve our time in "Babylon," but then move on!

Look closely at Jeremiah 51:48. How can you apply this to your spiritual life?

_____

_____

When Babylon fell, it was such good news that all rejoiced, both in heaven and on earth. When our enemy (Satan) falls, heaven and earth will rejoice too! It'll be such good news when the enemy of our soul is defeated, both in the daily battles of our lives and in the ultimate last battle at the end of the age.

The fall of Babylon occurred in 539 B.C., peacefully without a battle. A man named Cyrus, came as a liberator, not as a war-monger. Babylon was treated with the utmost respect by the new Persian monarch, King Cyrus.[3]

When **Babylon FELL...** **ALL** *rejoiced!* BOTH *heaven and earth.*

When our enemy— Satan **FALLS**, *heaven and earth* will *rejoice too!*

Cyrus' conquest of Babylon was seen as God's way of redeeming Judah from exile.

In 330 B.C., Alexander the Great also destroyed Babylon.[4] The prophecy also would be ultimately fulfilled in the end times, as described in Revelation 17 and 18. Many times prophecies have a duplicate meaning, both a near and far off fulfillment.

A couple assumptions can be drawn from the oracle to Babylon. First, God doesn't forget His people. Even though He may discipline them, He sees their suffering and wants to give them a new beginning. Second, God won't tolerate unjust power structures.[6] Ultimately, they won't endure. Yahweh has the last and final say in all things.

Finish the lesson by considering if it is time to leave your Babylon and move back to your Jerusalem. Has God accomplished His purposes in your Babylon? Are you ready to move on to the next step? If so, ask Him what He'd like to use you for in this upcoming season of your life. Be open to His plans. Rest in His presence!

NOTES

VIDEO QUESTIONS WEEK 5

1. Do you recognize any self-destructive paths you are on that need to change?
2. Have you ever experienced a season when God gave you a major wake-up call, like the Judeans? What did God teach you during that season?
3. Romans 6:23 says: "The wages of sin is death..." In what way can "small" sins eventually destroy us?
4. Read Hosea 6:1. Discuss what this verse means to you.

Video sessions are available for download at www.grassandflowers.org

WEEK SIX
TAKING CAPTIVITY CAPTIVE

DAY ONE
Message to the Exiles

DAY TWO
The Famous Verse

DAY THREE
Seeking God with all our Hearts

DAY FOUR
A Few Duds & Another Godly Prophet

DAY FIVE
Put No Confidence in the Flesh

DAY 1

Message to the Exiles

In Chapter 29, Jeremiah wrote several letters to the exiles in Babylon.

Start by reading Jeremiah 29:1-3. Who delivered the letters to the exiles (hint: verse 3)?

_____

The letters to the exiles were delivered after the first deportation in 597. It is likely the letters were sent in 595 or 594 B.C. However, the exact date is unknown. The Babylonian Chronicle hints at internal troubles in Babylon in 595 and 594 B.C. when it is believed there were thoughts of rebellion and revolt by some of the deported Jews."[1] The correspondence was probably sent after this by King Zedekiah to reassure Nebuchadnezzar that his loyalties still lay with him and he did not support any revolt his people may have been planning.

Read 2 Kings 22:4-10; reread Jeremiah 29:3. Who is Elasah's father most likely?

_____

Now read Jeremiah 26:24. Who saved Jeremiah's life here?

_____

It is believed Elasah may have been the son of Shaphan, the man who read the scroll of the Law upon its discovery during King Josiah's reign. If Elasah was the son of Shaphan then he also would have been the brother of Ahikam, the man who saved Jeremiah's life from the angry priests.[2]

The journey to Babylon was approximately 700 miles away from Jerusalem. Frequently, delegations were sent to Babylon during this period, despite the great distance. It is assumed by scholars that King Nebuchadnezzar was not oppressing the Hebrews while they were living in Babylon, because he allowed the letters to be delivered to them.[3]

Read Jeremiah 29:4-6, the beginning of the letter to the exiles. What did God tell the exiles to do in verse 5 & 6?

_____

_____

The exiles believed they'd be in Babylon briefly. The false prophets continued preaching to them, telling them they'd be going back home soon. The temple was intact in Jerusalem. Plus, Jerusalem was still inhabited by many Jews at this point. The majority of Jews were still in Jerusalem. Naturally, they believed that they'd be going back home soon.

However, God had a different plan. He did not want a premature return or quick fix. He knew the Jews needed to learn a lesson. It was time to let their failures teach them something valuable and develop their character. The Judeans had to lose what they thought was crucial to their identity to finally be able to find their God. The Judeans had to be "plucked up and broken down" before they could be "planted and built up" (Jeremiah 1:10).

The "good figs" lost everything sacred to them. Their once stable world collapsed. Yet, God reached down and told them, they weren't going to be leaving anytime soon. He advised them to settle down and become productive citizens. Plant gardens, marry, and have kids. They were to live responsibly and not waste their time while in Babylon because they were going to be there for awhile.

Exile means, "We are where we don't want to be."[4] Everything we hold dear is stripped away from us. "The accustomed ways we have of finding our worth and sensing our significance vanish."[5] It's a traumatic time. In the Hebrew, exile (galah) means "to uncover, remove, banish, captivity, expose, lay bare, reveal, shamelessly uncover, show, strip off, and be stripped."[6] The Hebrew and Chaldee Dictionary in my NASB Bible states the primary root of exile is "to denude (especially in a disgraceful sense); by implication to exile (captives being usually stripped)."[7] Exile was horrific, demoralizing, and shameful.

The Judeans faced not only one traumatic event, but a total loss of everything. "Disasters involve more than sad or tragic events. A disaster is 'disastrous only when events exceed the ability of the group to cope, to redefine and reconstruct' their world. They crush normal human responses; devour a sense of personal safety and daily routine; and devastate economies, cultures, and theological traditions. Disasters leave people numb, physically bereft, traumatized, rudderless, and without meaning."[8]

Exile is a devastating event for anyone to go through. Along with exile, comes battles, killings, destroyed homes, rapes, death for some on the march to exile, mistreatment, and torture. The bitterness and anger the Judeans had towards the Babylonians was intense.

Read Psalm 137:1-9. How does this psalm describe how the Judeans felt about their captors?

_____

_____

Obviously, the Judeans had major resentment towards the Babylonians. How often do you hear someone say, "How blessed will be the one who seizes and dashes your little ones against the rock" (Psalm 137:9)? I hope you've never heard that before and never will in the future. The Jews were crushed by this national catastrophe. Devastated, despairing, sorrowful, and angry were all descriptors of how they felt.

The Judeans had to be *"plucked up and broken down"* **BEFORE** they could be *"planted and built up."*
Jeremiah 1:10

Week 6

What kind of images stir up in your mind, when you hear the word captivity?

_____

_____

I imagine a lion in a cage, pacing back and forth. He wants to get out, but is unable. No matter how hard he tries to leave, he can't. He is stuck, frustrated, and going nowhere any time soon.

Read Jeremiah 29:7. What is the verse saying? Do you find anything unusual in God's request of His people?

_____

_____

_____

_____

PRAY

for our

ENEMIES?

The Judeans must have been thinking, "You've got to be kidding God? Is this some kind of joke? Pray for our enemies? Pray for those who treated us so poorly? They demoralized us. They don't deserve our prayers."

Read Romans 12:19-21. How are we to treat our enemies?

_____

_____

Name a time you followed God's advice and prayed for an enemy of yours? What was the result? No names please.

_____

_____

What did God say would happen if the Judeans would pray for their enemies (Jeremiah 29:7)?

_____

_____

Praying for Babylon's welfare would help them too! The Judeans were not to be puffed up and rebellious to the authorities placed over them. Instead, they were to pray for them. They were to pray for welfare, which in the Hebrew, welfare (shalom) means peace and prosperity.⁹

There are a lot of benefits of prayer. Prayer is relational. It requires honesty and a willingness to listen to God. It enables us to unload our burdens. Our desires become more like His through prayer. Prayer, while it helps others, also changes us. Praying for our enemies' well-being frees us from self-pity and anger. By forgiving our persecutors through prayer, our spiritual, emotional, and physical well-being is improved. "Studies have shown that people who are unforgiving and hostile suffer greater emotional and physical problems."[10]

> **Praying** for our **enemies' wellbeing, frees** us from **self-pity** and **anger.**

Hopefully, none of us have to experience the kind of exile the Jews went through. However, all of us at times have experienced or will experience "exile" in a sense.

Divorce, death of a loved one, losing your home or job, and war are all events that leave us asking why and throw us into a sort of "exile."

Perhaps, someone has deeply wronged you. The pain is so great you can't even imagine praying blessing on that person. That is the last thing you want to do. However, when you forgive them, and don't hold resentment any longer you become free. When you pray for them you see your enemy in a different light. You see them through God's eyes of mercy. It doesn't mean your enemy won't face judgment for their sin, but you can leave the judging up to God.

Write out Luke 6:27-28.

_____

_____

_____

Now skip down a few verses and read Luke 6:36-38. What happens if we don't judge people and choose to forgive them instead?

_____

_____

_____

Why should we show mercy to others if they hurt us?

_____

_____

Showing mercy to others and praying for them is really unthinkable in situations similar to what the Judeans faced. It reminds me of Christians who are persecuted, imprisoned, tortured, mistreated for their faith, yet they still pray for their captors. It doesn't make sense. However, it is exactly what God did for us. Humankind persecuted Jesus and refused His kindness, yet He still prayed and died for all people, taking their sins upon Himself, so they wouldn't have to die, but could have eternal life. He shows mankind unconditional love when they don't deserve it.

Our enemies have hurt us, but we're supposed to turn the other cheek and bless them, not curse them. Read Matthew 5:43-48. If we don't love our enemies and pray for them we are no different than whom?

_____

_____

Ray Pritchard offer several suggestions for how we can love our enemies:

- Greet them kindly. Don't avoid them.
- Disarm them by doing something they'd least expect.
- Do good to them.
- Refuse to speak evil of them.
- Thank God for them. Remember God allowed them on your path for a reason.
- Pray for them.
- Ask God to bless them.[11]

We are called to be a blessing and a light to the world. We are to share the love of Christ. The Judeans, even though they'd messed up big time, were to be an example to the Babylonians of how to live right. Isn't it nice to know if we've messed up we can still be redeemed and used by God?!

Psalm 67:1-2 states:

_____

_____

_____

The next verses you are about to read are a stark contrast from Psalm 67. Isaiah 13:15-19 describes what is going to happen to Babylon because of their mistreatment of the Judeans. So, while we are to forgive our enemies, at least a day will come when they have to pay for their ill-treatment of others, if they don't repent.

Read Isaiah 13:15-19.

God literally answered the Jews' prayers. Judgment came upon the

Babylonians for their mistreatment of the people of God. "Assuredly, the evil man will not go unpunished, but the descendants of the righteous will be delivered" (Proverbs 11:21). God always has the last say in a matter. So, don't waste your time being angry and bitter towards your enemies. It will only cause you grief. Instead, pray for their welfare and you will be blessed too.

DAY 2

The Famous Verse

Week 6! We're more than halfway through the study! It's been a blast doing this study with you and the best is yet to come. So, hang in there and enjoy!

Write out Jeremiah 29:11.

_____

_____

_____

Jeremiah 29:11 is one of the most popular verses in Scripture. However, most people who quote Jeremiah 29:11, know very little about the context. God was saying in this verse, "Out of all the chaos, calamity, and exile you've faced I still know the plans I have for you...and the plans are good...and I'm telling you this so you don't lose hope...you've got a future...you won't be in Babylon forever." What good news this must have been for the Jews. They probably had felt abandoned by God. Some of them most likely realized if they had just listened to God in the first place, they would have avoided this calamity.

Campbell Morgan stated, "If there is the making of a traitor in me, I shall certainly be placed in circumstances which will give me the opportunity to discover it, to yield to it; or to master it by flight to the refuge and the strength of my Lord's love."[1] The Jews were given a chance to learn from their mistakes and return to God's comfort. God had not stopped loving them. It was His mercy and love for them that brought them into exile — to make them aware of their sin and become spiritually healthy people again.

Many carry shame and regret as a result of dwelling on their past mistakes. This creates a paralysis which prevents further growth in Christ. Our hope is in Christ and we must allow Him to lead us forward. We must become victors, not victims. Suffering is supposed to make us grow up, not make us wallow in despair and misery. We're to use our suffering to draw closer to God for comfort, and then pass on the gift of comfort to others when they face similar situations. We're to let trials do their full work, whittling out our impurities, so we may be more like Him.

Wiersbe states, "One of the first steps in turning tragedy to triumph is to accept the situation courageously and put ourselves into the hands of a loving God, who makes no mistakes."[2]

Lauren is a woman who has allowed God to turn her tragedy into a triumph. Twenty weeks pregnant with her second child, she and her husband, Brett found out the baby had triploidy, a chromosomal disorder that causes physical deformities and mental delays. Usually, a child does not survive past the first week of life with this condition. They were told she could abort the

For **I know** the plans I have for You,' declares the *Lord,* 'plans for **welfare** and not for calamity to give you a *future* and a *hope.*

Jeremiah 29:11

child due to the complications they would have to face, but they chose not to listen to the doctors. She states, while she carried the baby almost the full pregnancy (36 weeks), it was very difficult knowing the child would likely not survive. They named their precious little boy, Truett, which means "little truth." At 36 weeks, Truett died in utero and a stillbirth was induced.

They had a funeral for Truett. Lauren and Brett, despite their deep grief, made the funeral into a celebration of Truett's brief life. They wanted there to be an opportunity for family members and friends to hear about Jesus and the abundant life He has to offer. The service was beautiful. Some commented on how incredible it was that she and her husband lifted their hands in praise to God amidst their tears during the songs. Lauren's sister was so moved by their witness of faith she made the decision to follow Christ that day. Lauren said to me, "If we had taken the easy way out, just aborted the baby, there would never have been a funeral. And if there had never been a funeral, there wouldn't have been an opportunity for many to hear about Jesus and my sister would not have come to know Jesus." Instead of feeling sorry for themselves, Lauren and Brett used their grief to touch others' lives. They would have preferred to have their baby healthy and happy in their arms, but they realized it was not what God had planned. Lauren said she thought of how God sacrificed His one and only Son for the good of others. It reminded her of her one and only son who had died ("little truth"), allowing others to know Jesus and find freedom. Lauren and her husband were in a place they didn't want to be in (exile), but they saw how God used it for good. As Lauren says, "God doesn't promise we won't have hardships, but He does say that He will never leave us or forsake us amidst the trial." At the end of the funeral, Lauren's sister pointed out to a beautiful double rainbow over the church. Lauren felt it displayed God's promise to them. He was in the midst of these circumstances; there was purpose in the suffering.

Three years later, Lauren and Brett have now adopted a little girl. Jeremiah 29:11 has rung true for them, "For I know the plans that I have for you, declares the Lord, plans for welfare and not for calamity to give you a future and a hope." Out of their grief and loss, God brings continued life. We may never know exactly why God chooses the path He has created for us. However, we can trust He knew what He was doing and there is a greater and higher purpose for things He does than we can imagine.

In our moments/days/years of weakness, we find our most precious times with God. The Judeans had the opportunity in their weakest moments and years of their lives to come to know God again.

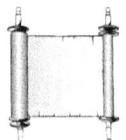

Read Romans 5:3-5. What does suffering produce?

_____

_____

Last summer we went to California for our family vacation. A couple of the national parks we went to had some of the largest trees in the world — the sequoias. We learned controlled fires are often used to maintain the forest's health, where fire crews actually start fires. After years of suppressing fires, people realized allowing a more natural fire cycle to occur proved more helpful than prevention. It averts the likelihood of more serious fires occurring, thins shade tolerant understory trees, and encourages new sequoia reproduction.[4] People have found out, fire, in moderation, is actually good for the sequoias.

I copied this quote off of a plaque from the Sequoia National Park Visitor Center, "Rising from the Ash — Seedlings: Thousands of seeds sprout in the ashy soil left by fire. This soil absorbs and holds moisture well. New roots easily penetrate it because it is loose and crumbly. Seedlings are much more likely to survive where fire burned hottest." And on another plaque it read, "Healing adaptation: Rapid growth often occurs after a fire. With competing trees burned away, surviving sequoias get more light, moisture, and nutrients. Trees may grow thicker annual rings for as long as 100 years."[5]

Fire would seem to be a destructive force to be avoided at all costs. However, fire actually is beneficial for these trees. It reminds me of trials. While it seems like you'd want to avoid trials at all costs, it is the very thing that helps us to grow and mature. Competing idols are like the competing trees. When idols are no longer in our way, we grow better. An environment is created through trials that chokes out things competing for our attention with God.

"By forces seemingly antagonistic and destructive nature accomplishes her beneficent designs – now a flood of fire, now a flood of ice… and again in the fullness of time an outburst of organic life…"[6] Just like nature benefits from catastrophe and suffering, we as humans do as well. In fact, in nature, growth occurs best after catastrophe and suffering. And many times it does the same for us.

How do you respond when catastrophe strikes? Do you complain or try to escape from reality or do you seek God in it?

_____

_____

Don't get me wrong, we don't have to like suffering and we may never completely understand why God allowed a traumatic event(s) to occur while here on Earth. Believe me; I've never understood why my mom died at such a young age. In my mind, whatever good has come from it hasn't seemed worth the loss. Even if hundreds of people came to know Jesus from her death, it still wouldn't have seemed worth it to me. I don't understand God's ways many times (Isaiah 55:8-9). However, I do know this – I will trust Him. He knows what He is doing. There is a greater purpose in what He did than I can see with my own eyes.

Life here on Earth is fleeting (like a drop of water in an ocean); compared to the time we'll spend in eternity (the ocean). I'll be with Jesus and my mom for eternity. I will live for Him while here and have faith that the Creator has good

Week 6

Trials
*HELP us
to both GROW
and mature.*

plans for me. In the center of suffering, through my mom's struggles with cancer, her death, and later the postpartum depression I dealt with, I came to know God more intimately than I would ever have without the suffering. I learned He listens, He cares. He is my counselor, comfort, joy, and salvation. Like Joseph, I say what was meant for evil, turned out for good! My pain has allowed me to comfort others in their suffering. In fact, if my mom hadn't had cancer I would never have been a nurse. It was through her battle with cancer and seeing the nurses take care of her in the hospital I realized what I wanted to do with my life.

Reflection

Are we allowing our trials to be used for God's glory?

God allows us to go through hardships and deep suffering for many reasons. Trials purge us of sin, test our faith, humble us, prepare us to minister to others, and help us to understand His character better.[7] Our pain teaches us, whether we like it or not. The question is: Are we allowing our trials to be used for God's glory? Or are we resentful toward them and allowing them to destroy us?

What suffering have you been through that has allowed you to comfort others in similar predicaments?

_____

_____

_____

I hope you are using your "exile" experiences for good. Before you leave today, write out this one last passage and then pray for the ability to see opportunities to help others in their distress.

Write out 2 Corinthians 1:3-4.

_____

_____

_____

_____

_____

Have a great day ladies! "For I know the plans I have for you, declares the Lord, plans for welfare and not for calamity to give you a future and a hope" (Jeremiah 29:11). Next time you hear or read this well-known verse, remember the context of it. Hope came out of suffering for the Judeans. Hope has and will offspring from your suffering as well.

Face to face with Christ, my Savior,

Face to face – what will it be,

When with rapture I behold Him,

Jesus Christ who died for me?

Refrain:

Face to face. I shall behold Him,

Far beyond the starry sky;

Face to face in all His glory,

I shall see Him by and by!"

Only faintly now I see Him,

With the darkened veil between,

But a blessed day is coming,

When His glory shall be seen.

What rejoicing in His presence,

When our banished grief and pain;

When the crooked ways are straightened,

And the dark things shall be plain.

Face to face – oh, blissful moment!

Face to face – to see and know;

Face to face with my Redeemer,

Jesus Christ who loves me so.

Hymn written in 1898 by Mrs. Frank A. Breck[8]

DAY 3

Seeking God With All Our Hearts

Read Jeremiah 29:12-14.

According to Ray Pritchard, we find ourselves in one of two places when we are discouraged. We either begin by assessing our problems or we look to God instead of our problems. When we look to God during times of discouragement, we find hope. However, when we focus on our problems only, we become more discouraged and are no better off by dwelling on them.[1]

Like the Judeans in Babylon, what do we do when we're caught in circumstances that don't pan out for us like we think they should? God invited the Judeans in Jeremiah 29:12-13, to call upon Him and seek Him in their calamities. He calls us to do the same. In our "Babylon," we are forced to slow down long enough to hear God and if we're wise, we'll choose to seek God in our "Babylon."

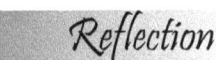

Will you choose to seek God during your difficult circumstances?

Will you choose to seek God during your difficult circumstances? Don't seek things that only temporarily satisfy. Only God can bring true and lasting satisfaction. Choose to not become bitter in your exile/tragedy. We can opt to be miserable in our circumstances or to learn something through our experiences. We need to open our eyes up to see what God has for us in each situation He places us in.

When tragedy comes and we pray for healing and it doesn't happen how we expect, we have to remember sometimes there is a greater purpose in it all.

Have you found your greatest blessings have come from the most painful times in your life? Explain.

_____

_____

Let's look up some verses about seeking God. Read Deuteronomy 4:29-31 and Isaiah 55:6-7. How do these verses describe God? What happens when we seek God?

_____

_____

When we seek God with our whole heart, we are received kindly by God, pardoned, and He promises He won't fail or forget us. Plus, in Jeremiah 29:14, God goes on to say we'll be brought out of exile and our fortunes restored. We are blessed by God when we seek Him unreservedly.

Week 6

Fill in the blanks:

"And without faith it is impossible to please Him, for he who comes to God must believe that He is, and that He is a _____ of those, who _____ Him" (Hebrews 11:6).

"...and if My people who are called by My name _____ themselves and _____, and _____ My face and _____ from their wicked ways, then I will _____ from heaven, will _____ their sin, and will _____ their land" (2 Chronicles 7:14).

"...the Lord is with you when you are with Him. And if you _____ Him, He will let you _____ Him; but if you forsake Him, He will forsake you... And all Judah rejoiced concerning the oath, for they had sworn with their _____ and had sought Him _____, and He _____ them _____ Him. So, the Lord gave them _____ on every side" (2 Chronicles 15:2b, 15).

The Lord wanted His people to come back to Him. He gave them opportunity through this trial to find Him again, if they'd seek Him earnestly.

If we have to work hard for something we usually appreciate it all the more when we obtain it. Or when we've lost something that is valuable to us and can't find it, when we do find it after an extensive search, we appreciate it all the more. It's just like seeking and looking for God. When we do find Him again after being away from Him, it is such a relief to be back in His presence. He longs for us to remain there.

I think God allows us to get so miserable, lonely, and desperate at times, so we'll come back to Him. When we realize nothing else satisfies us, we begin to yearn for a taste of living water again. When we find that living water again, it deeply refreshes us and we realize what we've missed.

Right now, we're in a church that, in my opinion, is huge! About 1,200 attend services each Sunday. You may not think 1,200 people is a lot if you come from a mega church, but if you come from a small church, like me, you will probably agree that 1,200 people is a large congregation! While there are many wonderful and friendly people in this church, it's been more difficult to find accountability and a sense of family/coziness that comes along with what we've experienced in smaller churches. The only way we can have this "feel" is to engage in small groups. When we first joined the church, we got involved in a small group, whom we adored, but because of busy schedules and then later a night of the week that we couldn't meet on, we found ourselves no longer able to attend. For a brief time not belonging to a small group was fine, but long term we began to miss the community we had enjoyed. At one point, I cried out to God and specifically told Him I couldn't go to this church any longer (despite knowing He had called us there), unless He provided us with an intimate group of believers to hang out with on a regular basis. I felt so lonely at that point, despite having many people surrounding me in the church. I knew God heard my prayer when the very next day at a church event, He opened the door up to meet a woman who was in the same predicament. This woman couldn't find a small group that met on a day her and her family could meet either. She, like I, had struggled without a small group. I knew instantly God had brought us together. God, thankfully, heard my prayers. He heard the desperation in which I cried out to Him and showed me that yes this mattered to Him too. Shortly after meeting this sister in Christ, God laid it on both my and my husband's heart that we were to start a small group. This woman's family became a part of our small group and we were able to reach out to many others who needed a place to grow with other believers. If I hadn't become discouraged, lonely, and unable to find a small group, we would never have started our own small group. God had a reason for why no other doors opened. How good it was to seek God with my whole heart and be rewarded for doing it. Sometimes, the times we see God move the clearest is in our moments of utter desperation.

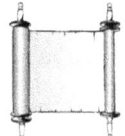

Can you think of a time you sought God wholeheartedly and found Him? Explain your experience.

_____

_____

_____

We can complain about our **CIRCUMSTANCES** or **we can** *find out* what God has for us **TO DO IN** our **circumstances.**

We can complain about our circumstances or we can find out what God has for us to do in our circumstances. God was trying to tell His people they were going to be in Babylon for awhile, so it would behoove them to stop whining and find Him there.

As Eugene Peterson so wisely said, "Throw yourselves into the place in which you find yourselves, but not on its terms, on God's terms. Pray. Search for that center in which God's will is being worked out (which is what we do when we pray) and work from that center."²

When we seek God diligently, we are praying. We are talking to Him. We're seeking Him for direction and peace in our lives. Plus, when seeking Him, we're listening to Him and worshiping Him. Seeking Him changes our attitudes. We keep our gaze on Him, instead of the circumstances around us. We start to thank Him for what He has given us, instead of focusing on what we no longer have. Sometimes keeping our gaze on Him can be very difficult, especially when we've lost someone or something of great value to us. He knows and understands how hard it is. He is there to comfort and reassure us. We also can get just plain angry with Him. He can take it, thankfully!

When a horse is trained, a bit is placed in his mouth in order to direct him. The horse doesn't like this at first, but in the end it is good for him, in order that he may become a useful horse. The same goes for us. Suffering isn't pleasant one "bit" (no pun intended!), but if we're going to become useful for God, we will have to allow God to mold us to become useful for His Kingdom.

Look at what happened with the Judeans when they took their minds off of their pain and began looking to God. "In an effort to separate themselves from their captors the exiles began practicing their religious observances with renewed fervor. Having no temple, they gathered together in synagogues (assemblies), and began writing on scrolls many of the oral traditions that had circulated for centuries."[3]

The time spent in Babylon was used wisely by many of the Judeans. "They settled down to find out what it meant to be God's people in the place they did not want to be – in Babylon. The result was that this became the most creative period in the entire sweep of Hebrew history...They learned how to pray in deeper and more life-changing ways than ever. They wrote and copied and pondered the vast revelation that had come down to them from Moses and the prophets, and they came to recognize the incredible riches of their Scriptures... They were pushed to the edge of existence where they thought they were hanging on by the skin of their teeth, and they found that in fact they had been pushed to the center, where God was. They experienced not bare survival but abundant life."[4]

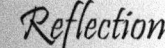

Are you letting God's Word generate hope in you?

God offered riches much greater than material goods, when He told the Judeans to seek Him wholeheartedly. He gave them hope. And how badly they needed hope during that time. He promised them their fortunes would be restored. By these promises God gave, it confirmed to them their suffering would not be for naught. His word generated hope in them.

Do you let God's Word generate hope in you? Slow down and talk to God today. He would love to fellowship with you and He promises to listen fully, if you'll seek Him with your whole heart.

DAY 4
A Few Duds and Another Godly Prophet

The last couple of days we've covered Jeremiah 29:1-14. Today, we're wrapping up the chapter and taking a quick glimpse at a new prophet on board. Chapter 29 consists of a variety of interactions between people via letters.[1] In the first 14 verses, which we've already examined, Jeremiah spoke to the exiles, giving them hope and encouragement. In the next passage, verses 15-23, Jeremiah addressed the false prophets in Babylon. In verses 24-32, Jeremiah concentrates on what Shemaiah said about him and how he responds back to Shemaiah's accusations.

Read Jeremiah 29:20-23. What are the names of the two false prophets mentioned here?

_____

What happened to these two prophets because they taught fallaciously?

_____

Besides falsely prophesying, what other kind of corruption did these men involve themselves in?

_____

Shemaiah referred to Jeremiah as a Madman.

These were not holy prophets; they predicted the future inaccurately and were involved in blatant sin. It sounds like they let their positions of power go to their heads, like so many do. Besides committing adultery, it is thought they were involved in a political upheaval of some sort, possibly trying to cause a revolt; otherwise Nebachadnezzar would never have burned them to death if they had only been adulterers.[2] Roasting people in the fire was a punishment commonly used by the Babylonians.[3] Ahab and Zedekiah's punishment was a warning to all the exiles. The exiles even used their names in a curse, warning others not to rebel.

Read Jeremiah 29:24-29. Who was Shemaiah speaking to in these passages?

_____

What was Shemaiah trying to say to the person he was addressing?

_____

Shemaiah, did not take kindly to Jeremiah; he referred to Jeremiah as a madman. He wished Zephaniah, the priest, would use his authority to silence Jeremiah. Zephaniah didn't directly address Shemaiah or Jeremiah concerning the matter. Instead, he simply read the letter to Jeremiah. It isn't known if Zephaniah was supportive of Jeremiah or not, but he did not punish Jeremiah. Maybe Zephaniah recalled the fate of Pashur earlier on and decided not to make the same mistake.[4] There are three other times Zephaniah is mentioned in Jeremiah. Two times Zephaniah, the son of Maaseiah, consulted with Jeremiah per the request of King Zedekiah (Jeremiah 21:1; 37:3). Lastly, he was referred to in Jeremiah 52:24-27, during the fall of Jerusalem when he was brought before the King of Babylon, along with others, to be killed.

What did Jeremiah do when he heard Shemaiah's unkind words (Jeremiah 29:31)?

_____

What was going to happen to Shemaiah because of his rebelliousness (Jeremiah 29:32)?

_____

_____

God takes His words seriously. He doesn't let anyone go unpunished if they have spoken falsely. A liar may not seem to reap the consequences of his actions immediately, but judgment eventually comes. Shemaiah's punishment must have been a reassurance to Jeremiah that God saw what was going on, as Jeremiah risked his life daily preaching God's word.

Unlike *Jeremiah*, E z e k i e l **never** *prophesied* in *Jerusalem*, he only *prophesied* in **Babylon**.

Another prophet was raised up in Babylon around this same time. He also put his life on the line, like Jeremiah did. His name was Ezekiel. Ezekiel wrote the book of the Old Testament named after him. The book of Ezekiel comes right after Lamentations, which is directly after Jeremiah. Ezekiel was taken to Babylon in 597 B.C., during the second deportation, along with all the other exiles.

Read Ezekiel 1:1-3. What year did God announce to Ezekiel his call to be a prophet?

_____

King Jehoiachin was exiled in the same deportation as Ezekiel in 597 B.C. Ezekiel's first prophecy was believed to have been in the summer of 593 B.C.[5] Unlike Jeremiah, Ezekiel never prophesied in Jerusalem, he only prophesied in Babylon. In Ezekial 1:1, the "thirtieth year" may refer to Ezekiel's age, meaning he would have been 30 years old when he began prophesying.[6]

What occupation did Ezekiel hold before becoming a prophet (Ezekial 1:3)?

_____

Ezekiel was a priest. Having been a priest, he had probably heard about

Jeremiah. Ezekiel, like Jeremiah, prophesied about the coming destruction of Jerusalem and the temple. He also spoke of God's mercy towards His people after the destruction of Jerusalem.

Read Ezekial 2:1-10 first. Then read Ezekial 3:16-21. What is Ezekial's job description according to Ezekial 3:17?

_____

_____

What type of stern warning did God give Ezekiel concerning the job He had given him (Ezekiel 3:18-21)?

_____

_____

Are we held just as accountable when God gives us a job to do? Explain your answer.

_____

_____

God calls each of us to spread the gospel. We are to speak the truth. We are not held accountable for what men do with the message they receive, but we are responsible in telling them the message and warning them.

What does 2 Timothy 4:2 state?

_____

_____

Just like Ezekiel, we have to first hear the words from God and then give the words of God to the people He instructs us to share with. There is not an option as a Christian to not tell others about Christ. It is our responsibility to warn them of God's future judgment.

I think in this day and age "Christians" have become used to not saying anything about Jesus. Many are fans of Christ, but few are followers.[7] As Christians we can't just stand on the sidelines and cheer Jesus on, we have to participate in "the game," along with Him. He didn't call any of us to be just spectators. If you compared a football game to following Jesus we're supposed to be out on the playing field with our team and following all the commands of our head coach Jesus, not on the bleachers watching the game.

Read Matthew 16:27. What is going to happen when Christ returns?

Preach the **WORD;** *be ready in season and out of season; reprove, rebuke, exhort, with [a] great* **PATIENCE** *and* **INSTRUCTION.**

2 Timothy 4:2

Week 6

_____

_____

Now, go back and read Matthew 16:24-25, the verses preceding what we just read. What does Jesus expect from us?

_____

_____

How can or do you practically apply this to your life, denying yourself and losing your life for Christ's sake?

_____

_____

We're held accountable for our actions or inactions, like Ezekiel. If you are not convinced of this, read the parable of the talents in Matthew 25. In the end, God will either say, "Well done good and faithful servant" or "You wicked, lazy servant. Throw that worthless servant outside, into the darkness, where there will be weeping and gnashing of teeth" (Matthew 25:21, 26, 30 NIV).

Write out Romans 14:12.

_____

_____

> **We're held *accountable* for our actions and inactions.**

We will give an account of ourselves to God. That's a sobering thought. Instead of living for ourselves, why not live for Him! There are a lot of things we're holding onto we could let go of here on earth. Most of the things we fret about or things we try to obtain for ourselves (material possessions, status symbols, etc.) won't do us a bit of good in eternity. Following Christ is all that will matter in the end. "For what will it profit a man if he gains the whole world and forfeits his soul" (Matthew 16:26)?

Take a look at yourself and think about what Jesus will hold you accountable for when you meet Him face to face. We're not only held responsible for our actions, but even our very words (Matthew 12:36-37). Spend some time asking Him who He expects you to be sharing the Gospel with. Allow Him to equip you for those moments.

DAY 5

Put No Confidence in the Flesh

Another big turning point occurs in Judah's history as we open the Word today. We will witness King Zedekiah unwisely breaking his covenant with King Nebuchadnezzar and see the dire consequences of that action. Before you begin, however, put all other thoughts aside and seek God's face. Become aware of Him, not giving your attention to worries and distractions, but instead giving Him all of your focus. Trust and thank Him that He will supply you with all of your needs. Know that He already knows everything that's going to happen to you today and nothing will take Him by surprise. He will be your protector and guide, if you allow Him.

Begin by reading 2 Kings 24:18-20. What did King Zedekiah do in 2 Kings 24:20b?

_____

Now read 2 Kings 25:1-3. What happened to Jerusalem after Zedekiah rebelled?

_____

_____

Read Jeremiah 52:1-5, which gives the same account as 2 Kings. When did the siege begin and end?

_____

_____

Judah had made an alliance with Egypt. The Egyptians encouraged the Judeans to rebel against Babylon. The new pharaoh, Pharoah Hophra, in Egypt, promised to help King Zedekiah stand up against the Babylonians. King Zedekiah felt with Egypt backing him up he could break the covenant with Babylon and be protected by the Egyptians, even if Babylon attacked. However, it was not in his or his country's best interest to rebel against King Nebuchadnezzar. Quickly, Nebuchadnezzar retaliated by assailing Jerusalem and the surrounding cities. The siege was thought to be from the 10th month of 588 B.C. (maybe January) to the summer of 586 B.C.[1] The siege lasted roughly 18 months.[2]

Read Ezekial 17:12-20. Who did King Nebuchadnezzar make a covenant with (verses 12-14)?

Week 6

Who then broke the covenant that was made?

_____

Repeatedly God warned Judah not to rebel against Babylon. However, once again Judah didn't listen. If King Zedekiah had kept the oath with Nebuchadnezzar he never would have been placed under siege by King Nebuchadnezzar. Zedekiah, as a vassal king, was safer following King Nebuchadnezzar and would have been blessed by God if he had not rebelled. However, King Zedekiah placed more of his trust in his allies than God. He trusted man more than God.

Putting our confidence in man, instead of God, is easy to do, isn't it? We trust what we see with our own eyes more easily than that which is invisible. However, that's the whole point of faith. We have to trust in what we don't see. Having faith in God, was a hard lesson for Zedekiah to learn. According to Warren Wiersbe, Judah's final collapse was caused by, "The leaders really didn't believe (have faith in) the Word of God. During the dramatic rise and fall of empires in that stormy era, Judah looked around for allies instead of looking up for divine assistance. Instead of repenting and turning to God, they hardened their hearts against the Word and trusted their own wisdom."[3] Wow! Doesn't that sound familiar? How many times have we done that as a nation or individually?

Take a look at how Nebuchadnezzar reacted to King Zedekiah's insubordination and ridiculous reliance on man instead of God. Read Nebuchadnezzar's reaction to King Zedekiah's insubordination:

"Josephus recorded the encounter: 'When he was come, Nebuchadnezzar began to call him (Zedekiah) a wicked wretch, and a covenant-breaker, and one that had forgotten his former words, when he promised to keep the country for him. He also reproached him for his ingratitude.'"...Nebuchadnezzar also said, "God is great who hateth that conduct of thine (Zedekiah), and hath brought thee under us."[4]

Even Nebuchadnezzar, a heathen, recognized Judah had broken their covenant with God. Nebuchadnezzar recognized God frowned upon Zedekiah's actions and God was the one bringing Judah under Babylon's control because of their insubordination. If only Zedekiah had listened to God, instead of man.

Now we're going to dive into Jeremiah 34, which consists of prophecies given during the siege of Jerusalem.

Start by reading Jeremiah 34:1-7. How is Zedekiah's death described?

_____

Repeatedly **God warned** _Judah_ **NOT to REBEL** _against_ **Babylon.**

Even Nebuchadnezzar a heathen **recognized** _Judah_ **HAD** _broken_ **THEIR COVENANT** _with_ **God.**

Nebuchadezzar, must have found some relief in the fact that he would die in peace rather than by the sword. Israel would even lament his death. It is speculated that maybe Zedekiah repented and conducted himself well in captivity to be honored so after his death, because if he was a completely dishonorable king he likely would not have received this honor.[5]

Looking back at Jeremiah 34:7 answer this true/false question:

T or F	Lachish and Azekah were the only cities in Judah Nebuchadnezzar had captured at this point.

Lachish was a city located 23 miles southwest of Jerusalem. Azekah, also southwest of Jerusalem, was 11 miles northeast of Lachish.[6] The Babylonian armies fought against all the cities of Judah so that no city could attack them when they laid siege to Jerusalem. The only two cities in Judah that remained operational at that point were Lachish and Azekah, but they too would eventually be destroyed.[7]

Continuing on, read Jeremiah 34:8-22. Summarize what happened in these passages.

_____

_____

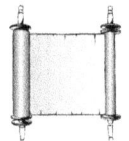

Zedekiah
didn't **FREE**
the **SLAVES**
BECAUSE it was
the **RIGHT**
THING TO DO,
he **ONLY** did it
TO GET
WHAT HE WANTED!

Zedekiah was seeking to gain God's favor by freeing the slaves. He basically was bribing God. Zedekiah didn't free the slaves because it was the right thing to do, he only did it to get what he wanted, maybe hoping the siege would end. Or maybe he was concerned about the scarcity of food and didn't want slave owners to have to worry about feeding their slaves. Also, he may have considered by releasing the slaves they'd be more willing to fight against Babylon, if needed.

God even reminds the Judeans they had once been slaves themselves in Egypt. You would think this would give them more reason to not own slaves and oppress them. However, it didn't.

Where had the Judeans made a covenant with God that they'd release the slaves (Jeremiah 34:15)?

_____

How did they "seal the deal" with God to free the slaves (Jeremiah 34:18-19)?

_____

suffer the same fate as the animal cut in half.[8] God said He would give them into the hands of their enemy Babylon and they would be destroyed by the sword, pestilence, and famine (Jeremiah 34:17). They faced the curses of the covenant they broke. God was watching out for the slaves and when they were mistreated He was not going to stand by and allow it to happen. Judgment came down on those who unjustly handled their slaves.

"Slavery" was actually chosen by some, it was a way those that owed debts could actually pay off their debts.[9] Slavery in those days had a different meaning than nowadays. The Israelite who became a "slave" was actually a hired hand and treated with great respect (read Leviticus 25:39-43). There was a contract between slaves and their owners.[10] The contract was to protect the exploitation of slaves. However, in King Zedekiah's day, that contract was not being honored and the slaves were treated unfairly.

Read Exodus 21:1-2, one of the first judicial laws given after the Israelites came out of Egypt.

Read Deuteronomy 15:12-18. Circle the things that were to occur if you owned a Hebrew slave. Do not circle any statements that are false:

> The Israelites were to set their slaves free in the seventh year, after 6 years of service.
>
> The Israelites were to remember their time of slavery in Egypt.
>
> The slave owner didn't have to give their slave anything once the 6 years of service was completed.
>
> The slave owner was to give generously to the slave once he left.
>
> Once the seventh year came, the slave could no longer ever serve his master again, even if he wanted to.
>
> The slave at the end of the seven years had the option to stay or leave.
>
> The master of the slave would be blessed when they released their slave and shouldn't view it as a hardship to themselves.

The rule of seven being the number that represented rest was throughout the Old Testament. God rested on the seventh day when He made creation. All God's people (slave and free) are to rest on the Sabbath, the seventh day of the week (Deuteronomy 5:12-15). And the slaves were to be released and given freedom in the seventh year.

God's intention for those who were enslaved was they'd be released from their debt after 6 years and given freedom. God expected they would be treated kindly and fairly when they were hired on by another Israelite for the 6

Campbell Morgan described the wrong done to the slaves like this, "The withdrawal of liberty profaned the name, it defamed the character of God to the men who were wronged; it denied the honour of God in the mind of those who were forced back again into slavery; and it degraded His authority in their case. These men who in His name had given the toilers freedom, were defaming the holy name..."[11]

By re-subjecting their fellow countrymen to slavery, which defamed God's character, the Judeans brought doom upon themselves. While the siege was temporarily lifted, because Pharoah Hophra attacked the Babylonian armies and distracted them briefly, the siege was not lifted for long. The Judeans would be given into the hands of their enemies because of their deplorable behavior.

Take a moment to reflect on your own behavior towards others. Is there anyone you are not treating fairly?

_____

_____

Maybe you, like the Judeans, are holding bondage over someone by not forgiving them, holding them up to too high of expectations, or not respecting them in some other way. By doing this, you are no different from the Judean who freed his slave briefly, only to take his fellow countryman right back and enslave them again when they were deserving of freedom. Maybe someone owes you something, financially or otherwise, and they are not able to pay you back. Can you free them of that debt? Is God asking you to let them have a fresh start and to not hold anything against them? Or do you need to free your spouse from all that you think he is supposed to give you, but is unable to? Are you too demanding with your kids? Maybe you've freed a person from "slavery" once, but you've taken them right back into "slavery" because you didn't see any immediate reward in releasing them. The question is, "Are you treating others as God has commanded?"

God's Word says, "...You shall love the Lord your God with all your heart, and with all your soul, and with all your mind. This is the great and foremost commandment. The second is like it, 'You shall love your neighbor as yourself'" (Matthew 22:37-39). "You shall not hate your fellow countryman in your heart; you may surely reprove your neighbor, but shall not incur sin because of him. You shall not take vengeance, nor bear a grudge against the sons of your people, but you shall love your neighbor as yourself; I am the Lord" (Leviticus 19:17-18).

Pray and ask God to reveal to you someone He has "freed," yet you are still carrying a "yoke of slavery" over them, not freeing them, like the Judeans were supposed to have done with their fellow countrymen. Release that

> By re-subjecting their **FELLOW COUNTRYMEN** to **SLAVERY** the **JUDEANS** BROUGHT **DOOM** UPON THEMSELVES.

NOTES

_____

_____

_____

_____

_____

_____

_____

_____

_____

_____

_____

_____

_____

_____

VIDEO QUESTIONS WEEK 6

1. What spoke to you in this video teaching?
2. How can you apply Isaiah 54 to your life.
3. What does "enlarge your tent" mean to you personally in Isaiah 54:2?
4. Do you feel like the beauty that God describes you as in Isaiah 54:11-12? Explain.
5. How do you apply the verse "No weapon that is formed against you shall prosper..." (Isaiah 54:17)?

Video sessions are available for download at www.grassandflowers.org

WEEK SEVEN
TAKING CAPTIVITY CAPTIVE

DAY ONE
Obstinate People

DAY TWO
The Pit

DAY THREE
Nothing Is Too Difficult for God

DAY FOUR
Call to Me

DAY FIVE
Restoration

DAY 1

Obstinate People

Come to God with a thankful heart. Rest in His presence. Allow His arms to envelope you in His love. Listen to what He is whispering to you. Allow His voice to become louder and your voice to lessen. It's amazing the peace you'll receive when you do this.

Open up to Jeremiah 37. Read Jeremiah 37:1-10.

The siege has just been lifted. The Babylonians' attention turns from Jerusalem to Egypt. For a brief second Jerusalem felt they might be protected by the Egyptians and not have to face Babylon's wrath. The inhabitants of the city were ecstatic. Yet, there was still grave concern. King Zedekiah sought out Jeremiah, sending two individuals to find him to tell him to pray for the city. Jeremiah's response was the same as usual. He stated disaster was coming and not to be deceived by the siege being lifted. The Chaldeans (the Babylonians), he stated, would be back again with vengeance. Even if the Egyptians left only wounded Chaldean soldiers after their battle, the Chaldeans would still return and set fire to the city. No matter how well Egypt warred against Babylon, the Judeans were doomed.

Before the siege, Zedekiah had sent Pashur, son of Malchijah (not the Pashur who put Jeremiah in the stocks) and Zephaniah, the priest to inquire of the Lord, hoping Babylon would withdraw.

Read Jeremiah 21:8-9. What did Jeremiah prophecy in this encounter?

_____

_____

_____

The only way the inhabitants of Jerusalem could save themselves at this point was to defect to Babylon. They could not defend their cities. However, to the Judean officials it seemed treasonous to defect to Babylon. They wanted to defend their city. They believed those who were willing to defect to Babylon were hostile to Judah's war efforts.

Zedekiah's inquiries set the stage up for the next scene you're about to read.

Read Jeremiah 37:11-16. Why was Jeremiah being arrested?

_____

_____

_____

The atmosphere in Jerusalem was tense. Despite the siege being lifted, the government was afraid many would defect to Babylon. While the gates of Benjamin were open so people could come and go, an alert for those who spoke seditious words was heightened by the government. And even though Jeremiah was not a traitor, he was viewed as one because of his prophecy that told individuals to save themselves by surrendering to Babylon. Jeremiah, however, was just pointing others to safety. He was not a Babylonian sympathizer.

What did the officials do to Jeremiah?

_____

Jeremiah's *suffering*
FORESHADOWS
Christ's
suffering.

Jeremiah tried to defend himself to Irijah, but Irijah was unwilling to listen to Jeremiah. Irijah's mission was to stop those who presented a threat to the war's efforts. Irijah performed his job duty, leaving out any room for hearing the truth. In Irijah's mind, he thought he was doing the right thing.

Irijah handed Jeremiah over to the officials who were brutal with Jeremiah. He received beatings and was put in a dungeon for a long time. Jeremiah's suffering was a foreshadow of Christ's sufferings. Jeremiah, knowing the risk he placed himself in by speaking the truth was willing to do it to save as many people as he could from the torture and torment Babylon would place on Jerusalem if they didn't comply and surrender. Jesus did the same for us. He was ridiculed, humiliated, scorned, beaten, and eventually crucified so we could be saved from our ultimate enemy, Satan. Jesus wants to protect us just like Jeremiah wanted to protect his countrymen.

Look back at Jeremiah 37:2. What wouldn't King Zedekiah, his servants, and the Judean people do?

_____

Zedekiah, the government officials, and the inhabitants of Jerusalem refused to listen. They couldn't accept the reality of Yahweh's rule and King Zedekiah thought his own ingenuity would save them.[1] King Zedekiah had sent Jehucal and Zephaniah, the priest to Jeremiah asking for prayer, but he wasn't willing to take Jeremiah's advice.

Have you ever known anyone like that? They are at the end of their rope and ask for help, but they won't take heed to any godly advice you given? Write down a situation you've seen similar to this. Remember do not write down or mention any names.

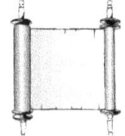

_____

_____

I have a friend whose world is falling apart. He cries out for help to others, but refuses to let go of his own perceived strength and intellectual reasoning power, despite his "strength" has gotten him nowhere. His incessant struggles to succeed never bring him lasting satisfaction. There is no peace in his life. The smartest thing he could do would be to follow God's commands. He would avoid much needless suffering. The Christian life is not pain-free, but at least the suffering a Christian experiences is not futile and has hope and eternal value in it. Whereas, a person who doesn't believe in Jesus, suffers for what purpose in the long run, if he doesn't allow himself to be drawn to Christ in it?

If we resist God's commands, we eventually face death. If we follow God's commands and surrender, we find life. That's the paradox of the Gospels. This is what my friend, mentioned above, cannot fathom and what Zedekiah and the Judeans refused to acknowledge. Zedekiah wasn't hearing what he wanted to hear to from the lips of Jeremiah. The people would rather fight to the bitter end, than surrender to God's ways in this situation. Being obstinate with God was not an admirable quality in the Judeans, nor is it in us. They and we won't win by being stubborn with Him!

Read Jeremiah 21:6-7. Jerusalem's obstinacy would cause them to suffer greatly. What would they face because of their adamancy?

_____

_____

What do you think "the sword, famine, and pestilence" represent in spiritual terms today for us, if we continue to rebel against God?

Sword represents:

_____

Famine represents:

_____

Pestilence (disease) represents:

_____

Those who do not bow down to God's sovereignty face "the sword, famine, and pestilence" spiritually. In my opinion, *"the sword"* spiritually represents war with the enemy. Satan seeks to kill and fight against us in whatever situation he can. However, thankfully if we abide in Christ, we have the Sword of the Spirit to fight back and be victorious against the enemy's schemes.

Famine is a state of extreme scarcity of food. Spiritually, a person who doesn't follow Christ is in a state of famine spiritually and can never be satisfied for long with what the world has to offer. They are starving for a satisfaction that lasts. They need the Bread of Life (John 6:47-51a).

Pestilence is defined as "a contagious or infectious epidemic disease that is virulent and devastating. One who rebels against God becomes sick spiritually — they have a diseased heart (or a spiritual "pestilence" they are dealing with). Disease (pestilence) can bring mental, physical, and spiritual ailments. All three conditions (the sword, famine, and pestilence) bring eventual death if not stopped.

How would your friend or acquaintance you mentioned above have fared if they had simply surrendered to God? How about the Judeans?

_____

_____

Sure, the Judeans may still have had to go to Babylon, but they wouldn't have been tortured and tormented to the extent they were. They wouldn't have watched their loved ones being slaughtered by the sword. They wouldn't have seen their women raped and children abused. They wouldn't have been haunted by watching many die of starvation and disease. They might have even been allowed to remain in Judah to care for their land. Also, their temple and their holy city may not have been burned down. Everything they loved and held dear wouldn't have been stripped from them.

Resistance to Babylon destroyed Judah. However, remember the ultimate reason the Judeans were destroyed was because of their resistance to God. God just used Babylon to punish them.

Interestingly, Zedekiah sought Jeremiah's counsel. Zedekiah must have realized that Jeremiah's words held truth in them. Zedekiah was too afraid to follow God's Words however.

Read Jeremiah 37:17-21. What is Zedekiah seeking from Jeremiah?

_____

How did Zedekiah go about asking Jeremiah?

_____

Zedekiah was too afraid of what others would think if he spoke to Jeremiah openly. He spoke to Jeremiah in secret. Jeremiah didn't placate the truth. He spoke boldly despite it could put him back in the dungeon. Jeremiah also took this opportunity to try to get out of the cruel and unwarranted imprisonment he was in.

What two things did Jeremiah mention to Zedekiah to defend himself?

_____

_____

Basically, Jeremiah was saying, "I've been telling you the truth all along Zedekiah. The prophecies I've spoken have come true so far, but I'm being punished still. That doesn't make any sense. What about all those guys who prophesied Babylon would never come against us and we were safe? Where are those guys? Shouldn't they be the ones locked up, not me? Please don't let me die in prison."

Zedekiah compassionately responded to Jeremiah's plea, knowing Jeremiah was speaking the truth. The dungeon Jeremiah was in must have been a foul and dangerous place to be incarcerated in if Jeremiah was afraid he would die there.[2] Zedekiah probably did not want to be held responsible for Jeremiah's death.

King Zedekiah kindly sent Jeremiah to the court of the guard house, and made sure he received daily bread until the famine became too severe to provide it. The court of the guard house was used for those who didn't require strict confinement.[3]

Read Jeremiah 32:2. Where was the court of the guard located?

_____

While Zedekiah was wise in seeking counsel from Jeremiah and releasing him from the dungeon, Zedekiah was not good at taking godly advice.

Read Proverbs 19:20-21. How do these verses apply or not apply to King Zedekiah?

_____

_____

"Many are the plans in a man's heart, but the counsel of the Lord, it will stand" (Proverbs 19:21). We are wise to listen to God's counsel. What He says goes. We can make all the plans we want, but if they aren't His will, it will fail. Zedekiah was insistent on doing things his way, despite the consequences laid out before him. How foolish! Yet, we, like Zedekiah, often prefer our own ingenuity to God's wisdom.

How about you? Do you ever feel God is putting the brakes on some of your plans? Are you listening to His counsel? Or are you attempting to ignore what He's whispering to you?

_____

_____

We are **wise** *to* **listen** *to God's* counsel.

Before we leave today, reread Proverbs 19:20. Listen to what God is specifically telling you. If you want to be wise, don't just ask God for advice; apply His recommendations to your life. It may not make sense initially, but it is the best route to go. Learn from King Zedekiah's mistakes.

DAY 2

The Pit

It is argued by some that Chapters 37 and 38 may be different accounts of the same event.[1] However, there are enough differences in each story that we will discuss both accounts. If they are the same events, there are certainly many more details given in Chapter 38. Also, there are enough differences to make many believe these accounts aren't the same events. Either way, today we'll dig into Chapter 38 to see what petrifying circumstances Jeremiah finds himself in.

Read Jeremiah 38:1. What are the names of the four individuals Zedekiah sent this time to Jeremiah?

_____

Gedeliah may have been the son of Pashur, the fellow who put Jeremiah in the stocks. Jucal (Jehucal) was thought to be the same guy sent to Jeremiah in chapter 37:3, when Zedekiah asked Jeremiah to pray to the Lord on Jerusalem's behalf. Pashur was the man who Jeremiah had encountered in Jeremiah 21:1, when King Zedekiah sent him to ask Jeremiah what the Lord was thinking.[2] Lastly, Shephatiah, the son of Mattan, is not mentioned elsewhere in the book of Jeremiah.

What does Jeremiah say will happen to those who surrender to Babylon? Read Jeremiah 38:2-3.

_____

What does having your own life as booty mean?

_____

_____

Having your life is better than not having your life. You will lose all, but you will have your life, if you surrender to the Babylonians.

So, why did so few take this suggestion?

_____

_____

Now read Jeremiah 38:4-5.

The officials obviously didn't want Jeremiah messing with the military morale. They felt he was discouraging the men of war and all of the people in the city.

Thus says the Lord,
"He who **stays**
in **this city**
will *die by the* **sword**
and by **famine**
and by **pestilence,**
but he who *goes out*
to the *Chaldeans*
will **LIVE** and
have his **own life**
as **booty** and
stay alive."

Jeremiah 38:2

Does it surprise you what Zedekiah states in Jeremiah 38:5?

_____

_____

In Chapter 37, Zedekiah showed a compassionate side of himself. Here, however, his cowardice side is revealed. King Zedekiah was a vacillating, weak-willed leader.

Compare what Zedekiah stated in Jeremiah 38:5 to what Pontius Pilate stated in Matthew 27:24. What are the similarities between the two men and their statements?

_____

_____

_____

Zedekiah resembles Pontius Pilate (John 18:28-19:19), because he wouldn't commit one way or another. Pontius Pilate didn't find Jesus guilty of anything, but he didn't know what to do with the people who insisted Jesus be crucified. Zedekiah was intimidated by the officials, as Pontius Pilate was intimidated by the Jews who wanted to crucify Christ. Zedekiah didn't want to know what the officials did with Jeremiah. Like Pilate, Zedekiah washed his hands clean.[3]

Read Jeremiah 38:6-13. The officials wanted Jeremiah to be put to death (verse 4); however instead of killing him outright they decided to place him in a cistern to die slowly.

In Genesis 37:18-24 and 26, Joseph's brothers plotted to kill him, but Reuben and Judah didn't want Joseph's blood to be on their hands, so instead they threw him in a pit. They did not want to be accused of murdering their brother. The same went for Jeremiah, the officials hoped he would die without bloodshed, so they would not be accused of violating one of the Ten Commandment, "Thou shalt not murder."[4] As if letting Jeremiah suffer a slow death was any less of a crime.

How do you envision the pit in which Jeremiah was thrown?

_____

_____

Grab a concordance and look up the word pit (the Hebrew word for pit is bowr). Write down the description of the word pit.

_____

_____

I envisioned a pit to be much larger and more spacious than what Jeremiah experienced. According to J.A. Thompson, "A typical cistern was dug out of limestone rock and consisted of a narrow neck perhaps 3 feet across and 3 or 4 feet in depth opening into a much longer bulbous cavity of varying depth. Water from catchment areas was directed to the opening."[5]

Jeremiah was let down into the mud. While he was no stranger to affliction, being in the pit had to be the worst torment Jeremiah had experienced so far. Jeremiah was placed under extreme conditions of suffering, yet he never once compromised the message given to him from God.

Jeremiah had been preaching to the Judeans for approximately 40 years. He was no longer a spring chicken! His age had to make the suffering that much greater. When I read Lamentations chapter 3, it reminded me of how Jeremiah must have felt in the pit. Some scholars think Lamentations chapter 3 was written by Jeremiah and others say it was written by the remnant of Jerusalem in Babylon after the siege. Either way, it is a passage that would be appropriate to examine now in the middle of Jeremiah's suffering in the pit. Raw emotions are expressed in Lamentations chapter 3 and must be close to how Jeremiah felt at that point.

When Jeremiah *came out of the pit* he was *no longer* **STUCK** in the pit — **mentally.**

Read Lamentations 3:52-55. Why do these verses make you think the author may have been Jeremiah?

_____

_____

Stones were placed over wells so people and animals wouldn't fall into them. While the quote, "have placed a stone on me," could have been referring to the heavy burden of suffering placed on Jeremiah or his people, I wonder if it could have been referring to a stone covering being placed over the top of the well Jeremiah was in? When it said, "waters flowed over my head," was this referring to Jeremiah having to deal with water coming into the well while in it? Or were the waters only a picture of the waves of affliction the sufferers in Jerusalem and/or Jeremiah felt?

Regardless, Jeremiah was in a distressing place. He must have had little strength, as it doesn't appear anyone fed him while he was in the pit, since the purpose of him being in there was to cause his death. I wonder if others heard his cries for help? I can't imagine he was completely silent in the pit.

Read Lamentations 3:1-9, 14-18. Does this sound like how Jeremiah might have felt? List some examples.

_____

_____

We've always seen Jeremiah be completely honest with God about his emotions. Jeremiah, who for the most part, stands firm in his walk with God, had days of despair too.

While I thought about verse 4, I wondered while Jeremiah was in the pit, if his skin wasted away. It would make sense being in a damp environment with no sunlight and having mud on his skin that his skin would have deteriorated. Also, when he was thrown or dropped into the pit, don't you wonder if it broke some of his bones? You would think being dropped into a deep cistern would cause his bones to fracture. He would have hit the sides of the cistern on the way down causing bruising, skin tears, abrasions, and likely multiple fractures.

In the middle of Jeremiah's distress though, while he vacillated between hope and despair, hope did win out. When Jeremiah came out of the pit, he was not still stuck in the pit mentally. He lived victoriously after that experience despite the great suffering he went through.

Read Lamentations 3:19-26. The Lord's mercy and His kindnesses, gives God's people and Jeremiah hope. It is in the context of suffering, in Lamentations 3:22-23, that two popular verses come forth to encourage us. Remember, next time you see these frequently quoted verses, what circumstances they originated from.

What does Lamentations 3:24 mean to you? What do you think it meant to Jeremiah?

_____

_____

_____

_____

Now skip over to Lamentations 3:56-59 and ponder what these verses meant to Jeremiah, if they were written by him?

_____

_____

God did rescue Jeremiah from the pit. He brought a kind eunuch to plead Jeremiah's case.

Read Jeremiah 38:7-13. Who is the hero that rescued Jeremiah from the pit? What nation is this hero from?

_____

_____

The Lord's lovingkindnesses indeed **NEVER CEASE,** for **HIS** *Compassions* never **FAIL.** They are new **EVERY** *Morning* **GREAT** is **YOUR** *Faithfulness.*

Lamentations 3:22-23

What is a eunuch? Look it up in a dictionary if you don't know off hand.

_____

_____

Ebed-melech has not been mentioned before in the book of Jeremiah. Very little is actually known about him. He was an extremely brave soul. Ebed-melech risked his life by going to the king and requesting Jeremiah be removed from the cistern. He, unlike Zedekiah, was not a coward.

Why was the king at the Benjamin gate? What took place there typically? Do you recall from any other readings what sorts of things occurred at the gate of this city?

_____

_____

> Ebed-melech
>
> **DARED**
>
> to **speak**
>
> the **TRUTH.**

The Benjamin gate was where kings and officials settled legal matters.[6] Ebed-melech spoke boldly at the Benjamin Gate, telling the king the men who had placed Jeremiah in the pit had acted wickedly and Jeremiah was going to die if he wasn't rescued quickly. How kindly Ebed-melech, with the help of others, lifted Jeremiah out of the cistern. Taking every precaution not to harm Jeremiah, he instructed Jeremiah to put the rags under his armpits so he wouldn't be injured by the ropes. Ebed-melech recognized Jeremiah's fragility from being left down in the pit so many days.

Later, after Jerusalem was captured by Babylon, God rewarded Ebed-melech by giving Jeremiah a word to give him.

Read Jeremiah 39:15-18. How did God reward Ebed-melech for his courageousness?

_____

_____

Ebed-melech did not place his trust in man, but in God. He dared to speak the truth. He spoke up when he saw one of God's people being mistreated. That took a lot of faith. He could have easily been imprisoned or killed for siding with a "traitor."

Read Jeremiah 38:14-28. How would you describe the interaction between Jeremiah and Zedekiah?

_____

_____

Zedekiah was in a pickle. He didn't know what to do or who to trust. Zedekiah was afraid of his officers and of the Judeans who defected to Babylon's side. He had to hide the fact he had met with Jeremiah.

Why was Zedekiah afraid of the Judeans who went to the Babylonian side?

_____

_____

Defeated kings were often tortured and killed.[7] This fact paralyzed Zedekiah despite he was reassured by Jeremiah that God would allow it to go well with him if he obeyed. Zedekiah could have still saved the city at this point. God's mercy continued to reach out to Zedekiah even till the very end.

Zedekiah went to the only man he could still trust – Jeremiah. Despite all of the intelligent men around Zedekiah in government, they still could not give him the direction he desperately needed; only God could do that through Jeremiah.[8] Unfortunately, Zedekiah could not grasp the security God offered him, because all he could worry about was the tremendous risks to him if he surrendered to Babylon. How true this is of us too. So many times God wants us to step out in faith, despite the risk, trusting Him. He gives us reassurances, but fear cripples our faith. So, while we may look down on Zedekiah for his foolishness, what would you have done in his situation? Unless your faith was rock solid, you may have crumbled under the tremendous pressure as well.

Think about your own life now. Is there any area of your life where you are letting fear reign, instead of faith? How could you allow God to turn this situation around and trust Him?

_____

_____

_____

Lord, help us to trust you more. Let us live like Ebed-melech who took risks and cared for someone being mistreated. May we not live by fear, but by faith.

See you tomorrow! Have a great day!

> Zedekiah could not grasp the security God offered him!

> Fear cripples our faith.

TAKING CAPTIVITY CAPTIVE

DAY 3

Nothing Is Too Difficult For God

Begin by reading Jeremiah 32:1-5.

Where was Jeremiah located at this point?

_____

What did King Zedekiah think about Jeremiah's predictions?

_____

_____

Zedekiah did not appreciate what Jeremiah repeatedly told him. Even though he sought Jeremiah's counsel, he really wished Jeremiah would amend his advice. Jeremiah didn't respond to Zedekiah's questions directly here, however. Indirectly, Jeremiah answered him by stating that salvation would ensue after judgment. In the next verses, you'll see how Jeremiah responds to God while he's imprisoned in the court of the guard.

Read Jeremiah 32:6-7. What did God tell Jeremiah to buy?

_____

Do you find this to be an odd request by God? Explain your answer.

_____

_____

Next read Jeremiah 32:8-15. Why did God have Jeremiah purchase this piece of land?

_____

_____

_____

Jeremiah chapters 30-33 are referred to as the "Book of Consolation" or the "Book of Comfort." These chapters were to offer Judeans hope. By Jeremiah purchasing the land from his cousin, it symbolized how God was going to restore the Jews' land to them and make them prosperous again, despite the judgment they were currently facing. From an onlooker's perspective, the purchase of land during the middle of a siege must have seemed completely illogical, a losing proposition.

Recently, in a Bible study group, my husband and I attend, one of the group members asked "How do you know if God is directing you to take a step of faith?" Jeremiah is an example of just that. He first received a word from God. God told him to buy his cousin's field. Jeremiah probably would not have bought the field if Hanamel had suddenly shown up without God giving him any warning.[1] Also, Jeremiah knew once the Babylonians did break down the walls of Jerusalem and take them captive to Babylon, it would be 70 years before they would return to the land. Jeremiah was an older man. He had prophesied for 40 years. The likelihood of him actually benefiting from that land was slim to nothing. Yet, after Jeremiah received the word from God, he humbly accepted by faith what God told him. When Hanamel arrived, he was prepared to make the real estate transaction. If God hadn't spoken to him, Jeremiah may have been angered by his cousin's untimely proposition.[2] After all, he was in prison and there was a siege (with the Babylonians probably having set up camp on the very land Hanamel was selling)!

So, first there were specific instructions given to Jeremiah by God. Even while in prison Jeremiah listened attentively. He could have easily been angry at God. Instead, he continued to seek God's face and be open to His instruction, even in prison. Circumstances did not dictate if he followed God or not. Many times it is within our *"prison walls"* God can speak the loudest and clearest. The instruction didn't make sense for the present circumstances in Judah, but long-term it made perfect sense.

Not only did Jeremiah have to be attentive to God's instruction, but he had to follow through with his faith in action. It wouldn't have done any good if he had just listened to God, but did nothing when the opportunity arose. He had to put his money down, which would have been quite precious to anyone during a time of a siege (starvation/suffering), for basic necessities just to survive, like paying for food. He had to make the purchase. He had to walk by faith, not by sight (2 Corinthians 5:7).

Many of us in the small group said, if God's telling you to do something He'll impress something upon you and then He'll confirm it. In this instance, God confirmed His will by bringing Hanamel to Jeremiah. As Morgan stated, "But he (Jeremiah) took no step until Hanamel came; and when Hanamel came he said, then I knew that was the word of Jehovah. In that simple way of telling the story, in the very incidentals of the narrative, we have a wonderful revelation of that mental mood which is the true mood of the man of faith; the sensitive mind that receives an impression even though at the moment of its reception he is not conscious, or perfectly certain, that it is the will of God. It is received as a suggestion in harmony with larger Divine intentions; and then faith waits for the verifying circumstance that sets its seal upon the spiritual impression."[3]

Look up Leviticus 25:25. What was a relative supposed to do if another relative became too poor and had to sell his property?

Jeremiah's cousin was probably strapped for cash. Hanamel had to sell the field and he first had to offer it to his nearest kinsman. Who knows if Hanamel had already tried to sell it to others closer to him in relation and they had refused to buy it due to lack of money or if they just viewed the transaction as absurd under the circumstances. However, God had saved this field for Jeremiah so His mercy could be revealed to all of the Israelites. Jeremiah was the kinsman redeemer to Hanamel, but his action spoke much louder than that, it was used as a symbol to remind His people that God Himself is the redeemer of the Jewish people. Jeremiah meticulously finalized the transaction with many witnesses surrounding him. His faithful scribe, Baruch, was there to make sure the deeds of purchase were stored securely so they would at least last 70 years when the captives would return and be able to see what God had promised them through Jeremiah's action.

Read Jeremiah 32:16-25. Immediately after Jeremiah purchased the field from Hanamel, he praised God, recounting how God had freed the Israelites from Egypt's cruel enslavement and brought them into a land flowing with milk and honey. Next, Jeremiah questions if he made the right choice by purchasing the land (Jeremiah 32:24-25). So often after we take a step of faith doubt follows quickly behind it. However, Jeremiah took his doubts to the right person, God himself. We must take our doubts to the Lord as well and be reaffirmed by Him. He alone can assuage our fears when we've risked our all, whether it is our reputation, our finances, our career, whatever it is God's asked us to lay down for Him.

A couple comes to mind who have risked everything, to serve Christ. They are called to serve in Ghana, Africa. Many, in Ghana, have still not heard the Gospel. My friends left the comfort of their home, the husband's career, their kid's schools and extracurricular activities, their extended family, and went over to a land far different from what they are accustomed to. Their "new" home does not have hot water all of the time; the air conditioning unit works, however, they rarely use it because they find it difficult to adjust to the heat outside if they use it. Numerous times throughout every week they are without electricity. Sometimes, they are without electricity, for up to four days. Without electricity, there is no hot water, access to the internet, or ways to charge their phones. Communication is very challenging during those unforeseeable outages. Besides not having as many conveniences as they had in the U.S., they also risk their health, as Ghana is a high risk malaria-infested area. Thankfully, they can take medicine daily to prevent malaria, but that is still one more sacrifice they have made to live there. The mom also has begun to home school their children. Their five children range in age from 3-16. The biggest sacrifice, however, has not been missing the conveniences they once had, but the sacrifice of relationships. They all agree this has been the greatest cost. However, Christ has become their all in all in part because of that and it has been well worth the cost for them.

Read Hebrews 11:1 and write it out. How is faith described?

I'm sure the family that went to Ghana, Africa had their doubts. They probably wondered at times if what they were doing was definitely God's will. Yet, they brought their reservations and questions to God. They didn't listen to man's answers, they listened to God. Some told them their plans were foolish and impractical. The enemy whispered in their ears, "Are you sure you want to do this? Are you sure you just can't stay here in America and do the very same thing? How are you going to handle it when you don't have all the comforts of home? What if ...?" The list could go on and on. Their obedience, however, has brought great blessing to Ghana and to them.

Jeremiah's obedience brought blessing to his people as well. People may have mocked Jeremiah for the purchase of land. It's no different than someone making fun of someone living by faith today. "The world laughs at us for our faith and our investments in the future, but one day God will keep His promise and vindicate us before people and angels. Instead of living for the sinful pleasures of this present world, we seek the joys of the world to come. We refuse to sacrifice the eternal for the temporal. The unbelieving world may ridicule us, but ultimately God will vindicate His people."[4]

God did not leave Jeremiah stranded with doubts after the risk he took. Instead, God spoke affirmation once again to Jeremiah, telling him to find security in Him alone, not in what others thought of him.

Read Jeremiah 32:26-44. What did God say in verse 27, 43, and 44 that should have assuaged Jeremiah's fears of purchasing Hanamel's property?

_____

_____

_____

"Behold
I AM the Lord,
the GOD
of all **flesh;**
Is **ANYTHING**
too **DIFFICULT**
FOR ME?"

Jeremiah 32:27

Fields will be bought again in the land of Benjamin, not just in Jerusalem and Judah, but specifically in the land of Benjamin, where the field he had just purchased resided. The very town Jeremiah grew up in, Anathoth. His purchase wasn't ridiculous.

God also answers Jeremiah's statement "Nothing is too difficult for Thee" (vs. 17) with "Is anything too difficult for me?" A rhetorical question. God is saying, "I am Jehovah," I made all of mankind...is anything really too difficult for Me? Jeremiah, I made the world, the universe. What I promise I will accomplish! Our problem is we lose our grasp of who God is, how awesome and powerful He is! In the Hebrew, the word Lord in verse 27 is actually Jehovah. The word Jehovah is a better descriptor of God than Lord because it describes His awe and glory more fully.[5] When we recognize how magnificent our God is, our questioning comes to a halt. When we remember He is the great "I Am," we realize nothing is too difficult for Him. When I stood in Yosemite National Park, I realized this fact: If He made those majestic mountains and gigantic redwoods then there is no problem too big that He can't fix.

Is there something in your life where you think there is no way God can change a particular person or situation? For instance, do you have the thought there is no way God can change your husband? Come on ladies, if you've been married long enough, you know you've had that thought! Or have you contemplated how in the world God could possibly get the attention of that family member of yours who has resisted God for so long? Or is there a situation or person at work that you can't possibly see God being able to transform? Do you place more of your "confidence" in people than your faith in God?

We're not to place our faith in people. Our faith is to be in God alone. If we're living just like everyone else around us, we're probably not living by faith.

What does Ephesians 3:20 declare to us?

_____

_____

Bring your burdens to the great "I AM." Bring your dreams and hopes to Him. Nothing is too difficult for Him. Expect more from God. Step out in faith, believing He's going to do what He said He's going to do.

"Attempt great things for God. Attempt something which as yet you cannot do. Any fool can do what he can do. It is only the Believer who does what he cannot do. 'Is anything too hard for the Lord?' Fall back upon omnipotence and then go forward in the strength of it."6

Jeremiah had to be thinking, "I have no idea how you are going to change these people God. It is absolutely ridiculous what I just did, purchasing that field. These people's hearts can't change. They are the ones who have relentlessly not listened to You and have mocked and persecuted me incessantly for 40 years. My actions appear crazy!" However, while obedience may appear foolish; it never is! His persistence and faithfulness to God brought many back to God eventually. It didn't happen right away though. Jeremiah never saw the results of his godly actions and hard work. He never saw the captives return to Israel and Judah. He never saw their hearts soften completely and fully to the Lord. He never saw them live for God with all their hearts.

Before we close for the day, I've listed a few suggestions for how to know if a word you sense God giving you is actually a word from Him. Many Christians struggle with this.

How to know if a word is from God:

Be still enough to hear God's voice. Be attentive to His spirit.

Pay attention to what God is saying specifically. Listen for any ideas He is impressing upon you. Write them down.

Wait. Wait to see if there is confirmation of this word given to you. Be cautious and do not act impulsively. Test to see if it's from God. Not all inner voices we hear are from God —it could just be you, the enemy, or bad indigestion!

It must line up with Scripture. Never do anything that contradicts God's written Word. In Jeremiah's case, the Scriptures weren't complete yet, but he knew what God had been saying all along about the Judeans and their return from captivity. What God told him to do in this instance certainly lined up with what God had said multiple times before to him. Also, he had the scroll of the Lord with early Biblical stories recorded in them. He knew Jewish history.

Recognize after you step out in faith and do what God commands that you will have doubts. The enemy will attack you. Faith believes in what we don't see. At some point, our choice will be questioned by ourselves and others. Faith is audacious. It doesn't make perfect sense. Jeremiah made the transaction when it seemed he could have made much better use of his money by buying bread for himself with the shekels of silver he used for the land. The longer the siege lasted, the less food there was and eventually many starved to death. Jeremiah even knew the grave conditions that were going to occur and yet he still bought the land. He did not act because it made sense, but because God told him to purchase the land.

Hold onto God's reassurances and promises concerning your step of faith, even if you see no fruit from your action immediately. Trust God will do what He said He is going to do. In the case of Jeremiah, it would be another 70 years before the acquired land could be inhabited again. However, surely Jeremiah's purchase gave the Jews hope in Babylon as they waited to be set free.

Your walk of faith will be open to public affirmation and scrutiny. Faith still has to go through normal channels in getting the action accomplished. Jeremiah had to have the deed drawn up and witnesses available. It was an official proceeding. His faith was open to public affirmation and scrutiny as well.

DAY 4

Call to Me

Read Jeremiah 33:1-13. List the promises God gave to Judah concerning restoration.

_____

_____

_____

God promised Judah He would heal them. Their sins would be forgiven. They would live in peace again and know truth. Their land and homes would be restored. Judah would be revered among the nations once more. Joy and gladness would once again reverberate throughout the land.

Now backtrack and hone in on verses 1-3 of Jeremiah 33. What does the Lord say He will do for Jeremiah, while Jeremiah is confined in the court of the guard?

_____

_____

_____

_____

What a privilege! God was telling Jeremiah, "Call to me...I have great things to tell you!" Just like God wanted to communicate with Jeremiah, He wants to talk to us too.

"Call to Me and I will answer you, and I will tell you great and mighty things, which you do not know" (Jeremiah 33:3).

The word *"call"* or *qara* in the Hebrew means, "...to summon His (God's) aid... Calling in this sense constitutes a prayer prompted by (a) recognized need and directed to One who is able and willing to respond... Basically, *qara* means 'to call out loudly' in order to get someone's attention so that contact can be initiated... Often this verb represents sustained communication..."[1]

God is inviting us to call out to Him. God desires for us to seek further revelation of who He is and what He wants to do. He wants to show us great and mighty things. Just as God shared blessings and promises that were going to happen to Judah in the future, He wants to do the same with us. God has many treasures He wants to give us, but we first have to call out to Him. If we don't do our part, sincerely calling out and seeking Him, we'll miss out on a lot.

Call to Me and I will answer you, and I will tell you GREAT and mighty things, which you do not know.

Jeremiah 33:3

Jeremiah must have felt quite alone in prison at times. Even in dire circumstances, I believe Jeremiah still had many moments of joy because he knew God intimately. Jeremiah had made God his dwelling place. He had a spiritual level of closeness to God that few have pursued. He sought after God with all his heart.

If we are to be like Jeremiah, we can't let others do the calling out to God for us. We must be the ones to pursue God. It's not enough for our pastor to call out to God for us. We must seek an intimate relationship with God ourselves. The greater intimacy we have with Christ, the more He'll reveal to us. Like a friend, the closer we are to them, the more we know about them. In marriage, the most intimate earthly relationship we can have, we don't know everything about the person on the first date, but the longer we spend time with them we get to know them quite well.

However, I have to say, even after 20 years of marriage, I still learn new things about my husband! That's funny because I thought by now I'd know everything about him! Just think if we can't know everything about our spouses after spending years with them, how could we possibly know everything about God? There is no end to the infinite things we have to learn about God.

God has so much more to reveal to you about Himself. His nature, His capabilities, His loving-kindness, His power, His majesty — it's endless what He wants to divulge to you. Treasures He wants to share with you. Not so you'll keep those treasures to yourself, but so you'll share them with others. Jeremiah wrote down the treasures God told him in Jeremiah 33, in order that thousands of captives would be encouraged. And eventually billions would be encouraged through his words. However, Jeremiah couldn't have encouraged others, if he hadn't taken the time to call upon God first.

What does Acts 26:16 state? Read this verse in the NIV translation of the Bible. Write out this verse.

_____

_____

_____

This verse is what the Lord told Saul (Paul) when he was converted on the Damascus road. He speaks the same to us. We are appointed to be servants and witnesses of what we have seen of Jesus and what He will show us in the future.

This past weekend I went to a women's retreat sponsored by our church. There were many words spoken that uplifted, and spurred me on in my walk with Christ. I didn't realize till after the event how much I needed this intense time with the Lord. I witnessed women giving words of hope to other women. I saw the retreat teacher obeying God's call, and sharing God's word with us. It was easy to tell she had spent time in the Lord's presence before speaking.

God has many **TREASURES** *He wants* **TO GIVE US** but we first have to **CALL OUT** *to* **Him.**

The worship leader, leading us into worship before our King, had just as strong of a relationship with Jesus, as the speaker. It spurred me on to witness these women's obedience. I saw how by them calling out to God, God gave them words to encourage others. How I want that to be said of me. However, I'm afraid all too often I don't take time out to call upon Him. God gently reminded me to spend time with Him, quiet time. That is where I can call out to Him and clearly hear Him. It is there He shows me (and anyone else for that matter!) great and mighty things that I (we) may share with others.

Why do you think He wants us to call to Him?

_____

_____

_____

God wants us to be thirsty for Him. If He gives us gifts all the time without us ever having to call out to Him, we won't appreciate Him as much. Just think if I constantly gave gifts to my kids. They would come to expect it and take it for granted. They wouldn't be as grateful for all they were given. However, if they sometimes had to seek me out and ask me for something, they'd probably show deep gratitude when I did give it to them. The thing is God actually does both – He gives us good things without us asking and He gives us good things when we do ask Him. I have to admit, the things I ask Him for, I appreciate more. I guess because I know that everything I ask for I'm not guaranteed to get. I have to spend time with Him and communicate with Him my need. The time spent with Him allows me to learn more of His character. Otherwise, I might not seek Him out. I'd take all the good things He gave me for granted if I always got everything I wanted.

God wants us to meditate on Him and know Him. If He gave answers quickly all of the time, we wouldn't spend time with Him. We'd be spoiled brats. Our time with Him transforms our minds. It allows us to see things from His perspective. Also, the things we may want may not be the best for us. Our vision is clouded.

We are to seek God for Himself and not for what we are going to get from Him. His gifts are good, but they are no substitution for Him and Him alone. If you search for something for a long time, is it not a sweeter experience when you find it?

What gets in our way of calling on Him?

_____

_____

Obstacles that prevent us from calling on God:

Thinking we're not good enough.

Read Psalm 86:5. What is God's approach when we call on Him?

_____

_____

_____

Do we have to be perfect when we call upon God? No, we don't have to be perfect! Take a good look at all the Old Testament Bible heroes that were close to God, yet far from perfection!

Don't let negative self-talk keep you from seeing how God sees you. Christ's blood has covered your sin. Jesus' work on the cross is a complete work; the Father only sees us through His son's perfect and completed work. He sees you as pure and righteous (Isaiah 61:10) and wants to pour out His love, encouragement, and vision into your life. He wants you to live abundantly. He wants you to know Him and His thoughts.

Not making time with God a priority. Excuse: lack of time.

Find daily time to call on the Lord. Ask God to show you great and mighty things. Write down in a journal what God is speaking to you when you call on Him. Put down the great and mighty things He reveals to you in His Word and speaks to you in your spirit in quiet moments of worship and prayer time. Listen to Him. There is so much He wants to share with you. Envision Him sitting by you or standing near you. Look into His face, His eyes.

Jeremiah wrote down everything the Lord shared with Him so generations after him could read God's promises and seek their God. Jeremiah not only "journaled" what God told him, he shared with the people by word of mouth as well.

If we want the mind of Christ, we have to fill ourselves with Him. We have to turn off the T.V., stop emailing, texting, running 100 mph, and abide in His Word. "If you keep My commandments, you will abide in My love; just as I have kept My Father's commandments and abide in His love. These things I have spoken to you so that My joy may be in you, and that your joy may be made full" (John 15:10-11).

Feeling distant from God.

God is near to us. Satan would like us to think otherwise. Our enemy tells us God is far away, distant, and could care less about us. Psalm 145:18 tells us, "The Lord is near to all who call upon Him, to all who call upon Him in truth."

What does Deuteronomy 4:7 say about God's closeness?

_____

_____

We are the ones who choose how close we want to be with God. He desires to be near us.

Not seeking God with our whole heart.

Jeremiah 29:12 "Then you will call upon me and come and pray to Me and I will listen to you. And you will seek Me and find Me, when you search for Me with all your heart."

"Starting from scratch, He made the entire human race and made the earth hospitable, with plenty of time and space for living so we could seek after God, and not just grope around in the dark but actually find Him. He doesn't play hide-and-seek with us. He's not remote; He's near. We live and move in Him, can't get away from Him" (Acts 17:26-28 The Message)!

"God doesn't play hide-and-seek with us" – don't you love how The Message paraphrases that verse? God wants to know us. He's not making it difficult for us to find Him. We're the only ones who make things difficult!

Lack of desire for God.

1 Peter 2:2-3, "like newborn babies, long for the pure milk of the word, so that by it you may grow in respect to salvation, if you have tasted the kindness of the Lord."

Jesus wants us to long for Him, yearn for Him. "The stiff and wooden quality about our religious lives is a result of our lack of holy desire. Complacency is a deadly foe of all spiritual growth. Acute desire must be present or there will be no manifestation of Christ to His people. He waits to be wanted."[2]

Do you hear that? "He waits to be wanted." Wow! If He could have it His way, He constantly would like to communicate with us. In fact, He's trying, but we let things get in our way from hearing Him.

If you are struggling with hearing from God when you call on Him, what are some things you can do to prevent that?

_____

_____

_____

HERE ARE SOME SUGGESTIONS FOR MORE CLEARLY HEARING GOD WHEN YOU CALL OUT TO HIM:

1. Know we have the right as children of God to come into His presence seeking Him. Draw near to Him. Confess your sins. Keep nothing hidden from Him. Realize we are justified in Christ. Because of Christ's atonement of our sin nature, we are fully cleansed. "Blessed are the pure in heart for they shall see God" (Matthew 5:8).

2. Expect to hear great and mighty things as He has promised. Live in the Spirit. Be cognizant of the spiritual realm. Cultivate your awareness of Him, become aware of His constant presence. Open His Word and expect to hear from Him.

Write out Psalm 34:10.

_____

_____

_____

3. Seek out Him with all your heart. Get rid of any idols in your life.

4. Ask God to give you the desire for Him, if you don't have it.

5. Exalt God. Come to Him in worship. Humble yourself. Kneel down at His feet. Maybe you can't physically kneel, but in your mind you can kneel down before His throne. I find a good way to seek God with my whole heart is to come before Him with praise and thanksgiving in His presence through worship. It is there I can take my eyes off myself and see Him clearly and get into a position to hear Him.

Read 1 Chronicles 16:9-11.

6. Keep it simple. Find a place you like to spend time with God and go there daily. Also, remember you can spend time with Him wherever you are...while driving in the car, on a walk, etc. Don't keep God out of your daily activities; let Him be a part of everything. Talk with Him 24/7.

7. Wait on Him. God's not into the mindset of us getting everything right away. Fast food, fast service, fast everything has made us accustomed to instant gratification. It's not always so with God. He doesn't want us to impatiently demand from Him. He wants us to wait on Him. When we're impatient, we miss out on opportunities where He can move and display His glory. He can display His loving-kindness when we wait on Him. Psalms 147:11 declares, "The LORD favors those who fear Him, those who wait for His loving-kindness."

Our aimless **PURSUIT** of pleasing men more than **GOD** keeps us from **HEARING** *God's* VOICE **CLEARLY.**

8. Be more concerned about God, than about man's opinions. Our aimless pursuit of pleasing men more than God keeps us from hearing God's voice clearly. "Who will make the once-for-all decision to exalt Him over all (versus man)? Such are these precious to God above all treasures of earth or sea. In them God finds a theater where He can display His exceeding kindness to us in Christ Jesus. With them God can walk unhindered, toward them He can act like the God He is."[3]

What does John 5:44 say?

_____

_____

9. Be assertive in seeking God. Yes, at first you may not feel like seeking God, but be diligent. Eventually, it will become easier and you will enjoy it. In fact, it will probably happen rather quickly if you have prayed for the desire to know Him better. When I first got back into running, it took a little time before I could run with ease and enjoy it again. I started by running 10 minutes and every other day added on 5 more minutes of running to the previous 10 minutes. Eventually I was up to running 40 minutes. From there I slowly increased my speed. It took time, but by being assertive, in a little less than 3 weeks I went from running 10 minutes and barely feeling like I could make it to running 3 miles and actually enjoying it! I had to make it happen though; I didn't always wake up feeling like going to the gym daily. And I still don't always feel like going to the gym. My PJ's and couch still call my name! However, the rewards of running have been great. You will find the same when you take time to hear God's voice.

I hated to even write this list down because I don't want you to go by a set of rules, but instead to form a constant communication with God. The list, however, helps us to know where we stand, why we may not be hearing from God, or point out our lack of desire for Him. May we become familiar with the sound of His voice as we begin or continue to call upon Him.

Lord, we long to know of the great and mighty things You want to reveal to us and accomplish in our lives. We cry out; we want to know You intimately. Show us the riches You want to restore to us. Not necessarily material riches, but spiritual riches. Give us spiritual treasures You have hidden just for us.

DAY 5

Restoration

Today's reading is going to cover chapters 30 and 31 in the Book of Consolation. It is thought these words were given to Jeremiah in a dream (Jeremiah 31:26). The Book of Consolation was written during the siege of Jerusalem, when things were not looking good at all for the Judeans. The words were given to the Judean community to give them hope during their darkest hour.

Read Jeremiah 30:1-17.

These first verses spoke of the terror and panic the Jews felt during the siege, war, and exile brought upon them. God acknowledges in these verses the utter seriousness of the calamity the community faced. Yet, He also gave them hope that the yoke Babylon placed on them would be broken and they would be saved out of this land of captivity.

How are the Judeans and their situation described in Jeremiah 30:12-13, 15?

_____

_____

How are their wounds, once incurable, later described in Jeremiah 30:17?

_____

_____

God was trying to tell the Judeans there was no way they could be cured unless God healed them. They were terminally ill, without hope, incurable. Nothing they could have done on their own would have restored them physically, mentally, or spiritually. They were doomed, and going to die. Their whole culture, way of life, and themselves would have disappeared if God had not had compassion on them and cured them.

The judgment brought upon the Judeans was meant to refine them, allowing them to come into a good relationship with God like never before. God removed the bondages and chains they were being held captive to. Once in Babylon, their whole outlook changed. God humbled them. They were then able to receive God's healing touch.

That reminds me of myself when I went into captivity— bound by Satan's lies, panicked by the frightening spiral downward of depression's grip, and humbled and humiliated by the lack of mental control I had. Not being able to control my emotions well made me ashamed and scared. However, it was there I learned I had no choice but to let God help me. He had to teach me the truth so I could not be pulled down by the lies being whispered into my ears. God's Word was what healed my mind. My "incurable wounds" were healed by

Him. And because of what He brought me out of I will be forever indebted to Him. It changed my relationship with Him forever. A willing obedience to follow Him stemmed from that experience. The situation had been serious, the depression had been deep, but it was not beyond hope. I put my hope in Him. I learned to not walk by my feelings (letting my emotions rule me) but let His Words govern me instead. That is why I carried Bible verses with me everywhere. This is what the Judeans must have done in Babylon – carried God's promises and hopes with them all day long as they were slaves in Babylon. The Book of Consolation was there to remind them, while on the brink of despair, that God had a hope and a future for them. They were going to be coming home.

> *I have Loved you* WITH AN *EVERLASTING* L O V E; Therefore I have *drawn* you with LOVING-KINDNESS. Jeremiah 31:3

Read Jeremiah 30:18-24. What stands out to you in this passage? Is there a verse that jumps off the page at you? Write it down and explain what it means to the Jews and yourself.

_____

_____

Read Jeremiah 31:1-7. This is my favorite chapter in the book of Jeremiah because it shows how God can take someone's mourning, their pain and turn it into joy and praise, and give them an abundant, fruitful life.

Reread Jeremiah 31:3, "I have loved you with an everlasting love; Therefore, I have drawn you with loving-kindness."

The word everlasting in the Hebrew is olam. Olam means "ages, always, ancient times, continual, days of old, eternal, eternity, forever and ever, long time, permanently, perpetually." I have not written all of the meanings of everlasting, but many of them.

Hear God say to you, "I have loved you with an everlasting love." Let that sink in. Apply the Hebrew meanings of the word everlasting *(olam)* to God's love for you. Bask in His presence a moment. For example, put the word permanent in place of everlasting in the verse so it reads, "I have loved you with a permanent love." Keep on doing this with the other descriptors of everlasting *(olam)*. Take it all in.

He loves you continually. His love for you never changes. It is permanent. Nothing you can do or say can change His everlasting love for you. He does not hold your past against you. He loves you.

God loved His people. Though the Judeans had been unfaithful to God, God still loved them. He reached out to them and drew them out of their misery with His loving-kindness. He reached down and healed them. God did not give up on them or stop loving them despite all their failures.[1]

Read Jeremiah 31:8-9. Who is God bringing home from the North Country and the remote parts of the earth?

_____

God is not bringing home warriors, the elite, prominent/key figures, the wealthy and the powerful. The great homecoming procession consisted of the blind, lame, pregnant, and women in labor. Social positions weren't important anymore. All those returning were on level ground.

God was bringing home the broken, wounded, and the vulnerable, those least valued in society. Women were considered lowly in public stature and held little political power in those days.[2] Yet, God mentioned them. He was bringing home those who were humble, injured, dependent on Him, those who acknowledged their weaknesses, those who were not valued, but had the most to give – they were fruitful (pregnant) and fertile (laboring women). "Blessed are the meek, for they will inherit the earth" (Matthew 5:5 NIV).

The proud had left for Babylon, but the humble returned. The wayward child had been chastised and refined.

How did it say the weak and wounded would walk home to Jerusalem (Jeremiah 31:9)?

_____

_____

It's not known whether they came home weeping for joy or with sorrow. However, we do know God led them by waters (providing strength/hydration for their journey) and that the path was without major obstacles. The path was straight and they didn't stumble. How nice to know if you are coming out of captivity and God's leading you home that there is a straight way without obstacles. He doesn't make it hard for us to return to Him. He helps us.

Read Jeremiah 31:10-14. What good gifts did God give to the survivors?

_____

_____

God provided protection, food, material goods, crops, herds, joy, satisfaction and their lives would be like a well-watered garden. They would flourish.

Let's look back at Jeremiah 31:11. We're going to look up the meanings of the words ransomed and redeemed. God ransomed and redeemed Judah from the clutch of Babylon, their enemy. God ransoms and redeems us from the hand of our enemy, Satan. Satan wants to destroy us completely. When I was in the pit of despair, he didn't just want to mess with me a little bit; he wanted to take me out of the picture completely. The depression became so great that at two separate times I was tempted to commit suicide. If you know me, you know I am not the suicidal type. I enjoy life and honestly am too chicken to go through with a suicidal plan, even if I had one.

However, on two occasions during the depression I was woken up in the middle of the night at 3 AM and heard a voice in my head tell me to commit suicide. I

Though the Judeans HAD BEEN *unfaithful to God,* GOD STILL LOVED THEM.

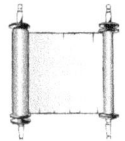

felt like I was suffocating and being strangled physically by evil. In my mind I had no reason to be suicidal. I had two great kids, a wonderful husband, and a promising life. I was depressed, but I didn't want to end my life. I recognized the voice in my head telling me to do this was not my own. It was a demonic voice. Now, if I hadn't known what spiritual warfare was I would have thought it was my own voice! Thankfully, God gave me discernment. I woke my husband up crying. I told him I knew what Satan was trying to do. I asked him to pray. He prayed and immediately the voices stopped. He prayed and declared out loud that the spirit of suicide must leave by the blood of Jesus. He commanded the demon to leave by the power of the Holy Spirit. And it left. The choking sensation and overwhelming presence of evil left instantly. I went back to sleep at once and slept peacefully the rest of the night. I woke up the next morning with no thoughts or inclinations of suicide.

We believed in the power of Christ's blood. We stood on His Word and the Lord redeemed me. The evil clutch on me was strong, but not stronger than my God. God redeemed me from the enemy.

I know patients struggling with anxiety and depression who tell me similar stories. Some understand the spiritual warfare they are facing, but some do not. Those not clearly understanding spiritual warfare are prey for the enemy. We cannot be ignorant of how our enemy attempts to destroy us. We must have our best defensive and offensive plays ready in this battle for our lives. Satan does not play fair or nicely.

If you have a Bible dictionary, look up what the word ransomed means. If you don't have a Bible dictionary, look online. Write a brief definition of ransom below.

_____

There was a price paid to release us from captivity and slavery to sin. The price was Christ's life. "(Jesus) gave Himself as a ransom for all..." (1 Timothy 2:6).

Read Isaiah 53:4-12. How are we described in this passage? How is Jesus described?

_____

_____

Christ took our sins upon Himself. He became our guilt offering. He bore our sins. He wants us to be free. We are healed by His stripes. Receive His forgiveness and love for you. Rejoice that He is a ransom for you. As Louis Stulman states ransoming/redeeming, "Conveys the sense of rescue or liberation from the bullies of this world."[3] Satan will try to bully us, but Jesus is fighting back for us, if we'll let Him.

Week 7

Connect each verse with the correct passage on the right:

Exodus 6:6	"But because the Lord loved you and kept the oath which He swore to your forefathers, the Lord brought you out by a mighty hand, and redeemed you from the house of slavery, from the hand of Pharaoh king of Egypt."
Deuteronomy 7:8	"And David...said to them, 'As the Lord lives, who has redeemed my life from all distress.'"
Deuteronomy 15:15	"Say, therefore, to the sons of Israel, 'I am the Lord, and I will bring you out from under the burdens of the Egyptians and I will deliver you from their bondage. I will also redeem you with an outstretched arm and with great judgments'."
2 Samuel 4:9	"And you shall remember that you were a slave in the land of Egypt, and the Lord your God redeemed you..."

Most of the verses describe Israel's release from slavery under the Egyptians. The Israelites had been oppressed for a longtime. The Judeans had been oppressed by the Babylonians. Satan has tried to oppress every one of us too. However, we can be redeemed by God's mighty hand.

What does it say the Judeans will do upon returning to their homeland (Jeremiah 31:12)?

_____

_____

What are we to do when we realize what God has redeemed us from?

_____

_____

Our redemption should cause us to rejoice. In Jeremiah 31:13, it states the people danced! "Here and elsewhere in the Bible dancing is an expression of great joy."[4] The dancing had stopped during the siege and after the destruction of Jerusalem. Lamentations 5:15 stated, "The joy of our hearts has ceased; our dancing has been turned into mourning." However, now the Jews' joy had returned and with it came dancing.

Read Psalm 30. Go ahead, it is short! Then, write out Psalm 30:11-12.

_____

_____

Are we to keep quiet when the Lord rescues us? How long are we to give thanks and praise to our God for His deliverance?

_____

Go back to the second half of Jeremiah 31:12. Verse 12 states, "...and their life shall be like a watered garden..." A watered garden is flourishing, fruitful, and beautiful. Wouldn't you like people to say that about your life?

Look at how Ezekiel described Jerusalem after its destruction compared to when it was restored? Read Ezekiel 36:35. What kind of garden would Israel and Judah look like?

_____

_____

When I think about the Garden of Eden I think of lush vegetation, flourishing trees, beautiful flowers, abundant fruit, peaceful conditions and a quiet, restful closeness to God found in the garden. Their lives would be like this. Our lives can be like this too.

Read Jeremiah 31:15-20. This piece of Scripture describes Rachel's response to Israel's waywardness, Ephraim's repentance, and lastly God's response to Israel's repentance.

Where is Rachel weeping?

_____

Read Jeremiah 40:1. What occurred in Ramah?

_____

_____

Ramah was 5 miles north of Jerusalem. It is where the exiles were gathered before the Babylonians transported them to Babylon. It is also thought to be the site of Rachel's burial.[5] Rachel was the mother of Joseph and Benjamin. Her son Joseph had two sons — Ephraim and Manasseh. The tribe of Ephraim belonged to Northern Israel. Ephraim was a surrogate name of Israel.[6]

Rachel is depicted in Jeremiah 31:15 as mourning the loss of her wayward children, but the Lord encourages her in stating that they will return and there is hope. Ephraim, who represents Israel, then speaks, and finally acknowledges his sin, his shame, and his discipline by the Lord. Ephraim longs to restore his relationship with his God and fully grasps the foolishness of his ways. He is like the prodigal son. God responds by calling Ephraim "My dear son" and "delightful child." God remembers him fondly, despite having chastised him, and God yearns for him to return and lavish mercy upon him.

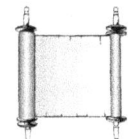

Read Jeremiah 31:21-22. What do you think the phrase "For the Lord has created a new thing in the earth, a woman will encompass a man" mean? Interpret it within the context we've just read concerning Israel (Ephraim) returning to God.

_____

_____

This is a verse interpreted differently by many scholars. I won't go into all of the various theories on this passage. I personally believe it means a new thing is about to happen. Israel (the woman) is going to embrace/cling to God (the man) like never before. Israel and Judah had never embraced God like this before, but because of the complete transformation in exile that occurred and the new covenant God was going to make with them, they would be able to for the first time really follow their God faithfully. It was new and different. They were new creatures. The old had gone, the new had come. They were survivors and they knew who had enabled them to survive. They were forever grateful to God for their transformation. The woman encompassing a man represented a new intimacy between man (God's bride) and God; a relationship that no longer was one-sided, but their affection was mutual.[7]

Read Jeremiah 31:27-30. The question begged to be asked – will the children of the parents who sinned and brought the exile upon the nation of Judah, do the same thing their parents did? The phrase "fathers have eaten sour grapes and the children's teeth are set on edge" was a popular proverb in Jeremiah's days. There was concern this cycle of sin might continue. However, God's response was this: each man bears responsibility for his own action. They couldn't make excuses any longer and blame their *"problems"* on their parents.

Some psychologists and TV talk show hosts constantly like to blame the generation before us for our own sin. We must, however, as individuals take responsibility for our own sin.

"...Will the people not be at the mercy of their parents' failures? The answer does not negate the principle the consequences of sin affect future generations are not necessarily victimized by their ancestors wrongdoings. Since every sinner suffers for his or her own sins, a new beginning is not doomed from the start."[8]

Read Ezekiel 18:20. Write down the general principles here concerning who pays for sins.

_____

_____

If you've blamed your parents for your own sin, will you fess up and acknowledge it before God right now? God doesn't want you playing the blame game. Spend time in prayer concerning this.

We've covered a lot of territory today. The next passage is the longest quotation of the Old Testament in the New Testament. It is an important concept for not only the post-exilic Jew, but for the Christian.

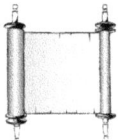

Read about the new covenant given to the Jews in Jeremiah 31:31-34. Then read Hebrews 8:7-13. Was this new covenant fulfilled immediately after the exile or would it not be fulfilled until Jesus death on the cross?

_____

_____

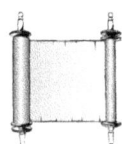

Scholars disagree on when the new covenant came into play. I'm not going to tell you what to believe one way or the other. I recommend reading Hebrews 9 for direction in this area. After reading Hebrews 9, has your answer changed or stayed the same?

_____

_____

NOW
the Covenant
IS WRITTEN
on men's
HEARTS.

The new covenant offered a new start. The Jews could now have a more intimate relationship with God. No individual or group was superior in their closeness to God.⁹ The average lay person could know God as much as a priest in the temple. Now instead of the covenant being written on stone tablets (Exodus 19:1-24:11), the covenant would be written on men's hearts. People would internally know what was right and have the desire to delight in God. They would no longer require someone else to teach them about God, they could know Him individually. A mediator is no longer required. In fact, knowing God would be like a marriage. There would be an intimate knowledge of Him.¹⁰ Lastly, the covenant would allow their sins to be forgiven. Christ's death on the cross made the way for no more animal sacrifices. His sacrifice covered all of our sins.

What does Luke 22:20 and 1 Corinthians 11:25 refer to?

_____

The new covenant, mentioned in Jeremiah, is the only place in the Old Testament it is mentioned.¹¹ This passage Jeremiah 31:31-34 is a BIG DEAL! Think about how many times the new covenant is referred to in the New Testament in comparison to the Old Testament. I wonder if the Jewish people understood the significance of the new covenant promised them?

Wrap up this lesson by celebrating the fact that we have access to the new covenant of Christ and what He did on the cross for us. Have a glorious day!

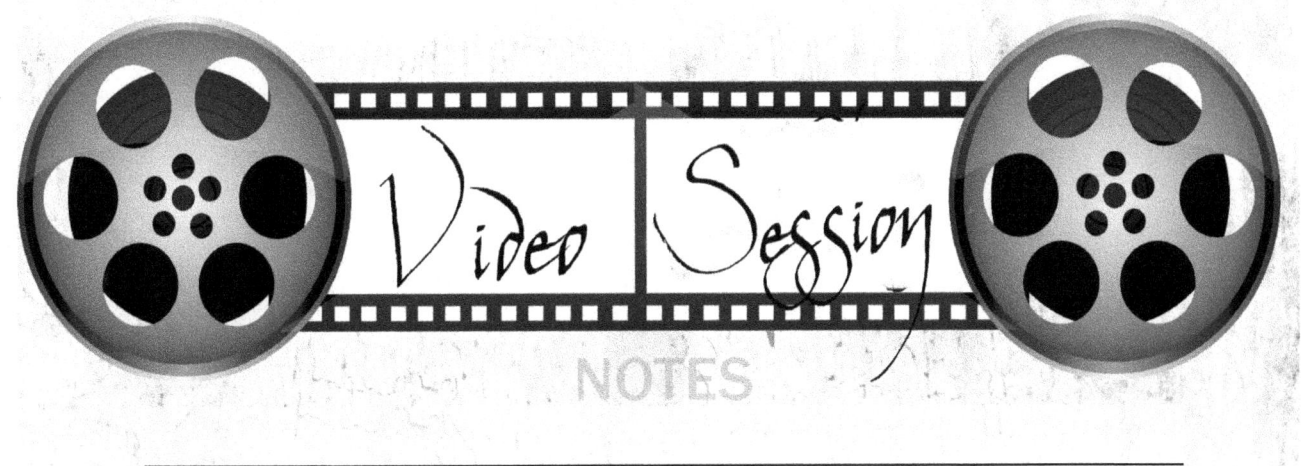

NOTES

VIDEO QUESTIONS WEEK 7

1. What are some of the challenges you face as a parent? If not a parent, what are some of the challenges of being a spiritual parent?
2. How does Jeremiah 32:38-42 speak to you concerning your children (or spiritual children)?
3. How can your past, if you were in bondage and the strongholds have been broken, bring a blessing upon your children (or spiritual children)?
4. What promises have been given to you by God for your children's future? Have you shared these promises from God with your children?
5. How are you accomplishing Psalm 78:4? "We will tell the next generation the praiseworthy deeds of the Lord, His power, and the wonders He has done."

Video sessions are available for download at www.grassandflowers.org

WEEK EIGHT
TAKING CAPTIVITY CAPTIVE

DAY ONE
The Fall of Jerusalem

DAY TWO
A Chance for a New Beginning

DAY THREE
Egypt & Jeremiah's Last Words

DAY FOUR
Wrapping It Up

DAY FIVE
Hope

DAY 1

The Fall of Jerusalem

It is an amazing journey we have taken these last 7 weeks! I am excited and a little sad; this will be our last week studying the book of Jeremiah. I hope you have enjoyed the journey as much as I have! We certainly have come to know one of the most courageous prophets in history. Plus, we've come to see how silly it is to not follow God and the messes we'll get into if we choose to follow our own way, instead of God's way.

We are now going to read about one of the most pivotal events in Israel's history. Besides, the Israelites being brought out of Egypt, there is no other greater event that changed the Jews' way of thinking in the Old Testament than when they went into Babylonian captivity and Jerusalem was destroyed. Some would even argue that the fall of Jerusalem had a larger impact on the Jews than the flight out of Egypt. Either way you look at it, the defeat and fall of Jerusalem in 587 B.C. was a life-changing experience for them.

Begin by reading Jeremiah 39:1-10.

Jeremiah had been warning the Judeans of impending judgment if they didn't turn from their ways for over forty years. God was patient with His people. Time had run out though. God never wanted to afflict His people, but if they would not listen then eventually divine judgment would come. When people turn to their own ways and stubbornly refuse to allow God to reign in their lives, eventually destruction will come. "We in our security need to be reminded that for us also there may come the eleventh year, and the fourth month, and the tenth day of the month, when God will hurl us from our place of privilege, as He surely will, unless we are true to Him." [1]

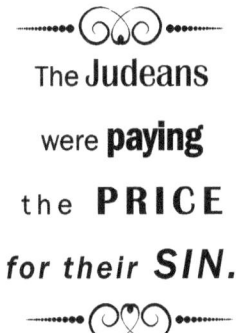

The Judeans were **paying** the **PRICE** for their **SIN**.

The siege had lasted for 18 months. Famine had become widespread in the city. Many people had already died of hunger.

Read Lamentations 4:3-12. What were the conditions like in Jerusalem right before Jerusalem fell?

_____

_____

_____

Conditions were horrible during the siege. In verse 3, the mothers were described as ostriches. Ostriches are known for deserting and not caring for their young; the infants and children in Jerusalem were starving. In verse 5, "those reared in purple" referring to the wealthy who no longer ate delicacies, but instead were living off of ash heaps. Their appearance had changed from nice complexions to "blacker than soot." Their skin was clinging to their bones. They were completely emaciated. Compassionate women had turned into monsters because of starvation, and cooked their own children for food.

The Judeans were paying the price for their sin. Not only did the sinners suffer, but their children as well. The babes suffered from the sin of their parents, even though they hadn't caused the disaster. Like a baby born to a mother addicted to crack, which didn't deserve the ill effects of his/her mother's sins, these babies paid for the consequences of their mother's and father's poor lifestyle choices. Humankind would do well to remember this phenomenon.

Besides the tragic effects of the famine within the walls of Jerusalem, it must have been just as terrifying when the walls came crumbling down and the Babylonians raided their homes and killed many by the sword.

Read Lamentations 5:11-12. What happened to the women, princes, and the elderly?

_____

_____

_____

Reread Jeremiah 39:3.

Once Jerusalem's walls came down, the Babylonians took authority over the city by setting up officials in the Middle Gate. Nergal-sav-ezer the Rab-mag was likely Neriglissar, who succeeded Nebuchadnezzar's son Evil-marduk as king after assassinating him (Evil-marduk was Neriglissar's brother-in-law).[2] Evil-marduk was the Babylonian king after King Nebuchadnezzar.

Reread Jeremiah 39:4. What did Zedekiah and his men do when they saw all of the prominent officials of Babylon make their presence known?

_____

_____

Zedekiah deserted his people. Zedekiah's refusal to bend to God's will, brought doom on himself and the Judeans by being defiant to Babylon. Zedekiah never acted on God's Word given to him by Jeremiah. He tried to save his own life, but he lost it. He faced a brutal end. "He who has found his life shall lose it, and he who has lost his life for My sake shall find it" (Matthew 10:39).

Read Jeremiah 52:7-11, which is another account of the fall of Jerusalem with a few more details. What else happened to King Zedekiah in this account that we didn't learn about in Jeremiah 39?

_____

_____

Jeremiah had warned Zedekiah of his fate and it came to pass just as he had prophesied. Zedekiah must have painfully pondered all of Jeremiah's words on the walk to Riblah. The walk to Riblah was 200 miles north of Jerusalem, giving Zedekiah plenty of time to think. King Nebuchadnezzar had his campaign headquarters set up there and was ready to put an end to this disloyal royal family.[3]

The last thing Zedekiah saw were his sons being killed before him, being forced to watch their executions before he was brutally blinded himself and then manacled and taken to Babylon, where he was imprisoned till his death.

Can you imagine the physical and mental anguish Zedekiah suffered? Try to describe the suffering Zedekiah went through in your own words.

_____

_____

_____

Read Jeremiah 52:12-16. Now that there was no longer a royal threat from Zedekiah and his sons, when did Nebuzaradan, the captain of the bodyguard, come to Jerusalem? Look at Jeremiah 52:6-7 and compare to Jeremiah 52:12.

_____

_____

What did Nebuzaradan burn down?

_____

Who did Nebuzaradan carry off into exile and who did he leave behind?

_____

_____

_____

When Nebuzaradan arrived one month later, he made sure every structure in Jerusalem was burned down. He left only some of the poorest people to till the land. Maybe these poor people were the same slaves who had once been mistreated by the wealthy Judeans. How ironic if that were the case! The poor could have been given the same land that was once their master's land. One author stated the poor were left behind to take care of the land agriculturally in order to feed the Babylonian soldiers who remained in Judah.[4]

Read Jeremiah 52:17-23.

Before the temple burned down, the Chaldeans collected all of the valuable temple artifacts. Besides the temple confiscations being extremely profitable to the Babylonians, it also was a statement to all the nations that the Babylonian gods had prevailed over the God of Israel.[5]

Some of the temple artifacts were so large the Chaldeans had to break them in pieces before carrying the bronze to Babylon where they could melt the bronze and make it into whatever article they wanted. The two bronze pillars, Jachin and Boaz, were each 27 feet high. The bronze basin had the potential to hold 11,000 gallons of water; it was 15 feet in diameter, and was supported by 12 bronze oxen (1 Kings 7:13-25).[6]

Now go back to Jeremiah 39:11-14 and read what Nebuzaradan did with Jeremiah. Describe how Jeremiah was treated.

_____

_____

_____

Jeremiah received

KIND treatment

by the Babylonians

BECAUSE

they considered him

a *LOYALIST.*

Did you notice the number of officials sent to release Jeremiah from prison? Jeremiah was treated like royalty. All of the leaders of the king of Babylon went to release Jeremiah from prison, as well as the highest officials and his good friend Gedaliah. Jeremiah was finally receiving the treatment he deserved! "The scene would put a Hollywood spectacular to shame. All of this pageantry in the march toward a Jewish prophet in his little prison. The name of Jeremiah means 'God exalts.' My how He exalts when He wants to say 'Well done, good and faithful servant'."[7]

Jeremiah received kind treatment by the Babylonians because they considered him a loyalist. However, God saved Jeremiah, because Jeremiah faithfully served the Lord.

Do you remember Gedaliah? He was the son of Ahikam, and the grandson of Shaphan, a family who supported Jeremiah throughout his years of prophecy. This family obviously had views similar to Jeremiah's views for Babylon to entrust Jeremiah to them.

Read Jeremiah 52:24-27. How many citizens, including leading officials, were taken to Riblah next and killed?

_____

_____

_____

All of the other Jews taken from Jerusalem were there to witness the execution of these citizens. Two ranking priests, three officers in the temple, one military officer, 7 members of the king's cabinet, and one scribe of the army, along with 60 other men (74 men total) were destroyed to prevent any political will for independence among the Jews.8 Seraiah was the grandson of Hilkiah, the priest who found the books of the law for King Josiah (2 Kings 22:8). Zephaniah was the one who threatened Jeremiah (look back at Jeremiah 29:24-29) and he made two calls on Jeremiah when the king asked him to consult with Jeremiah (Jeremiah 21:1; 37:3). It certainly was ingrained in the Judeans' minds, by witnessing these horrific acts, to not rebel against Babylon.

It is hard to imagine how much distress and despair the people must have felt at this point as they were led away in shackles having just witnessed these events. They were chained side by side to one another with the Babylonian soldiers forcing them to walk towards Babylon, extremely fatigued and hungry. From Jerusalem it was a 700 mile walk to Babylon. It must have taken them months to complete the journey.

Read Jeremiah 52:28-30. How many people were carried away into exile in 587 B.C.?

Barbara Szentmarjay
Shutterstock

_____

This number seems small compared to the colossal event that had occurred. It is suspected the reason for the small number is because only the adult males were counted in this number. In 2 Kings, the number is much larger and is believed to have reflected the women and children.

In the first deportation, it states in Jeremiah 52, only 3,023 were taken into exile in 597 B.C., but if you read the account in 2 Kings 24:14, 16, you'll see 10,000 captives and 8,000 men of valor and craftsmen/smiths were actually taken away.[9] It is likely that the other low counts in Jeremiah 52, including the 587 B.C. deportation and 581 B.C. deportation, also only reflected the adult males.[10]

Read Jeremiah 52:31-34 (the last words in the book of Jeremiah).

These words were oddly placed at the end of the book of Jeremiah. It is believed those words were placed here in order to give hope to the Jews. While in exile, around 562-560 B.C., when Nebuchadnezzar's son Evil-marduk ruled, Evil-marduk had compassion on Jehoiachin after Jehoiachin had been in prison for 37 years. Jehoichin was recognized as a king by Evil-marduk. The gesture symbolized to the Jews what God could do for them, just as Evil-marduk had freed King Jehoiachin, so could God free them. He was still a merciful God, despite all of their previous sin, and the hardships they had had to endure for their disbelief.

Go back now to Jeremiah 40. Read Jeremiah 40:1-6.

This may seem a little confusing at first. Jeremiah had already been released from prison and told he could live with Gedeliah, so why is he now in Ramah bound in chains? It is thought that when the soldiers were rounding up the Jews in Jerusalem they accidently rounded up Jeremiah in the crowd.

However, when Nebuzaradan released him at Ramah (Jeremiah 40:1), Nebuzaradan gave the choice to Jeremiah to either go with him to Babylon where he'd be treated kindly or he could go anywhere in the land of Judah and have whatever land he wanted. If he lived in Babylon, Jeremiah would have been indulged and given luxurious living by the Babylonians. Jeremiah was 65 years old and it would have been a great retirement package for him to take!11 Instead, Jeremiah choose to stay in his homeland with the "bad figs" and live by faith. He must have felt God called him to stay behind with the remaining Jews. He was also friends with Gedeliah so I'm sure he wanted to help him out in leading the people spiritually. Jeremiah never took the easy way out. He always followed God's path, even when it would have been much simpler and less painful to do his own thing. How impressive is that?

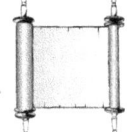

What will you do in your retirement years? Will you live a life full of comfort and ease, or will you sacrificially lay down your life for God's purposes?

_____

_____

_____

When you think about it, who wouldn't want to take a break and get pamperedin Babylon? Jeremiah had just been in prison for months with little food. He was probably emaciated and could use some king's food to fatten him up. Plus, wouldn't it be nice to just say once, "I told you so" to all of his fellow citizens who had once ridiculed him? Thankfully, Jeremiah was not like that. He remained humble and a servant to those in the greatest need. Once again, Jeremiah proved to be a hero in every sense of the word. Whoever labeled Jeremiah as the weeping prophet was way off! Jeremiah wasn't weak and pitiful, he was strong and courageous. He was not a wimp in any sense!

Close this day by meditating on God. Ask Him in what situations He would like you to be more courageous, sacrificing your security and comfort, in order to serve Him.

Week 8

DAY 2

A Chance for a New Beginning

Good day! Nice to have you back again! Start with prayer as usual.

Begin by reading Jeremiah 40:6. What did Jeremiah do after Nebuzaradan released him from Ramah?

_____

_____

Next read Jeremiah 40:7-12. What occurred in these passages?

_____

_____

Everyone heard Gedaliah was appointed to be their leader. Both the military and those Jews who had been driven away from Judah returned to Mizpah. The soldiers who returned, had probably fought in the war and retreated into the hills to hide when the city fell. Gedaliah challenged the military to become civilians and contribute to the economy.[1]

Notice how the remnant left in Judah was blessed. They were offered a new beginning. The Judeans had an abundance of food and wine; their land was flourishing. Peace and prosperity reigned under Gedaliah's leadership. Gedaliah expected the Jews to give their loyalty to Babylon as God had commanded the people to do in the first place. Gedaliah restored the unity among the people and laid their fears to rest. He was a heroic figure and offered the community an optimistic outlook once again.

Read on in Jeremiah 40:13-16, what was the warning Johanan gave Gedaliah and why do you think Gedaliah didn't take heed to the warning?

_____

_____

_____

Read Jeremiah 41:1-3. What happened?

_____

_____

It makes you wonder why Gedaliah hadn't listened to Johanan. Gedaliah had only been governor for 3-4 months. The community while improving, was still in a precarious state, having recently been through tremendous political

217

upheaval and turmoil. Johanan had not wanted to see the peace and unity of this recovering nation threatened. He did the best he could in giving Gedaliah a heads up. Either Gedaliah didn't believe Ishmael could perform such a hideous act or Gedaliah was so interested in building group unity he didn't want to disrupt the peace by killing Ishmael. Obviously, Gedaliah did not make the best choice.

The political climate was such as to expect a conspiracy. Ishmael was from the line of David, next in line for the throne, and had been passed over in favor of Gedaliah.² His alliance with the Ammonite king, Baalis, perpetuated his hatred of Gedaliah as well. Baalis may not have wanted to see Babylon control another nation or perhaps he didn't want to see Judah rise to prosperity again, making his own country more vulnerable. It doesn't give Ishmael's or Baalis's motives in the text, so we are left to our own imaginations as to what went through both of their heads.

The political CLIMATE *was such* as to EXPECT a *conspiracy*.

Read Jeremiah 41:4-10.

Ishmael was a ruthless assassin, a terrorist. The mass murder of the seventy men was horrific and inexcusable. "He (Ishmael) had violated oriental custom by murdering Gedaliah while partaking of his hospitality. Now he violated the Jewish custom concerning mourning (by killing the seventy men)."³

Read Deuteronomy 14:1 and compare it to what the 80 men who came from Shechem, Shiloh, and Samaria were doing (Jeremiah 41:5). Were these men following God's instructions?

_____

God commanded the Jews to not cut themselves or shave their beards to show their grief. It was a cultural rite of mourning though that the men from Shechem, Shiloh, and Samaria, had learned from other nations. Maybe they were ignorant of God's command to not cut yourself or shave your beards. Or perhaps they were so used to following other nation's customs they forgot God's laws and unknowingly sinned. It was clear, however, they came with repentant hearts and offerings for the Lord. The 80 men were likely mourning for the fall of Jerusalem.

It makes no sense that these 80 innocent men, trying to worship God, and Gedaliah, who was obeying God and trying to lead the nation back to health, would lose their lives. Why would the innocent suffer and God not intervene? Isn't that the question that comes to mind in situations like these? Louis Stulman attempts to answer the question, "This courageous text (Jeremiah 41) not only graphically depicts a chaotic world but it does so without reference to God. This is the only major literary unit in the book (of Jeremiah) in which God is absent...Besides distancing God from the massacre, the silence of God speaks on behalf of the victims (the 80 men and Gedeliah). It allows their voices to be heard. It preserves their story and their memory. Any utterance would trivialize their deaths. Any textual explanation would mute their cries."4 I agree there is no good answer as to why the innocent had to suffer. So, we will leave it at that. Many innocent lives were lost in those two days.

Continue by reading Jeremiah 41:11-18. Who rescued the Judeans?

_____

Where did they go once they were free?

_____

Geruth Chimham was not in the direction of Mizpah. Why did they go there instead of returning to Mizpah (Jeremiah 41:17-18)?

_____

Johanan was the Judeans' hero. The Judeans fled to Geruth Chimham, near Bethlehem, a few miles south of Jerusalem, because they were afraid King Nebuchadnezzar would kill them for their association with Ishmael.[5] Johanan had to have time to figure out what to do. Everyone was exhausted from the terror and tragedy they had just experienced. Their future was precarious.

Read Jeremiah 42:1-6. What is the demeanor of the Judean remnant in this passage?

_____

_____

The Judeans seemed earnest in seeking God and sincerely wanted God to give them guidance through Jeremiah. It appears they had faith at this point, and though they had once ridiculed Jeremiah, they now realized that he was a true prophet. They were willing to do whatever God told them to do.

Read Jeremiah 42:7-22. What are the two choices God offers the Judeans? What are the consequences of each choice?

_____

_____

The answer to Jeremiah's prayers didn't come immediately. There was a waiting period. It demonstrates the fact that we are not to expect God to answer our prayers on our timing, but on His timing.

When God finally did answer Jeremiah, the answer to their problem seemed simple. To stay put and settle in the land was without question their best option. In fact, they had already seen God was blessing them in the land during the 3-4 months when Gedaliah governed them. Fears remained, however. They were not sure how Nebuchadnezzar would treat them. They

*When we're **scared**, we typically come up with our **own solutions** and many times our **solutions** **DON'T ALIGN** with God.*

Week 8

had just witnessed the horrors of the fall of Jerusalem. Those images would not die easily in their minds.

God understood their dilemma. He knew their fear. He commanded them though to not be afraid. He would protect them from Nebuchadnezzar. In fact, He would cause Nebuchadnezzar to have compassion on them, not blaming them for Gedaliah's death. On the other hand, if they went to Egypt, they would die for their disobedience. God wanted them to stay in Judah.

Jeremiah seemed to know how the Jews were going to respond even before he finished his speech. Maybe he had overheard their fears over the last 10 days or them saying they were going to go to Egypt no matter what the old prophet told them. Or perhaps God revealed to Jeremiah how they would respond to his message.

The wait obviously didn't help the Jews, although it could have if they had allowed it. Instead of feeding their faith those 10 days, they were nourishing their anxieties. Perhaps, instead of trusting in one individual to find out for them what they were to do in this crisis, they should have all sought God fasting and praying. This is also true for the community of faith today. If there is a big decision to be made, all involved should seek God's face, not just the pastor or the leadership.

Have you ever prayed for guidance from God and during the time you were waiting for His answer (which seemed to take forever) you decided on your own what was best to do, but you came to find out when He finally did answer that that was not at all what He wanted you to do? What did you do? What were the consequences?

_____

_____

Obedience is usually not easy or comfortable. When hard times come, it's easier to run away. When we're scared, we typically come up with our own solutions and many times our solutions don't line up with God's solutions.

A year ago, my family faced a serious financial challenge due to some upcoming expenses in our near future. Our income needed to increase in order to meet the added expense. My husband is self-employed so our income is variable depending how much work he has. After he sent out several resumes and received no reply, I started getting a little scared. I decided maybe I should ask my employer if I could work more days. However, deep down I knew this was not what God wanted. So, I didn't go to my employer, but I was tempted! It would have been easier to take matters into my own hands and try to fix them. If I had fixed things, it would have happened promptly (if my employer had agreed) and my fears would have subsided quickly. I wouldn't have to trust God (which is hard) and I could have enjoyed the fruits of my labor immediately. However, then I had to ask myself would I have enjoyed it long-term and was it what God wanted? I knew running away from what God told me to do would not bring me peace or joy. God wanted me to finish writing the Bible study (you have in your hands) and if I had gone back to working more it would have been impossible to have finished it. We had to choose between "Judah" (God's will) or "Egypt" (our will). So, we waited. We remained in our "Judah," awaiting His redeeming power. Scared at times, but overall trusting and at peace. And I'm here to say, it paid off! Just days before some extra financial expenses were to begin, my husband received the work he needed. God answered our prayers and protected us. He accomplished what He said He would do. Just in the nick of time too! Isn't that how He works many times? I believe He waits till the last minute so we'll learn to rely on Him and pursue Him during that waiting period. If we hadn't obeyed however, we would have suffered the consequences. It may not have been immediate consequences, but long term we would have paid for our disobedient decision. The Jews didn't pay immediately for their decision to go to Egypt. It was 20 years later that famine, the sword, and pestilence robbed them of their existence and they died in Egypt, never seeing their homeland (God's promises) again. I don't want to miss out on God's promises, just because of my own anxieties. You and I can trust and believe Him when He's given us a promise. It just won't happen necessarily in our timing!

Maybe you are in a crisis right now or have a big decision to make. You feel anxious, uncertain, and scared. You are scared of the unknown, like the Jews were scared of what the Babylonians would do. The longer it's taking God to answer your prayers the greater your worry becomes. You are ready to make a rash and foolish decision just to end your anxiety. Slow down and think again, is that really best for you in the long run? Is it what God wants? Will you be accomplishing His purposes if you go this route?

Take a moment to ponder that thought. Write down any big decision you are thinking of and what you believe God is telling you to do concerning it.

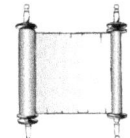

_____

_____

_____

Read Jeremiah 42:20 again, "For you all have deceived yourselves..." Jeremiah is speaking to the Jews after he just received God's answer concerning whether they are to go to Egypt or remain in Judah. It's funny, isn't it? When we want something to go our way, we often deceive ourselves. When we want God to follow our plans, instead of us following His plans, we deceive ourselves, believing God agrees with our viewpoint.

I know of someone who is doing just that right now. She is considering divorcing her husband. Neither one of them have done anything wrong to warrant a divorce, she just doesn't love him anymore. They are both Christians. She has prayed and feels God wants her to divorce him. Wow! Did you hear that? God wants her to divorce him? That's not what I read in the Bible. If He did say that almost every married person would get divorced at some point! When we want things to go our way, instead of His, we can even justify and rationalize that God said something when He didn't. That's why we have to go to the Bible because the voices in our head may not be God's voice. Satan has deceived her. She's rationalized her disobedience, justified her divorce. Nowhere in Scripture does it say God is alright with that kind of divorce. There are few times when God does OK a divorce, but this is not one of them.

This particular person has been warned that if she divorces she will be disobeying God and will not be under His blessing. However, in her pride, she feels nothing bad will happen to her and that she's doing the right thing. What a scary situation. This is the same situation the Jews faced. Either they could be under the umbrella of God's protection by staying in Judah and having faith God would help them, or they could go to Egypt and no longer have God's protection and suffer the consequences.

What about you? Have you made a foolish decision before because you were being deceived? Explain the situation.

_____

_____

_____

Read Jeremiah 43:1-7. What do you think about how they treated Jeremiah?

_____

_____

Ten days earlier, the Judeans seemed to have a lot of faith. They were willing to do whatever Jeremiah told them. Now, they were telling Jeremiah he was lying and God had not told him they couldn't enter Egypt. They even blamed Baruch persuading Jeremiah to lie, so they'd remain in the land and be killed by the Babylonians. Their logic had become screwed up and ill-founded. They justified their actions. They rationalized their disobedience.

It's amazing what fear will do. It caused them to be suspicious and distrust Jeremiah's and Baruch's motives. Fear is destructive. It led the Jews down the wrong path and it will lead you and I down the wrong path too. Fear opposes faith. We must choose faith in the midst of our fears. Faith leads to abundant life!

Let's pray. Ask God if there is something in your life you are running away from out of fear. Or are you looking for security in the wrong places? Inquire if you are justifying your actions. Invite Him to show you what is sinful in your life. Seek God's Word for what He would have you do in your situation. Don't allow the enemy to deceive you. Hold on to God's promises no matter how scared you may be and how impossible the situation may seem.

> **FEAR** opposes *faith*. We **MUST** choose *faith* in the midst of our **fears**. *Faith* **LEADS TO** **ABUNDANT** *life!*

Week 8

DAY 3

Egypt & Jeremiah's Last Words

Are you still reeling from the turn of events we read about yesterday? Can you believe the Judeans took off for Egypt after Jeremiah's warnings?

Read Galatians 5:1. Then write it out.

_____

_____

_____

The Judeans had been given the opportunity for freedom, or at least relative freedom under the Babylonian rule. The remnant in Judah had been given land, they were faring well. Abundant yields were coming from their crops and they were promised the protection of God from any harm if they remained in Judah. Yet, instead of choosing to stay in their land, they chose to go to Egypt.

Staying in Judah represented living in God's will — freedom. Going to Egypt represented living autonomously, leaving God out of the picture. This eventually would lead to living under bondage (the opposite of freedom). The funny thing was living in Egypt (bondage) looked so fun, secure, happy, and inviting at first. It was a deceiving image. Egypt was enticing. It looked way better than what God was offering them. That's how it works, isn't it? Satan makes *"his freedom"* look so good, but it only leads to oppression. His deceit is so deceitful! What the enemy offers looks better at first, but later on will come to bite us.

There were other times in the Jews' history when they yearned for the "security" of Egypt. One time was shortly after they were freed from slavery in Egypt, when Moses led them into the wilderness.

Read Exodus 14:11-12.

The Hebrews had just left Egypt, under cruel treatment from Pharaoh, and already were complaining that they wished they had never left Egypt. They protested because they were scared. The Egyptians were pursuing them to capture them, feeling they'd made a big mistake by letting the Hebrews go. Thankfully, Moses did trust God, unlike the Judean remnant left in Judah, and God brought victory.

Read on in Exodus 14:13-14. What did the Lord tell them to do here?

_____

_____

How is this situation similar to the Judeans who had been left in Judah?

_____

_____

It was there God did the miraculous! He opened the Red Sea so the Hebrews could walk through it in safety. Then God killed Pharaoh's armies in hot pursuit behind them. Just think if the Israelites hadn't listened and followed Moses, it would have been disastrous. The same could have happened with the Judeans left in Judah. If they had listened to Jeremiah and God, they would have seen the miraculous. They would have witnessed Nebuchadnezzar's compassion and would have prospered in Judah.

Another time the Hebrews were afraid and didn't trust God's promises, was when they were about to enter the Promised Land. Spies came back with stories of giants in the land. The spies were terrified and felt there was no way they could conquer them. The only two spies who spoke optimistically were Joshua and Caleb.

Read how the Hebrews responded to the spies' reports in Numbers 14:2-4. Once again, where did they want to go back to?

_____

Even though God had promised them the land of milk and honey, they followed their fears instead of God. The consequences were they had to wander in the wilderness for 40 years and never saw the Promised Land. These guys gave up the Promised Land, just like the remnant gave up Judah and lost all the promises God had given them.

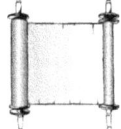

How about you? Have you given up the "Promised Land" God promised you? Have you gone back to "Egypt" or are you considering going back to "Egypt" (bondage) because you are too afraid of what lies ahead? Explain your answer.

_____

_____

_____

In our flesh, we desire to go back to our "Egypt." We have a tendency to return to what enslaves us. We go back to depression, anger, bitterness, overspending, addictions, you name it. Even if we know our "Egypt" will harm us, we'd rather be back there. We'd rather be in our comfort zone and feel immediately "safe," even though we're not out of harm's way there. We're terrified of the unknown and Satan scares us into thinking of all the terrible things that could happen if we just wait on God. We'd rather flee and take things into our own hands to make sure those "terrible" things in our imaginations don't happen than stay put. It's easier to fall back into our enslavement to our idols (anything we put before God), than to follow Him.

It reminds me of someone with a drug or alcohol addiction. There is a powerful draw back to the drug even when the person recognizes the harm it causes. Those who try to get rehab so many times will go back to their addiction. The person drawn back to the drug seems to lose their reasoning and forget about the long-term and serious consequences of the drug. They are consumed by the immediate comfort the drug offers. This is what the Jews were doing, getting a quick fix, thinking it would make things better at least for a little while. Not caring about the long-term consequences.

Have you ever heard of what FEAR stands for? F=false. E=evidence. A=appearing. R=real. Fear is false evidence appearing real. In the Judeans' minds the false evidence was building up and they couldn't hear God's voice while they were panicking. We can't usually hear much of anything from anyone when we're panicked. We do foolish things as human beings when we act out of fear.

If we **PUT** *our* **TRUST** in **ANYONE** *other than* **GOD,** they **will FAIL** us.

The Judeans in Egypt, they felt they would have roofs over their heads, food on their tables, and a routine. They would be distanced from Babylon. They would have a life of ease, and not have any fears. They wouldn't have to fight for what they had. Egypt offered them chariots and horses, a strong military presence. Egypt was a superpower among the nations. No other nation had been around longer than Egypt. It was a logical place to go in many ways. They would rather rest in the security of Egypt's power, than in God's might.

If we put our trust in anyone other than God, they will fail us. That is what happened eventually. The Judeans could have been courageous and faced their reality with God on their side; instead they went back to their idolatrous ways. Instead of valiantly facing reality with God on their side, they returned to false idols. They attributed more power to Egypt than they were rightly due.

Recently, I despaired over a particular situation in my life. It was making me physically ill from the anxiety it caused and I was beginning to lose sleep over it. I woke up one morning and opened my e-mail to a devotion that read, "So you wanna go back to Egypt?" It hit me like a ton of bricks! I knew what God was trying to say and I began laughing. Then I said to Him, "No God, I don't' want to go back to Egypt (bondage). This despair is going to lead me back to Egypt, isn't it? So, here it is God. I let go of it. I won't feel hopeless about this situation any longer. I will put my hope and trust in You and leave it in your capable hands. I'm done with it!" A huge weight was lifted from me immediately and I physically felt better after letting go of the burden. Over the next couple days, as I was tempted to pick up the burden again, I would repeat to myself, "So you wanna go back to Egypt?" And remind myself, "No way!"

Egypt was not a good place for me. And neither is it good for you. "Egypt" represents anxiety, insomnia, and depression for me. Not a state of mind I ever want to experience again!

What does your "Egypt" look like?

_____

How can you avoid going there?

_____

Read Jeremiah 43:8-13. What did Jeremiah tell the people when they first arrived in Egypt?

_____

_____

Jeremiah performed his **LAST** symbolic **ACT** in Taphanes.

The Judeans had blatantly defied God's will for them. They even took poor Jeremiah along with them, against his will, and against what he knew God wanted for all of them. Taphanes was a town along the border of Egypt. This town had a royal government house which was used for state visits from Pharaoh. It was not Pharaoh's permanent residence, just one of his palaces.[1]

Jeremiah performed his last symbolic act in Taphanes. He took large stones and placed them under the mortar pavement at the entrance of Pharaoh's palace. The stones symbolized Nebuchadnezzar would one day come and set up his throne there as a sign of his conquest of Egypt. The stones were left there to remind the Jews when it finally did happen that indeed God had warned them.

The very gods the Judeans wanted to worship were destroyed when Nebuchadnezzar came to Egypt. It was not going to be hard for Nebuchadnezzar to accomplish. He would sweep up the nation of Egypt like a shepherd wrapping himself with his cloak. The Egyptian temples and gods would be destroyed. Many would be killed by the sword or taken captive. Nebuchadnezzar would return safely to Babylon after he demonstrated his power.

Next read Jeremiah 44:1-8.

At this point, the Judeans had already been living in Egypt for awhile. They had spread out and had settled in many different towns. God reminded them of what He had done in Jerusalem because of Judah's sin. He asked them why they were committing the same sins, harming themselves. He reminded them to not follow their own ways or they would be cut off from Him and become a curse, without a remnant to leave behind.

Read Jeremiah 44:11-14. Do you think if the people had repented at this point, and returned to Judah God would have prevented this calamity from happening? Explain your answer.

_____

_____

Week 8

Instead of repenting, how did they respond to Jeremiah's speech? Read Jeremiah 44:15-19.

_____

_____

All of the men and women burning sacrifices to other gods defiantly answered Jeremiah. Their ultimate rebelliousness was not against Jeremiah however, but God. They had no remorse. The settlers had not learned anything from Jerusalem's fall. They defended their mixed up theology, stating when they stopped serving the gods, when King Josiah made them give up their gods, that's when things went wrong. Not the other way around. They were not going to listen to Jeremiah or God. They became cynical and pessimistic to their God, essentially divorcing Him.²

Read Jeremiah 44:20-30.

These are the last words we'll hear Jeremiah speak. How I've come to love this man's words. Unfortunately, his words hadn't changed much over the last 40 years. These Judeans were no better off than when they began. They had not listened to a word he said. Jeremiah sarcastically said to them, "Go ahead and confirm your vows to your gods. That's what you're going to do anyways. I can't stop you. But, listen one more time to what God is going to do to you." They would be destroyed for their disobedience and only a few would escape. They would then know only God's Word would stand.

Better to be on GOD'S side THAN FIGHTING against HIM.

We are just putty in God's hands. He's going to do what He wants. He will receive the glory in the end. Better to be on God's side than fighting against Him. God even said to them, "I'll be watching over you to harm you, not to do good to you." This seems contrary to the words we are accustomed to hearing God speak. His words were the complete opposite of what He spoke to the Jews taken into Babylon. "I know the plans I have for you, plans for welfare and not for calamity to give you a future and a hope" (Jeremiah 29:11).

In 567 and 566 B.C., Nebuchadnezzar invaded and ravaged Egypt.³ Pharoah Hophra had lost his throne in 570 B.C. and eventually lost his life to his relative Amasis who became the next pharaoh. Nebuchadnezzar came to deter Egypt from meddling in Asia. Nebuchadnezzar allowed Pharoah Amasis to retain his throne, but Amasis had to follow Babylonian policy and cooperate with King Nebuchadnezzar.⁴

Over and over again, God tried to reach these people. He was at the end of His rope with them. They absolutely refused to relent. How much better their lives would have fared if they had just stayed in Judah.

Let's try to learn from their mistakes. When we have a big decision to make or a crisis we're facing, let's not run back to our Egypt. Don't fall into that trap again. Refuse to let fear dominate your life. Trust Him even when things seem impossible. Stop, drop, and roll. You know the phrase used for putting out a fire. It can be used spiritually as well. I saw this posted on Facebook and modified it a little. STOP – reacting to your fears and worrying; DROP – your fears; ROLL – get on with your life, and find rest in Him.

Read Psalm 23.

"The Lord is my Shepherd, I shall not want." This sums it all up. We lack nothing in Him. He will protect us from our enemies. He will comfort us. We can have His joy and peace overflowing from us when we stand on His promises. We will go through the shadow of the valley of death, but He will be by our side. Pray and hear what God is speaking to you. Rest in His arms. Praise Him for who He is.

Week 8

DAY 4

Wrapping It Up

You've come a long way sister! We've been studying Jeremiah for 8 weeks now. Hopefully, you have learned some valuable lessons from Judah's history and Jeremiah's life to apply to your own life.

Bask in God's presence before you begin today's lesson. Ask God to reveal to you truths He wants you to take home from this study and apply to your life. Listen and write down anything that comes to mind.

_____

_____

_____

The Judeans suffered greatly for their sin, but thankfully that was not the end of the story. While the Judeans who went to Egypt met a bleak demise, the Judeans transported to Babylon learned their lesson and came back to Judah with a new heart and mind, 70 years later.

Read Ezra 1:1-4. Who freed the Judeans and allowed them to return to Jerusalem to repair the temple?

_____

Now read Isaiah 44:28 and 45:1-7. How is King Cyrus described by God?

_____

_____

King Cyrus was anointed by God and described as a shepherd. Isn't it interesting, despite Cyrus not being one of God's chosen people, God still used King Cyrus? Plus, God girded him with strength to conquer the nations. God revealed treasures to him.

Why did God do all this for King Cyrus? Read Isaiah 45:3 again.

_____

God did this so Cyrus would come to know Him! King Cyrus was a pagan king. He didn't follow the God of Israel. However, Cyrus respected gods of all different cultures. He respected Yahweh as well. He allowed conquered nations to keep their traditions. King Cyrus conquered the Babylonian Empire in 539 B.C. Amazingly, Isaiah wrote the prophecy in chapters 44 and 45 of Isaiah, 150-200 years prior to King Cyrus releasing the Jews. Isaiah, chapters 40-55 speak of Judah's return from exile, authorized by King Cyrus.

ISAIAH, Chapters 40-55 *speak of* JUDAH's *return* from **EXILE**, *authorized by* **KING CYRUS.**

Read Isaiah 44:21-23. How do you think this passage would make a Jew feel when they were returning home to Jerusalem?

_____

_____

> The *Lord* DISCIPLINED the JUDEANS severely, but THEY came through it TRIUMPHANTLY.

Isaiah 44:22 really leapt off of the page for me. Yesterday, as I was listening to the Christian radio, I heard one of the DJ's discuss how we are cleansed through Christ's shed blood when we confess our sins. Today, as I was driving through a severe fog, I couldn't see the car or the road in front of me. I could easily have run into someone. As I drove, the visibility vacillated back and forth. I'd go through a peak of sunshine, then I'd go through a thick cloud. This went on for over 4 miles. Some drivers pulled over on the side of the road because the visibility was so poor. It was the worst fog I've ever seen. So, when I read this verse, "I have wiped out your transgressions like a thick cloud" (Isaiah 44:22a), it made sense! I couldn't see anything in that fog except a big white cloud in front of me. That's how it is when Jesus forgives our sins! He can't see our sin anymore. We are white as the big white cloud in the fog after we're forgiven. We're as white as snow. We're pure and blameless in His sight because of what He did for us. He did this for the Jews returning to Jerusalem and He'll do it for us too, if we repent.

"He brought me up out of the pit of destruction, out of the miry clay; and He set my feet upon a rock making my footsteps firm. And He put a new song in my mouth, a song of praise to our God; many will see and fear, and will trust in the Lord" (Psalm 40:2-3). Just like David, the Judeans saw the miry clay they had come out of and a new song was put in their hearts. Their return to the Lord was a testimony to the Lord of what He had done. All of the nations saw it.

May we have as powerful a testimony as their testimony. May God receive all the praise and glory for the bondage He has brought us out of or is bringing us out of. May many come to see, fear, and trust in the Lord because of what He has done for us.

The Lord disciplined the Judeans severely, but they came through it triumphantly. What they went through reminds me of these verses.

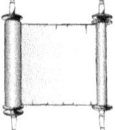

Read Psalm 118:17-21. Tell us how you can apply these verses to your life.

_____

_____

God gave me several verses to overcome postpartum depression. Psalm 118:17-21 was one of them. Victory came through God's grace as His Word drew me to Him and spoke truth into my life.

Now read Psalm 119:67-72.

In this Psalm, the writer speaks of how much better off he was to go through affliction because before affliction, when everything was going good, he went astray. However, during affliction he learned God's precepts.

How about you? Is this what you have experienced in your life too? Explain.

_____

_____

Write out Psalm 126:5-6.

_____

_____

_____

The Judeans' suffering from their sin was intense. They sowed many tears. However, because of their turning back to God they reaped great joy. They went from being life-takers to life-givers. God converted their sorrow and fear into praise and joy.

We now know what happened to the "good figs," but what happened to the Babylonians after the Jews were freed by King Cyrus? Study Isaiah 47:1-9.

_____

_____

_____

Babylon was described as a virgin. However, this did not relate to their moral condition, but instead to the fact they had become a world power unconquered at this point.[1] The whole passage depicts a country brought low from a haughty position. They were put to shame, stripped of their pride.

Read Daniel 5:30-31.

To understand these verses better you may want to read all of Daniel 5. The night Babylon was conquered by King Cyrus was when the Babylonians least expected it. It occurred when King Belshazzar (one of King Nebuchadnezzar's ancestors and predecessors) held a great feast in the middle of the city. Babylon was surrounded by "impenetrable" walls. While Belshazzar was holding the feast, the king saw a hand appear and write a message on the palace wall. Of course, this shocked Belshazzar and he immediately tried to find someone to interpret the writing. No one could decipher the writing until they brought in the God-fearing, interpreter of dreams, Daniel. Daniel revealed to Belshazzar, God would put an end to his kingdom. Belshazzar's kingdom ended that very night.

So, you may be wondering why did Darius the Mede receive the Babylonian Kingdom instead of King Cyrus? Darius the Mede was King Cyrus's uncle. Darius and Cyrus were partners in war and conquest. Therefore, Cyrus gave his uncle dominion over the Babylonian Kingdom, in partnership with himself.[2] Note the age of Darius. He was 62 years old. Darius was born in the eighth year of captivity, the year when King Jeconiah and all the nobles (the largest deportation) took place. God had designed at the very time He was bringing judgment upon His people; a day of salvation for them by bringing into the world King Darius.[3] God, even during judgment looked ahead to the day when He could restore His people back to their homeland.

What did God tell the Jews once King Cyrus released them? Read Isaiah 48:20-21.

_____

_____

_____

God told them to get out and tell others who saved them! They must flee! God provided for them on the way home. He even provided water in the desert for them and not just a trickle. The water gushed forth from the rock when they needed it. They were not thirsty at all. That is truly amazing considering they were in a desert and on a 700 mile journey!

Read Isaiah 52:1-2, 11-12. What does God tell the captives to do in this passage once freed?

_____

_____

God told them to shake off the dust. Clothe themselves in strength and in beautiful garments. Loose their chains. Touch nothing unclean. He tells them He'll be their rearguard. The warning to not touch anything unclean when they departed Babylon was God's way of saying don't take any of the Babylonian idols with you.[4]

We've seen the freedom and restoration the Judeans received 70 years after their captivity in Babylon. Plus, we have read the consequences the Babylonians faced for mistreating the Judeans. However, have you wondered what happened with Jeremiah? Although, there are no records of how Jeremiah died in the Bible, it is thought he was stoned to death.

What do you think about Jeremiah's life and death?

_____

_____

_____

_____

What will our country's demise be if we follow in Judah's steps? Do you think our nation is going in the same direction as Judah did before their nation fell?

_____

_____

_____

End this lesson with these thoughts: Isaiah 60:1 states, "Arise (from the despair that circumstances have held you captive and rise to new life)! Shine (be radiant with the glory of the Lord), for your light has come, and the glory of the Lord has risen upon you!" I added the words in parenthesis.

Your story is just as important as Jeremiah's story of Judah. God made us to tell about God's deliverance and the victory we live in through Him. He's taken us out of bondage and brought us into freedom. We are to tell others about what He has done.

Read Revelation 12:11. How do we overcome Satan?

_____

_____

Besides the blood of Jesus overcoming Satan, the word of our testimony also overcomes the enemy. Your testimony about what God has freed you from is really powerful. We are to testify of what God has done and is doing in our lives. The enemy will try to prevent us from testifying any way he possibly can. Be aware of his tactics, so you don't fall for them.

Read 2 Corinthians 1:4. What are we to do with our affliction?

_____

_____

God wants us to comfort others after He has comforted us. We are not to keep His comfort to ourselves. Ask God who you need to comfort today.

DAY 5

Hope

"In the first year of King Cyrus of Persia, the Lord fulfilled the prophecy He had given through Jeremiah" (Ezra 1:1a).

I know we read this verse yesterday, but read it again and let it sink in. God let his people return to Jerusalem! God used Cyrus, a secular king, to return his remnant to their homeland. Not only did God give the Judeans a fresh start, He also showed them great favor. God fulfilled the prophecy He gave to Jeremiah.

Take a moment and give God praise for His redeeming power and love, He is worthy to receive all praise and glory for what He has done and what He is currently doing in our lives. He has freed us and is fulfilling His purposes for us, just like He did for the Judeans.

Write down what God has done for you:

_____

_____

_____

The book of Ezra gives an account of the exiles return from Babylon. Ezra, was one of the leaders who led some of the remnant back to Palestine. Three groups returned from exile. These groups were led by Zerubbabel, Ezra, and Nehemiah, respectively. Ezra's group left Babylon in 457 B.C.

As I read through the first few chapters of Ezra, several principles leapt off the pages concerning what happens when we, like the Judeans, leave areas of bondage in our lives. (Note: I used the NLT version of the Bible for some of this lesson.)

1. God's favor will be on us.

Read Ezra 1:2-5. List the ways God showed favor on his people through King Cyrus.

_____

_____

Has God done the same for you when He brought you out of captivity?

_____

_____

In the first YEAR of KING CYRUS of Persia, the *Lord* FULFILLED the **prophecy** He *had given* through Jeremiah.

Ezra 1:1a

When we've made serious mistakes and our lives are in shambles, God doesn't leave or forsake us. He is faithful. He yearns for us to walk in the truth. He wants to bless us.

2. Unity among believers will accomplish great feats.

Read Ezra 3:1.

When the families returned to Jerusalem, look at how beautiful a picture it was. Notice what verse 1 says in Chapter 3, "...all the people assembled in Jerusalem with a unified purpose" (NLT). The unity of God's people accomplishes much. What a delight it is to watch a united group of people work together. The Judeans goal was to obey God and walk hand-in-hand in accomplishing what God had asked of them. Have you ever been in a church like this? Or on a mission trip team where everyone served Jesus well together? What a beautiful thing it is when we take the focus off of ourselves and work cohesively as a team.

3. It will be scary to rebuild our lives, but do it anyways.

Read Ezra 3:3.

"Even though the people were afraid of the local residents they rebuilt the altar at its old site" (Ezra 3:3 NLT). When leaving a place of bondage in our own lives, it is often frightening to rebuild. It is easy to be afraid of what others might think of us. Just remember we're taking back the territory the enemy took from us. We have a right to that "piece of property!" However, don't think for a second the enemy won't put up a fight for your inheritance. The Devil doesn't want you to live in freedom.

At this point in Ezra, we don't know how the "locals" reacted to the Jews returning to Jerusalem and rebuilding their altar. Maybe the Jews had unfounded fears at this point. But they were probably perceived as intruders. Remember, it had been 70 years since the Israelites had been in Jerusalem. I'm sure the locals didn't like them coming in and taking over! Just like our enemy doesn't like it either.

4. Praise and sometimes sorrow for what one has lost accompanies restoration.

Read Ezra 3:10-13.

Once free, people will hear about it! You can't keep quiet! Notice how the praise and weeping was heard from far away. Those who remembered the old temple, the elderly, wept. They remembered what they had lost. And those who were younger, couldn't stop praising Him! They were so excited to see the land they had only heard about.

I have a friend who the Lord restored after years of going down the wrong path. She was full of thankfulness and praised God for her restored life. However, she also wept for what she had lost. Due to her previous promiscuous lifestyle, she had chosen to have several abortions. She was like the Judeans. However, once her freedom was restored she praised God and wept. Godly remorse is a part of the restoration process.

5. People/Enemies/Adversaries will attempt to hinder the work God has laid out for you to do. The enemy will come to discourage, frustrate, and frighten you.

Read Ezra 4:4-6, 23-24. What did the enemies of the Judean people do to stop them from rebuilding the temple of God?

_____

_____

Write out how the enemy has tried to frustrate your efforts to live in freedom. What have you done about it?

_____

_____

_____

Write out 2 Thessalonians 3:3.

_____

_____

_____

6. God will use others to encourage us and support us as we accomplish the task God has laid out for us.

Read Ezra 5:1-2.

God used prophets to encourage His people to get back to the task He had laid out for them. Haggai and Zechariah, mentioned in these verses, are the same prophets who wrote the books in the Bible. Ezra 5:2 states, "... and the prophets of God were with them supporting them."

Do you see who God has put in your path to encourage and support you as you strive to live for God? Name them.

_____

_____

_____

7. When the enemy halts our progress to accomplish God's tasks, He will reveal to others and ourselves plans He has for us again and the plans will be accomplished.

Read Ezra 5:3-6:13.

King Darius found King Cyrus' decree. It was not only God who was their commander over the project, but also authority figures placed over them. God used those in authority to accomplish His purposes. God will do the same for you. He will command you what to do and place those in authority over you to accomplish what His purposes are. How refreshing that is!

When I returned to writing this book, I knew God was telling me to cut back working so many hours at my workplace to enable me to have more time to write. I had initially started writing the study two years earlier, but found it difficult to find time to write while working 30-40 hours/week at my job. Through prayer and confirmation from God, I knew I must work less in order to finish writing this study. It was not an easy decision, as it would require stepping out in faith and leaving our financial situation up to God again. Thankfully, authority figures over me at work agreed to let me cut back my hours. They didn't have to do that, but they kindly did. Not only did they allow it, but they were thankful to still have me work with them. God had already prepared their hearts. I'm grateful for God's provision and for finding favor from those in authority over me to follow God's call to write.

God, through King Darius, not only told Tattenai and his colleagues they were to allow the Jews to rebuild the temple, but they were also to help them! You won't be left on your own if God asks you to do something! Notice how those opposing the Jews ended up "carried (carrying) out the decree with all diligence" (Ezra 6:13b). Those opposing us, may end up helping us! The enemy may use people to frustrate God's plans, but God uses people to further His plans. Tattenai, the governor of the province, ended up helping the Judeans. Remember what Tattenai and his colleagues first said, "Who issued you a decree to rebuild this temple and finish this structure" (Ezra 5:3)? It may be that Tattenai and his colleagues were law abiding citizens and didn't want anything, not in the rule book, to be done unless it was issued. Ever been around someone like that? You know you're supposed to be accomplishing a project, but someone keeps trying to slow you down or stop you? They think they are doing the right thing. They are following the rules, but not being led by the Spirit!

8. You will be successful in the plans God has for you through the encouragement God gives you through others.

Read Ezra 6:14.

"And the elders of the Jews were successful in building through the prophecy of Haggai the prophet and Zechariah the son of Iddo" (Ezra 6:14). God may use preachers, books, magazines, nature, visions, dreams, the media, or

> And the ELDERS of the Jews were **SUCCESSFUL** in **BUILDING** through the prophecy of **Haggai** the prophet and **Zechariah** the son of Iddo.
> Ezra 6:14

actual prophets giving you words of knowledge to help you accomplish what He's asked of you.

9. It will take WORK and SACRIFICE to accomplish what God plans for you.

Finish reading Ezra 6:14-22. How long do you think it took the Judeans to rebuild the temple (relook at Ezra 1:1-3 and Ezra 6:15).

_____

The Jews didn't rebuild the temple overnight. It took years. The Judeans had to work hard to build the temple. It was labor intensive. Don't expect what God calls you to do to be easy!! I'm sure, like us, the Judeans had other things vying for their attention. For instance, taking care of their own personal possessions and keeping up with the status quo. However, they put God first, building His temple instead.

We no longer worship in temples. As New Testament Christians we are called the temple of God. As the temple of God, do we invest into developing ourselves for God or do we mainly focus on attaining things for ourselves?

_____

_____

The Judeans, along with God's help, did a marvelous job of rebuilding the temple and their lives. God took them from captivity into freedom. "God empowered His chosen people to overcome all opposition, even against impossible odds."[1]

The book of Ezra covers over a 100 year period from 536-432 B.C. Between chapter 6 and 7 of Ezra, almost 60 years passed.[2] If you continue to read the rest of Ezra, you will be disappointed to find out the Judeans did not continue obeying God's commands. This reminds us we must remain vigilant to the fact that we can easily be enslaved by sin again.

Write out Galatians 5:1.

_____

_____

We must stand firm in Christ to not be enslaved again. The question you may be asking is "Well, how do we do that?" I've included a list below to give you ideas of how to do just that.

Remember we are humans, so we will sin. However, we can remain free from sin ruling over us and causing us to slip into areas of bondage (such as anxiety, depression, despair, anorexia, alcoholism, perfectionism, etc.). When you are in bondage, you are controlled by the bondage. You can't get

Walk by the *Spirit.*

free from it on your own. It takes control of your life, in a sense. And to be freed from it, the power of God must assist you.

Read my list of ideas below. These are concepts I used to get out of postpartum depression myself.

How to Take Captivity Captive:

Read God's Word daily.

Seek God. If a person or nation doesn't value God's wisdom, they will fail. Joshua 1:8 states, "This book of the law shall not depart from your mouth, but you shall meditate on it day and night, so that you may be careful to do according to all that is written in it; for then you will make your way prosperous, and then you will have success." You will never become prosperous according to God's standards until His word becomes valuable to you. Learn to hear God's voice in the solitude. "Be still and know that I am God" (Psalm 46:10). God's wisdom is the only solution for man's problems. "Sustain me according to Thy word, that I may live; and do not let me be ashamed of my hope" (Psalm 119:116).

Take your thoughts captive.

"For though we walk in the flesh, we do not war according to the flesh, for the weapons of our warfare are not of the flesh, but divinely powerful for the destruction of fortresses. We are destroying speculations and every lofty thing raised up against the knowledge of God, and we are taking every thought captive to the obedience of Christ" (2 Corinthians 10:3-5). Recognize the battle for our souls. Let God's reality/perspective become your reality/perspective. You have to walk in the truth of God's Word, not according to the lies you hear from the enemy. Don't let the enemy define you. Let God define you. Refute the enemy's lies with God's truth. When I am struggling with negative thought processes, I go back to Scripture and remind myself of what God says about me. I stand on His promises. It doesn't matter how I feel. I take my thoughts captive and stand on God's Word. Never go by your feelings, go by the truth.

Be thankful.

Write down your blessings. It's amazing how taking the time to write down all the blessings you can think of changes your perspective. You'll realize how much you have to be grateful for!

Rejoice!

Laugh, dance, sing, and worship God. Imagine how God perceives you as you worship Him. You are beautiful to Him. There is no more shame. You are forgiven and set free. Envision yourself as white as snow, the gorgeous bride of Christ. Imagery can play a powerful role in how you view God and yourself. Other images I like to think about as I'm worshiping are: Jesus

Be *Thankful.*
Col. 3:16

> Rejoice in the *Lord* Always; again I will say *Rejoice*.
> Phil. 4:4

holding me in His hands or arms, dancing with me; Angels surrounding me; God, protecting me, like a mother chick protecting her babies under her wings; and God as my rock (my protector/strength, sure foundation, immovable). Allow yourself to feel His supernatural peace as you worship. When you focus on praising Him, your mind is unable to dwell on your problems. Instead, you are able to lift up your anxieties to Him.

"Rejoice in the Lord always; again I will say, rejoice" (Philippians 4:4)! If we abide in Jesus, our joy will be made full (John 15:11). "A joyful heart is good medicine, but a broken spirit dries up the bones" (Proverbs 17:22).

Think about God's unconditional love for you.

"The Lord's loving-kindnesses indeed never cease, for His compassions never fail. They are new every morning; great is Thy faithfulness" (Lamentations 3:22-23). Whether we're cranky, happy, or depressed, His love doesn't change for us. We are of great value to Him. He chose us! (Romans 9:11; Ephesians 1:4-6). He will never leave nor forsake us. An insecure view of God's love for us makes us insecure people. If we realize His love for us and take it at face value, it will change our attitudes and actions.

Write down promises (Scriptures) God has given you and meditate on them. Remind yourself of them throughout the day. Write them on index cards. Post them on your refrigerator. Put them in your pocket. Read them aloud while at a stop light in your car. Memorize the Scripture.

Don't dwell on the past.

Our past is over. You are a new creation; walk in the light of your new identity. The only reason we share our past is it to give hope to others so they may know God can deliver them from their past. God is in the business of restoring the broken. Our changed lives are evidence of His power. There is no more condemnation for those who are in Christ Jesus (Romans 8:1).

Expect God to give you victory over areas of bondage. Believe.

"But when Jesus heard this, He answered him, "Do not be afraid any longer; only believe, and she will be made well" (Luke 8:49-51). This passage is referring to when a father came seeking Jesus for a healing for his daughter and she died while he waited to speak to Jesus. She was brought to life again though by Jesus. The passage provided me great comfort as I sought to climb out of the pit of postpartum depression. It reminded me to not be afraid, to believe, and I would be made well eventually, even though I felt like I was emotionally dead at times. Sometimes we are not healed right away, but this slow process of healing allows us to be taught our unhealthy ways and to grow in Christ. Just like it takes time for a physical wound to heal, so does an emotional wound take time to heal. Believe God's promises for you (Joshua 1:5-6), even if you have not seen them fulfilled yet.

See obstacles as opportunities.

Paul, in the New Testament, was amazingly resilient. He was imprisoned, stoned, shipwrecked, beaten, yet he knew what he believed. His beliefs are what allowed him to bounce back. Paul understood his purpose on earth and kept his eyes on eternal goals (2 Corinthians 4:7-18). Sometimes God calms the storm, but sometimes the storm remains and He teaches us how to be calm in the storm. Before clay is put through the fire, it is soft and useless. However, once it is shaped and comes through the fire, it can be used for something. "Behold I have refined you, but not as silver; I have tested you in the furnace of affliction" (Isaiah 48:10).

The answers to life's problems are not found in asking why, but in being content with the fact that God is in control. God has a reason for what He does. We don't have to know the reasons all of the time. Many times we won't ever know the reason He does things on this side of heaven. I'm not sure, even if we did know the answers to our questions, it would satisfy us because we still live in our flesh and have a hard time keeping an eternal perspective. We have to make a choice to rejoice even when we don't know the answers to our questions. God's perspective is completely different than ours. Any onlooker at the cross would have thought it was surely a defeat, but in the end it was the ultimate victory. Think like Paul, "I am overflowing with joy in all our affliction…" (2 Corinthians 7:4-7).

Give Him all your worries.

I am a natural born worrier. My two favorite Bible verses of all time are about not worrying. Here they are: "Cast(ing) all your anxiety upon Him, because He cares for you" (1 Peter 5:7). "Be anxious for nothing, but in everything by prayer and supplication with thanksgiving let your requests be made known to God" (Philippians 4:6-7). We can't handle our worries. Jesus told us to take up His cross daily, not our cross (Matthew 16:24). "For My yoke is easy and My load is light" (Matthew 11:30).

Testify about Jesus.

"They overcame him (Satan) by the blood of the Lamb (your guilt, shame, and sin have already been taken care of on the cross) and by the word of their testimony; they did not love their lives so much as to shrink from death" (Revelation 12:11). Do you care about Him so much that you are passing on His abundant life? Or are you just saying, "Oh, I love my Bible study so much, what can I get out of it for me?"

Dwell on These Things!

What do you fill your mind with? Philippians 4:8 says, "Finally, brethren, whatever is true, whatever is honorable, whatever is right, whatever is pure, whatever is lovely, whatever is of good repute, if there is any excellence and if anything worthy of praise, let your mind dwell on these things." Just like we should put healthy food into our bodies to make us strong physically, we

---

BUT IN
ALL THESE THINGS
WE
OVERWHELMINGLY
CONQUER
THROUGH HIM
WHO LOVED US.

ROMANS 8:37

need to put the best "nourishment" we can find emotionally and spiritually into our minds and spirits if we want to flourish mentally and spiritually. If we're only putting junk into our minds, that's all we'll get out of it. However, if we're putting in God's Word, we'll have a reservoir of spiritual energy to face the Goliaths in our life.

For WHEN

I am weak,

then **I am STRONG.**

2 Corinthians 12:10

I am weak; but God is strong!

We must understand our utter dependence upon the Lord. 2 Corinthians 12:10, "...for when I am weak, then I am strong." God made us to need Him. We can't live without Him. God wants our strength to be in Him. Only He can do the impossible in us. Stand firm in God's strength. It is not your strength, but your weakness God will use. Sometimes we are made with disabilities so we can lean on God for our ability. When we get too strong it's easy to fall back into self reliance and self confidence. King Uzziah did that. Read about it in 2 Chronicles 26:5, 15-16.

Please God, not man.

Put no confidence in the flesh. Put all your confidence in God. Don't be distracted from God's purposes for you by people or possessions. Many times these two things (people and possessions) keep us from accomplishing all that God wants us to do. By this I am not meaning to neglect your family or loved ones. God wants us to take care of our families and each other. However, He needs to be first in our lives.

Stop trying to maintain such tight control of your environment.

If you are a mom, let the house be messy at times. Don't fret about keeping things all neat and tidy. Enjoy your kids. If you can't stand a messy home, pay a maid to come in biweekly or once a month to have your house clean for one day. When your kids go down to nap or take their quiet time, don't use the whole time you are away from them to clean your house. Use that time to spend with the Lord or take a nap yourself.

Help others.

"...God of all comfort; who comforts us in all our affliction so that we may be able to comfort those who are in any affliction with the comfort with which we ourselves are comforted by God" (2 Corinthians 1:3b-4).

Affirm out loud your confidence in the Lord, especially during times of discouragement.

If you don't have some fight in you, you'll lose. Declare God's Word. The Lord will deliver you from your enemy, if you rely on Him. God never intended for you to lose to the enemy. God is for you, not against you. Expect to win.

Enjoy close friendships.

Our friends can help lift us up out of the mire. Just to know you are not alone is huge. Also, to be able to rebound ideas off of someone else is key to the healing process. Friends can offer sound advice. Being honest and transparent with someone is healing. Friendship also provides accountability to stay on the right track. Make sure to keep your friendships God centered. This prevents codependency which can be just as unhealthy as the bondage you are trying to get out of. If you don't make God the center of your relationship, you will just exchange one bondage for another.

Exercise daily.

Exercise is one of my favorite activities. Exercise boosts our moods, releases endorphins to diminish our perception of pain (both physically and emotionally), calms us, increases our immunity, combats diseases, and helps us to sleep better. It also provides a distraction from negative thought patterns and increases our self-esteem. What better "medicine" could you ask for? In fact, some doctors are now prescribing exercise, just like they prescribe medicines. Exercise has been found to significantly improve patients' anxiety and depression, even more so than antidepressant medicine. Just sitting around and hoping your depression or anxiety will go away, won't help things. Get out and exercise daily, even if it is just for a short period of time.

Eat right.

By eating healthy, it offers our body the necessary nutrition needed to function well. A balanced diet gives us energy and helps us to feel our best. Include an abundance of vegetables, fruits, and whole grains in your diet. It will improve your health significantly. Avoid processed foods. A low-fat diet is best.

Get enough sleep nightly.

A good night's sleep improves our memory, helps us to stay more focused, lowers our stress, and maintains a healthy weight. It also keeps us more emotionally stable if we get adequate sleep.

Enjoy nature.

A walk in the woods is often therapeutic. Nature relaxes us and is conducive to thinking insightfully. It helps to distress us and connect with God.

Make time for yourself. Have a hobby.

Hobbies allow us to express ourselves giving us quiet time typically, decreasing the distractions around us. Hobbies keep us active. Often it reveals a talent or passion we have that we can end up using to help others and serve God.

Join a support group.

Support groups decrease people's sense of isolation. They allow people to relate with others who have similar problems and can identify with them.. Support groups can suggest new ways to deal with our problems and be a shoulder to cry on when needed.

Get counseling, if necessary.

Counseling provides a safe environment to talk. Counselors work with individuals on changing self-defeating behaviors and how to manage their emotions better.

I hope my list of how to take captivity captive helps you. It is not conclusive, but it should give you a good start to taking captivity captive. Recognize the thief came to destroy, but Jesus came to give us abundant life (John 10:10). You have two choices: Either allow the enemy to destroy you or live life to the fullest following Christ's lead. "…greater is He who is in you than he who is in the world" (1 John 4:4b). May we each say this, "I shall (will) walk in the presence of the Lord, in the land of the living" (Psalm 116:9).

Freedom in Christ is a right of all Christians. Your circumstances may make it look like freedom is impossible, but with God all things are possible. If He came to give us abundant life, shouldn't that be our focus, to live an abundant life in Him? "If you abide in My Word, then you are truly disciples of Mine; and you shall know the truth, and the truth shall make you free… If therefore the Son shall make you free, you shall be free indeed" (John 8: 31a, 32, 36). We have to abide in His truth (His Word) to remain free or become free.

There is nothing I cherish more in this life than my freedom in Christ. He is the only one who can give me joy and peace in all circumstances. He is the One that satisfies my soul.

How I have enjoyed this study with you. Who would have known the book of Jeremiah could be so rich and meaningful to our lives?! I never would have guessed it before I began studying Jeremiah. I will never be the same from the lessons I've learned from both Jeremiah and the people of Judah. I will never again think of the book of Jeremiah as boring and irrelevant. I hope the same is true for you.

I know if you seek God with your whole heart, you will find the freedom you so long for. It is not a dream or a mirage. You, with God's help, are able to take captivity captive!

"Bless our God, O peoples, and sound His praise abroad, who keeps us in life, and does not allow our feet to slip. For Thou hast tried us, O God; Thou hast refined us as silver is refined. Thou didst bring us into the net; Thou didst lay an oppressive burden upon our loins. Thou didst make men ride over our heads; we went through fire and through water; Yet Thou didst bring us out into a place of abundance" (Psalm 66:8-12).

Thank you Lord! We love you! May we continue taking captivity captive the rest of our lives!

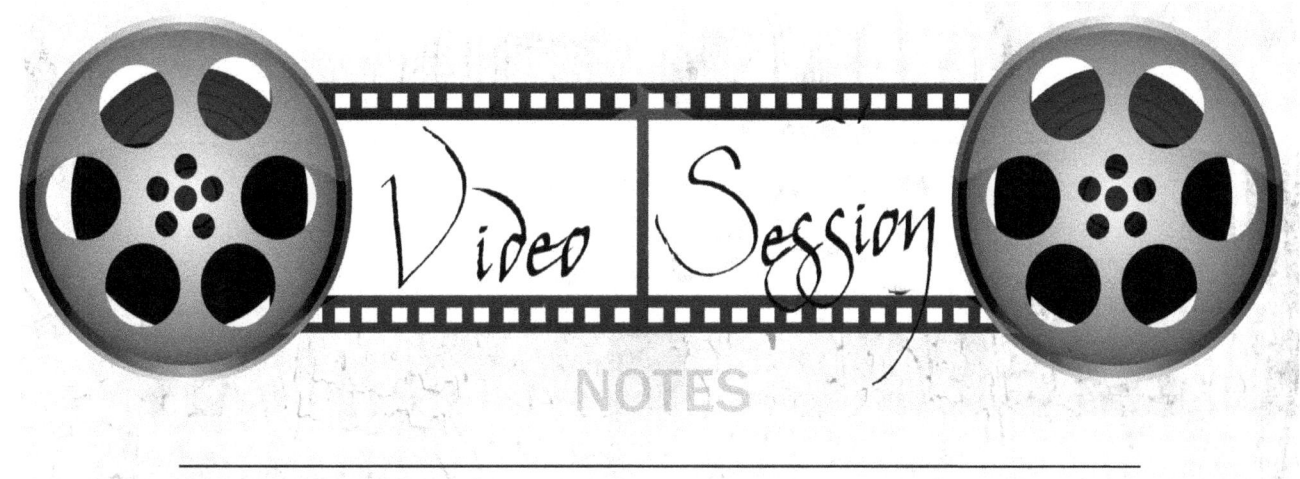

NOTES

VIDEO QUESTIONS WEEK 8

1. Discuss how 1 Peter 2:9 applies to you.
2. One of the biggest challenges that keep us from following God's purposes is the fear of man. How can we avoid stumbling into this common fear?
3. How can you apply Isaiah 52:1-3 to your life?

Video sessions are available for download at www.grassandflowers.org

Addendum 1

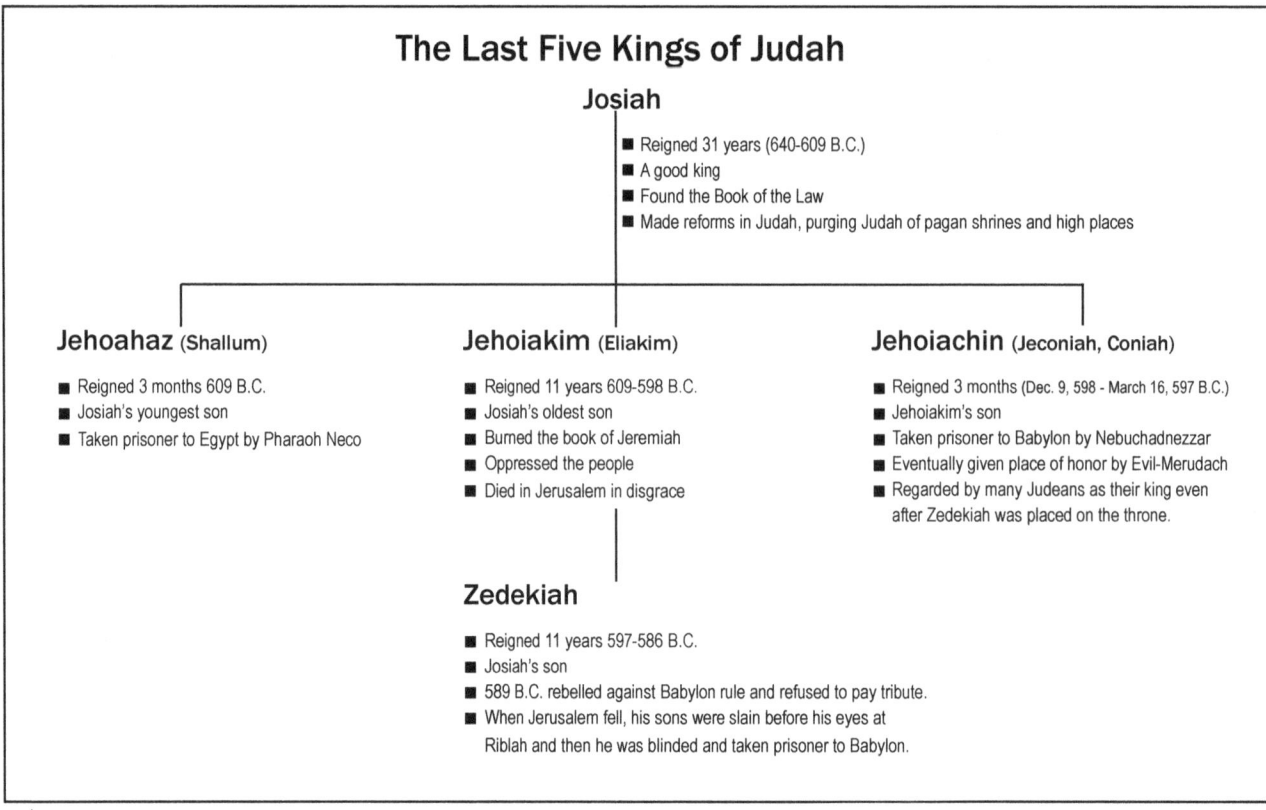

The Last Five Kings of Judah

Josiah
- Reigned 31 years (640-609 B.C.)
- A good king
- Found the Book of the Law
- Made reforms in Judah, purging Judah of pagan shrines and high places

Jehoahaz (Shallum)
- Reigned 3 months 609 B.C.
- Josiah's youngest son
- Taken prisoner to Egypt by Pharaoh Neco

Jehoiakim (Eliakim)
- Reigned 11 years 609-598 B.C.
- Josiah's oldest son
- Burned the book of Jeremiah
- Oppressed the people
- Died in Jerusalem in disgrace

Jehoiachin (Jeconiah, Coniah)
- Reigned 3 months (Dec. 9, 598 - March 16, 597 B.C.)
- Jehoiakim's son
- Taken prisoner to Babylon by Nebuchadnezzar
- Eventually given place of honor by Evil-Merudach
- Regarded by many Judeans as their king even after Zedekiah was placed on the throne.

Zedekiah
- Reigned 11 years 597-586 B.C.
- Josiah's son
- 589 B.C. rebelled against Babylon rule and refused to pay tribute.
- When Jerusalem fell, his sons were slain before his eyes at Riblah and then he was blinded and taken prisoner to Babylon.

Deportations From Judah to Babylon

605 B.C.
- Only mentioned in Daniel 1:1.
- Believed to be when Daniel and his friends were taken to Babylon.

597 B.C.
- Largest deportation of the Judeans.
- 10,000 people deported including King Jeconiah.

588-586 B.C.
- Siege on Jerusalem for 18 months before more Judeans were taken captive to Babylon.

581 B.C.
- Only 745 people were transported to Babylon.

Addendum 2

TIMELINE
Tracing Judah's Captivity

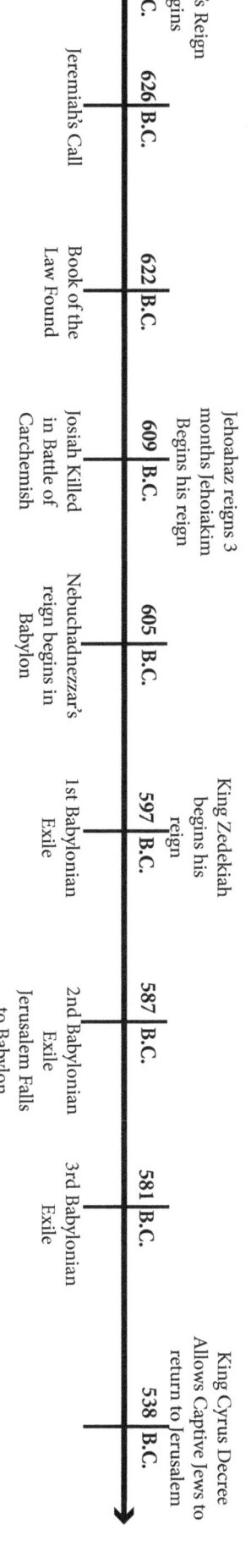

- **640 B.C.** — Josiah's Reign Begins
- **626 B.C.** — Jeremiah's Call
- **622 B.C.** — Book of the Law Found
- **609 B.C.** — Josiah Killed in Battle of Carchemish; Jehoahaz reigns 3 months, Jehoiakim Begins his reign
- **605 B.C.** — Nebuchadnezzar's reign begins in Babylon
- **597 B.C.** — 1st Babylonian Exile; King Zedekiah begins his reign
- **587 B.C.** — 2nd Babylonian Exile, Jerusalem Falls to Babylon
- **581 B.C.** — 3rd Babylonian Exile
- **538 B.C.** — Persians Conquer Babylon, King Cyrus Decree Allows Captive Jews to return to Jerusalem

Addendum 3

The World in the Days of Jeremiah

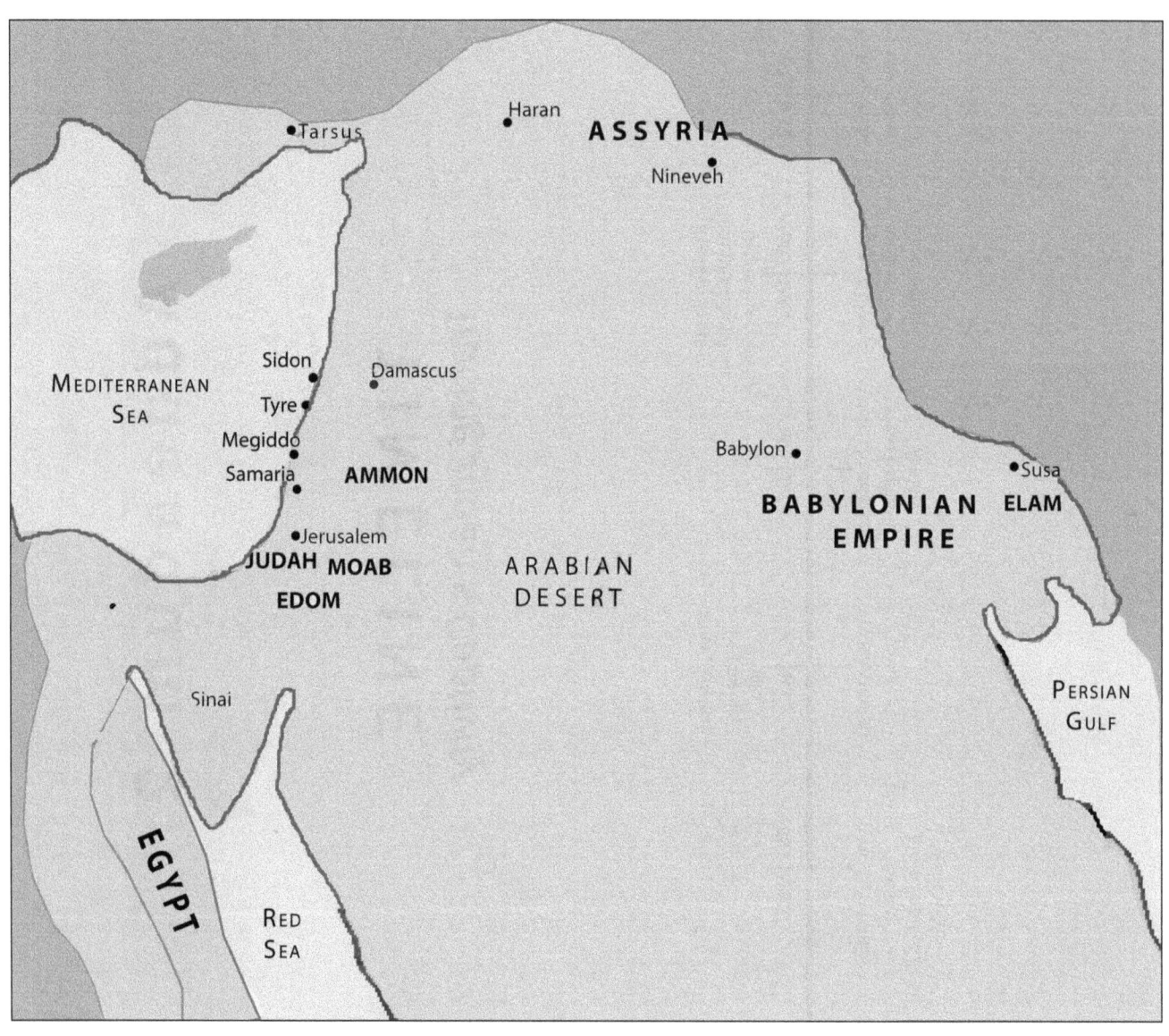

ENDNOTES

WEEK ONE

DAY 1 - SET APART

1. Warren Wiersbe, *Be Decisive* (Colorado Springs: Victor, 2005), p. 12.
2. Elmer A. Martens, *Cornerstone Biblical Commentary* (Wheaton: Tyndale, 2005), p. 311, 313.

DAY 2 - CREATED FOR A PURPOSE

1. W. Don Wilkins (ed.), *The Strongest NASB Exhaustive Concordance* (Grand Rapids: Zondervan, 1998), p.1268.
2. Warren Wiersbe, *Be Decisive* (Colorado Springs: Victor, 2005), p. 22.
3. Warren Wiersbe, *Be Decisive* (Colorado Springs: Victor, 2005), p. 22.

DAY 3 - THE ALMOND ROD & THE BOILING POT

1. Warren Wiersbe, *Be Decisive* (Colorado Springs: Victor, 2005), p. 20

DAY 4 - KING JOSIAH - A REFORMER

1. W. E. Vine, *Vine's Concise Dictionary of Bible Words* (Nashville: Thomas Nelson Publishers, 1999), p. 18.
2. W. E. Vine, *Vine's Concise Dictionary of Bible Words* (Nashville: Thomas Nelson Publishers, 1999), p. 18.
3. W. E. Vine, *Vine's Concise Dictionary of Bible Words* (Nashville: Thomas Nelson Publishers, 1999), p. 189.

WEEK TWO

DAY 1 - GUARD AGAINST SIN

1. New American Standard Exhaustive Concordance Project Staff, *The Strongest NASB Exhaustive Concordance* (Grand Rapids; Zondervan, 2000), p. 1372.

DAY 2 - TEMPLE SERMON

1. James Ussher, *The Annals of the World* (Green Forest, AR: Master Books, 2003), p. 95.
2. New American Standard Exhaustive Concordance Project Staff, *The Strongest NASB Exhaustive Concordance* (Grand Rapids; Zondervan, 2000), p. 1486.
3. Elmer A. Martens, *Cornerstone Biblical Commentary* (Wheaton: Tyndale, 2005), p. 348.
4. K. Owen White, *The Book of Jeremiah* (Grand Rapids: Baker Book House, 1961), p. 26.
5. Elmer A. Martens, *Cornerstone Biblical Commentary* (Wheaton: Tyndale, 2005), p. 351.

DAY 3 - TEMPLE SERMON (CONTINUED)

1. Warren Wiersbe, *Be Decisive* (Colorado Springs: Victor, 2005), p. 41.

DAY 5 - THE BABYLONIANS

1. Timothy B. Cargal et al., *The Chronological Study Bible NKJV,* (Nashville: Thomas Nelson, 2008), p. 715.
2. David N. Freeman (ed.), *Eerdmans Dictionary of the Bible* (Grand Rapids: Wm. B. Eerdmans Publishing Co., 2000), p. 139.
3. David N. Freeman (ed.), *Eerdmans Dictionary of the Bible* (Grand Rapids: Wm. B. Eerdmans Publishing Co. 2000), p. 139.
4. Marc Van De Mieroop, *A History of the Ancient Near East* (Malden, MA: Blackwell Publishing, 2004), p.260.
5. David N. Freeman (ed.), *Eerdmans Dictionary of the Bible* (Grand Rapids: Wm. B. Eerdmans Publishing Co. 2000), by Weissbach, 46, no. 3:22-26.
6. http://www.bible-history.com/babylonia/Babylonia The Ziggurat.htm.
7. Chris Scarre (ed.), *The Seventy Wonders of the Ancient World: The Great Monuments & How they were Built* (London: Thames & Hudson Ltd., 1999), p. 27.
8. Chris Scarre (ed.), *The Seventy Wonders of the Ancient World: The Great Monuments & How they were Built* (London: Thames & Hudson Ltd., 1999), p. 29.

9. Chris Scarre (ed.), *The Seventy Wonders of the Ancient World: The Great Monuments & How They were Built* (London: Thames & Hudson Ltd., 1999), p. 29.
10. Marc Van De Mieroop, *A History of the Ancient Near East* (Malden, MA: Blackwell Publishing, 2004), p. 260.
11. Encyclopedia Brittanica, eb.com
12. Mark Hitchcock, *The Complete Book of Bible Prophecy* (Wheaton: Tyndale, 1999), p. 97.

WEEK THREE

DAY 1 - THE LINEN SASH

1. Elmer A. Martens, *Cornerstone Biblical Commentary* (Wheaton: Tyndale, 2005), p. 374.
2. New American Standard Exhaustive Concordance Project Staff, *The Strongest NASB Exhaustive Concordance* (Grand Rapids: Zondervan, 2000), p. 1479.
3. New American Standard Exhaustive Concordance Project Staff, *The Strongest NASB Exhaustive Concordance* (Grand Rapids: Zondervan, 2000), p. 1379.

DAY 2 - THE SCROLL

1. New American Standard Exhaustive Concordance Project Staff, *The Strongest NASB Exhaustive Concordance* (Grand Rapids: Zondervan, 2000), p. 1466.
2. Elmer A. Martens, *Cornerstone Biblical Commentary* (Wheaton: Tyndale, 2005), p. 475.
3. Timothy B. Cargal et al., *The Chronological Study Bible NKJV*, (Nashville: Thomas Nelson, 2008), p. 719.
4. Eugene Peterson, *Run with the Horses* (Downers Grove, IL: Intervarsity Press, 2009), p. 207.
5. Eugene Peterson, *Run with the Horses* (Downers Grove, IL: Intervarsity Press, 2009), p. 127.
6. F.B. Meyer, *Jeremiah: Priest and Prophet* (London: Morgan and Scott, 1957), p. 108.
7. John Foxe, *Foxe's Christian Martyrs of the World* (Uhrichsville, OH: Barbour Publishing, 1989), p. 69.
8. F.B. Meyer, *Jeremiah: Priest and Prophet* (London: Morgan and Scott, 1967), p. 109.

DAY 3 - THE DROUGHT & JEREMIAH'S MINISTRY CRISIS

1. John Guest, *The Preacher's Commentary Series, Volume 19: Jeremiah, Lamentations* (Nashville: Thomas Nelson Publishers, 1988), p. 116.
2. John Guest, *The Preacher's Commentary Series, Volume 19: Jeremiah, Lamentations* (Nashville: Thomas Nelson Publishers, 1988), p. 117.

DAY 4 - THE RECHABITES - LIVES OF INTEGRITY

1. Timothy B. Cargal et al., *The Chronological Study Bible NKJV*, (Nashville: Thomas Nelson, 2008), p. 730.
2. J.A. Thompson, *The New International Commentary on the Old Testament: The Book of Jeremiah* (Grand Rapids: Wm. B. Eerdmans Publishing Co., 1980), p. 616.
3. John Bright, *Jeremiah* (New York: Doubleday, 1965), p. 190.
4. J.A. Thompson, *The New International Commentary on the Old Testament: The Book of Jeremiah* (Grand Rapids: Wm. B. Eerdmans Publishing Co., 1980), p. 617.
5. John Bright, *Jeremiah* (New York: Doubleday, 1965), p. 189.
6. Quote from Billy Graham, from *Prayers and Promises for Men: A Topical Devotional* compiled by Criswell Freeman.
7. Eugene Peterson, *Run with the Horses* (Downers Grove, IL: Intervarsity Press, 2009), p. 140.

DAY 5 - JEREMIAH'S LIFESTYLE & THE SABBATH DAY

1. J.A. Thompson, *The New International Commentary on the Old Testament: The Book of Jeremiah* (Grand Rapids: Wm. B. Eerdmans Publishing Co., 1980), p. 403.
2. Matthew Henry, *Matthew Henry's Commentary Volume 4, Isaiah to Malachi* (Peabody: Hendrickson Publishers, 2000), p. 403-404.

ENDNOTES

3. J.A. Thompson, *The New International Commentary on the Old Testament: The Book of Jeremiah* (Grand Rapids: Wm. B. Eerdmans Publishing Co., 1980), p. 404, paraphrased from Hillers, Treaty-Curses and the OT *Prophets*, p. 68f.
4. J.A. Thompson, *The New International Commentary on the Old Testament: The Book of Jeremiah* (Grand Rapids: Wm. B. Eerdmans Publishing Co., 1980), p. 405.
5. J.A. Thompson, *The New International Commentary on the Old Testament: The Book of Jeremiah* (Grand Rapids: Wm. B. Eerdmans Publishing Co., 1980), p. 407.
6. Matthew Henry, *Matthew Henry's Commentary Volume 5, Matthew to John* (Peabody: Hendrickson Publishers, 2000), p. 88.
7. Spiros Zodhiates, *Hebrew-Greek Key Word Study Bible: New American Standard Bible* (Chattanooga: AMG Publishers, 1990), p. 1082.
8. James Strong, *A Concise Dictionary of the Words in The Hebrew Bible in the Authorized English Version* (in the back of the Hebrew-Greek Key Word Study Bible NASB) (Chattanooga: AMG Publishers, 1990), p. 112.
9. The Lockman Foundation, *The Strongest NASB Exhaustive Concordance* (Grand Rapids: Zondervan, 1998), p. 1463.

WEEK FOUR

DAY 1- GARBAGE!

1. Warren Wiersbe, *Be Decisive* (Colorado Springs: Victor, 2005), p. 89.
2. Warren Wiersbe, *Be Decisive* (Colorado Springs: Victor, 2005), p. 89.
3. John Guest, *The Preacher's Commentary Series, Volume 19: Jeremiah, Lamentations* (Nashville: Thomas Nelson Publishers, 1988), p. 142.
4. Warren Wiersbe, *Be Decisive* (Colorado Springs: Victor, 2005), p. 90.
5. Warren Wiersbe, *Be Decisive* (Colorado Springs: Victor, 2005), p. 90.
6. Derek Kidner, *The Message of Jeremiah: Against Wind and Tide* (Leicester, England: Intervarsity Press, 1987), p. 79.
7. Matthew Henry, *Matthew Henry's Commentary on the Whole Bible: Volume 4, Isaiah to Malachi* (Peabody: Hendrickson Publishers, 2000), p. 423.
8. Derek Kidner, *The Message of Jeremiah: Against Wind and Tide* (Leicester, England: InterVarsity Press, 1987), p. 80.
9. Matthew Henry, *Matthew Henry's Commentary on the Whole Bible: Volume 4, Isaiah to Malachi* (Peabody: Hendrickson Publishers, 2000), p. 423.
10. Derek Kidner, *The Message of Jeremiah: Against Wind and Tide* (Leicester, England: InterVarsity Press, 1987), p. 80.
11. Warren Wiersbe, *Be Decisive* (Colorado Springs: Victor, 2005), p. 91-92.
12. F.B. Meyer, *Jeremiah: Priest and Prophet* (London: Morgan and Scott, 1957), p. 89.
13. Eugene Peterson, *Run with the Horses* (Downers Grove, IL: Intervarsity Press, 2009), p. 105

DAY 2 – THE KINGS

1. David N. Freeman (ed.), *Eerdmans Dictionary of the Bible* (Grand Rapids: Wm. B. Eerdmans Publishing Co. 2000), p. 679.
2. Derek Kidner, *The Message of Jeremiah: Against Wind and Tide* (Leicester, England: Intervarsity Press, 1987), p. 87.
3. Derek Kidner, *The Message of Jeremiah: Against Wind and Tide* (Leicester, England: Intervarsity Press, 1987), p. 87.
4. J.A. Thompson, *The New International Commentary on the Old Testament: The Book of Jeremiah* (Grand Rapids: Wm. B. Eerdmans Publishing Co., 1980), p. 484.
5. Timothy B. Cargal et al., *The Chronological Study Bible NKJV*, (Nashville: Thomas Nelson, 2008), p. 737.
6. David N. Freeman (ed.), *Eerdmans Dictionary of the Bible* (Grand Rapids: Wm. B. Eerdmans Publishing Co. 2000), p. 678.

7. Clyde T. Francisco, *Studies in Jeremiah* (Nashville: Convention Press, 1961), p. 98.
8. David N. Freeman (ed.), *Eerdmans Dictionary of the Bible* (Grand Rapids: Wm. B. Eerdmans Publishing Co. 2000), p. 1175-1176.
9. Warren Wiersbe, *Be Decisive* (Colorado Springs: Victor, 2005), p. 103.
10. Warren Wiersbe, *Be Decisive* (Colorado Springs: Victor, 2005), p. 104.
11. W. Don Wilkins (ed.), *The Stongest NASB Exhaustive Concordance* (Grand Rapids: Zondervan, 1998), p. 532.

DAY 3 – A GOOD LEADER

1. G. Campbell Morgan, *Studies in the Prophecy of Jeremiah* (Eugene, Oregon: Wipf & Stock Publishers, 1955), p. 124.
2. **www.blueletterbible.org**
3. G. Campbell Morgan, *Studies in the Prophecy of Jeremiah* (Eugene, Oregon: Wipf & Stock Publishers, 1955), p. 125, 128.
4. David N. Freeman (ed.), *Eerdmans Dictionary of the Bible* (Grand Rapids: Wm. B. Eerdmans Publishing Co. 2000), p. 1208.

DAY 4 – THE COMING RIGHTEOUS BRANCH

1. Clyde T. Francisco, *Studies in Jeremiah* (Nashville: Convention Press, 1961), p. 101.
2. J.A. Thompson, *The New International Commentary on the Old Testament: The Book of Jeremiah* (Grand Rapids: Wm. B. Eerdmans Publishing Co., 1980), p. 487.
3. J.A. Thompson, *The New International Commentary on the Old Testament: The Book of Jeremiah* (Grand Rapids: Wm. B. Eerdmans Publishing Co., 1980), p. 490.
4. Ann Spangler, *Praying the Names of God: A Daily Guide* (Grand Rapids: Zondervan, 2004), p. 280.
5. David Couchman (Focus Radio). (2011). *The Parable of the Wedding Feast* (Matthew 22:1-14). Retrieved February 27, 2011, from: www.facingthechallenge.org/matthew22.php.
6. David Couchman (Focus Radio). (2011). *The Parable of the Wedding Feast* (Matthew 22:1-14). Retrieved February 27, 2011, from: www.facingthechallenge.org/matthew22.php.

DAY 5 – FALSE PROPHETS

1. New American Standard Exhaustive Concordance Project Staff, *The Strongest NASB Exhaustive Concordance* (Grand Rapids: Zondervan, 2000), p. 1440.
2. Neil T. Anderson & Dave Park, *The Bondage Breaker Youth Edition,* (Eugene, Oregon: Harvest House Publishers, 2001), p. 171.

WEEK FIVE

DAY 1 – A TURNING POINT

1. http://freedomnowministries:blogspot.com/2012/01/understanding-spiritual-bondage.html.

DAY 2 – THE YOKE OF BABYLON

1. Louis Stulman, *Abingdon Old Testament Commentaries: Jeremiah* (Nashville: Abingdon Press, 2005), p. 246.
2. W.E. Vine, *Vine's Concise Dictionary of Bible Words* (Nashville: Thomas Nelson Publishers, 1999), p. 425.
3. John Guest, *The Preacher's Commentary Series, Volume 19: Jeremiah, Lamentations* (Nashville: Thomas Nelson Publishers, 1988), p. 188.
4. Brueggeman, 1998:43, from Elmer A. Martens, *Cornerstone Biblical Commentary* (Wheaton: Tyndale, 2005), p. 436.
5. John Bright, *Jeremiah* (New York: Doubleday, 1965), p. 201.
6. Warren Wiersbe, *Be Decisive* (Colorado Springs: Victor, 2005), p. 122.
7. http://biblesco.com/christian-life/yoke-bible-definition-word-study/

ENDNOTES

DAY 3 – ORACLES TO THE NATION

1. Derek Kidner, *The Message of Jeremiah: Against Wind and Tide* (Leicester, England: Intervarsity Press, 1987), p. 175.
2. Eugene Peterson, *Run with the Horses* (Downers Grove, IL: Intervarsity Press, 2009), p. 182-183.
3. Elmer A. Martens, *Cornerstone Biblical Commentary* (Wheaton: Tyndale, 2005), p. 506.
4. Louis Stulman, *Abingdon Old Testament Commentaries: Jeremiah* (Nashville: Abingdon Press, 2005), p. 358.
5. Louis Stulman, *Abingdon Old Testament Commentaries: Jeremiah* (Nashville: Abingdon Press, 2005), p. 359.
6. Elmer A. Martens, *Cornerstone Biblical Commentary* (Wheaton: Tyndale, 2005), p. 509.

DAY 4 – ORACLES TO THE NATION (CONTINUED)

1. J. A. Thompson, *The New International Commentary on the Old Testament: The Book of Jeremiah* (Grand Rapids: Wm. B. Eerdmans Publishing Co., 1980), p. 708.
2. Louis Stulman, *Abingdon Old Testament Commentaries: Jeremiah* (Nashville: Abingdon Press, 2005), p. 365.
3. John Bright, *Jeremiah* (New York: Doubleday, 1965), p. 323.
4. J.A. Thompson, *The New International Commentary on the Old Testament: The Book of Jeremiah* (Grand Rapids: Wm. B. Eerdmans Publishing Co., 1980), p. 716.
5. Warren Wiersbe, *Be Decisive* (Colorado Springs: Victor, 2005), p. 169.
6. Derek Kidner, *The Message of Jeremiah: Against Wind and Tide* (Leicester, England: Intervarsity Press, 1987), p. 143.
7. Information from Josephus, *Antiquities,* in Derek Kidner, *The Message of Jeremiah: Against Wind and Tide* (Leicester, England: Intervarsity Press, 1987), p. 144.
8. Louis Stulman, *Abingdon Old Testament Commentaries: Jeremiah* (Nashville: Abingdon Press, 2005), p. 368.
9. J.A. Thompson, *The New International Commentary on the Old Testament: The Book of Jeremiah* (Grand Rapids: Wm. B. Eerdmans Publishing Co., 1980), p. 720, ref. #15.
10. Louis Stulman, *Abingdon Old Testament Commentaries: Jeremiah* (Nashville: Abingdon Press, 2005), p. 368.
11. John Bright, *Jeremiah* (New York: Doubleday, 1965), p. 336.
12. John Bright, *Jeremiah* (New York: Doubleday, 1965), p. 336.
13. J.A. Thompson, *The New International Commentary on the Old Testament: The Book of Jeremiah* (Grand Rapids: Wm. B. Eerdmans Publishing Co., 1980), p. 728-729.
14. Louis Stulman, *Abingdon Old Testament Commentaries: Jeremiah* (Nashville: Abingdon Press, 2005), p. 368.

DAY 5 – BABYLON'S FUTURE

1. Warren Wiersbe, *Be Decisive* (Colorado Springs: Victor, 2005), p. 175.
2. Warren Wiersbe, *Be Decisive* (Colorado Springs: Victor, 2005), p. 178.
3. John Bright, *Jeremiah* (New York: Doubleday, 1965), p. 360.
4. Warren Wiersbe, *Be Decisive* (Colorado Springs: Victor, 2005), p. 176.
5. Louis Stulman, *Abingdon Old Testament Commentaries: Jeremiah* (Nashville: Abingdon Press, 2005), p. 385.

WEEK SIX

DAY 1 – MESSAGE TO THE EXILES

1. J.A. Thompson, *The New International Commentary on the Old Testament: The Book of Jeremiah* (Grand Rapids: Wm. B. Eerdmans Publishing Co., 1980), p. 544.
2. Louis Stulman, *Abingdon Old Testament Commentaries: Jeremiah* (Nashville: Abingdon Press, 2005), p. 251.
3. John Guest, *The Preacher's Commentary Series, Volume 19: Jeremiah, Lamentations* (Nashville: Thomas Nelson Publishers, 1988), p. 195.

4. Eugene Peterson, *Run with the Horses* (Downers Grove, IL: Intervarsity Press, 2009), p. 145.
5. Eugene Peterson, *Run with the Horses* (Downers Grove, IL: Intervarsity Press, 2009), p. 144.
6. New American Standard Exhaustive Concordance Project Staff, *The Stongest NASB Exhaustive Concordance* (Grand Rapids: Zondervan, 2000), p. 1377.
7. James Strong, *A Concise Dictionary of the Words in the Hebrew Bible in the Hebrew-Greek Key Word Study Bible NASB* (Chattanooga: AMG Publishers, 1990), p. 27.
8. Christine Roy Yoder, Kathleen M. O'Connor, E. Elizabeth Johnson, & Stanley P. Saunders (ed.), *Shaking Heaven and Earth: Essays in Honor of Walter Brueggemann and Charles B. Cousar* (Louisville, KY: Westminster John Knox Press, 2005), p. 60.
9. Derek Kidner, *The Message of Jeremiah: Against Wind and Tide* (Leicester, England: Intervarsity Press, 1987), p. 100.
10. Chester L. Tolson & Harold G. Koenig, *The Healing Power of Prayer* (Grand Rapids: Baker Books, 2003), p. 78.
11. http://www.keepbelieving.com/print.htm?sermon=817

DAY 2 – THE FAMOUS VERSE

1. G. Campbell Morgan, *Studies in the Prophecy of Jeremiah* (Eugene, Oregon: Wipf & Stock Publishers, 1955), p. 155.
2. Warren Wiersbe, *Be Decisive* (Colorado Springs: Victor, 2005), p. 124.
3. http://www.Leopold.wilderness.net/pubs/271.pdf
4. Plaque from the Sequoia National Park Visitor Center.
5. Copied from a display in the Sequoia National Park Visitor Center, quote by John Muir, 1877.
6. http://www.keepbelieving.com/print.htm?sermon=822
7. http://www.hymnary.org/text/face_to_face_with_christ_my_savior

DAY 3 – SEEKING GOD WITH ALL OUR HEARTS

1. http://www.keepbelieving.com/sermon/2008-04-30-What-You-Seek-You-Find/
2. Eugene Peterson, *Run with the Horses* (Downers Grove, IL: Intervarsity Press, 2009), p. 150.
3. Robert Laha, *Interpretation Bible Studies: Jeremiah* (Louisville, KY: Westminster John Knox Press, 2002), p. 67 (an excerpt from Celia Brewer Marshall, *A Guide through the Old Testament* (Louisville, KY: Westminster John Knox Press, 1989), p. 114.)
4. Eugene Peterson, *Run with the Horses* (Downers Grove, IL: Intervarsity Press, 2009), p. 152-153.

DAY 4 – A FEW DUDS & ANOTHER GODLY PROPHET

1. Warren Wiersbe, *Be Decisive* (Colorado Springs: Victor, 2005), p. 123.
2. J.A. Thompson, *The New International Commentary on the Old Testament: The Book of Jeremiah* (Grand Rapids: Wm. B. Eerdmans Publishing Co., 1980), p. 549.
3. J.A. Thompson, *The New International Commentary on the Old Testament: The Book of Jeremiah* (Grand Rapids: Wm. B. Eerdmans Publishing Co., 1980), p. 549, from Hammurabi, Code 25, 110, 157; Daniel 3:6.
4. Derek Kidner, *The Message of Jeremiah: Against Wind and Tide* (Leicester, England: Intervarsity Press, 1987), p. 102.
5. Spiros Zodhiates, *Hebrew-Greek Key Word Study Bible: New American Standard Bible: New American Standard Bible* (Chattanooga: AMG Publishers, 1990), p. 1082.
6. Timothy B. Cargal et al., *The Chronological Study Bible NKJV* (Nashville: Thomas Nelson, 2008), p. 765.
7. Kyle Idleman, *Not a Fan* (Grand Rapids: Zondervan, 2011), p. 24.

DAY 5 – PUT NO CONFIDENCE IN THE FLESH

1. Elmer A. Martens, *Cornerstone Biblical Commentary* (Wheaton: Tyndale, 2005), p. 767.
2. Roy L. Honeycutt, Jr., *Jeremiah: Witness Under Pressure* (Nashville: Convention Press, 1981), p. 427.

ENDNOTES

3. Warren Wiersbe, *Be Decisive* (Colorado Springs: Victor, 2005), p. 140-141.
4. John Guest, *The Preacher's Commentary Series, Volume 19: Jeremiah, Lamentations* (Nashville: Thomas Nelson Publishers, 1988), p. 227, excerpts from *Flavius Josephus, Antiquities of the Jews, 3 vols.* (Grand Rapids: Baker Book House, 1984), 3:72.
5. Matthew Henry, *Matthew Henry's Commentary on the Whole Bible: Volume 4, Isaiah to Malachi* (U.S.A: Hendrickson Publishers, 2000), p. 491-492.
6. Elmer A. Martens, *Cornerstone Biblical Commentary* (Wheaton: Tyndale, 2005), p. 467, 468.
7. J. A. Thompson, *The New International Commentary on the Old Testament: The Book of Jeremiah* (Grand Rapids: Wm. B. Eerdmans Publishing Co., 1980), p. 613.
8. Louis Stulman, *Abingdon Old Testament Commentaries: Jeremiah* (Nashville: Abingdon Press, 2005), p. 291.
9. J. A. Thompson, *The New International Commentary on the Old Testament: The Book of Jeremiah* (Grand Rapids: Wm. B. Eerdmans Publishing Co., 1980), p. 611.
10. G. Campbell Morgan, *Studies in the Prophecy of Jeremiah* (Eugene, Oregon: Wipf & Stock Publishers, 1955), p. 218.
11. G. Campbell Morgan, *Studies in the Prophecy of Jeremiah* (Eugene, Oregon: Wipf & Stock Publishers, 1955), p. 219.

WEEK SEVEN

DAY 1 – OBSTINATE PEOPLE

1. Walter Brueggemann, *A Commentary on Jeremiah* (Grand Rapids: William B. Eerdmans Publishing Company, 1998), p. 355.
2. J. A. Thompson, *The New International Commentary on the Old Testament: The Book of Jeremiah* (Grand Rapids: Wm. B. Eerdmans Publishing Co., 1980), p. 635.
3. J. A. Thompson, *The New International Commentary on the Old Testament: The Book of Jeremiah* (Grand Rapids: Wm. B. Eerdmans Publishing Co., 1980), p. 635.

DAY 2 – THE PIT

1. J.A. Thompson, *The New International Commentary on the Old Testament: The Book of Jeremiah* (Grand Rapids: Wm. B. Eerdmans Publishing Co., 1980), p. 637.
2. John Guest, *The Preacher's Commentary Series, Volume 19: Jeremiah, Lamentations* (Nashville: Thomas Nelson Publishers, 1988), p. 249.
3. Derek Kidner, *The Message of Jeremiah: Against Wind and Tide* (Leicester, England: Intervarsity Press, 1987), p. 124.
4. J. A. Thompson, *The New International Commentary on the Old Testament: The Book of Jeremiah* (Grand Rapids: Wm. B. Eerdmans Publishing Co., 1980), p. 638.
5. J. A. Thompson, *The New International Commentary on the Old Testament: The Book of Jeremiah* (Grand Rapids: Wm. B. Eerdmans Publishing Co., 1980), p. 638.
6. Louis Stulman, *Abingdon Old Testament Commentaries: Jeremiah* (Nashville: Abingdon Press, 2005), p. 310.
7. Elmer A. Martens, *Cornerstone Biblical Commentary* (Wheaton: Tyndale, 2005), p. 484.
8. Walter Brueggemann, *A Commentary on Jeremiah* (Grand Rapids: William B. Eerdmans Publishing Company, 1998), p. 365.

DAY 3 – NOTHING IS TOO DIFFICULT FOR GOD

1. Warren Wiersbe, *Be Decisive* (Colorado Springs: Victor, 2005), p. 136.
2. Derek Kidner, *The Message of Jeremiah: Against Wind and Tide* (Leicester, England: Intervarsity Press, 1987), p. 112.
3. G. Campbell Morgan, *Studies in the Prophecy of Jeremiah* (Eugene, Oregon: Wipf & Stock Publishers, 1955), p. 191.
4. Warren Wiersbe, *Be Decisive* (Colorado Springs: Victor, 2005), p. 138.
5. www.spurgeongems.org., sermon #2020, p. 4.

TAKING CAPTIVITY CAPTIVE

DAY 4 – CALL TO ME

1. W.E. Vine, *Vine's Concise Dictionary of Bible Words* (Nashville: Thomas Nelson Publishers, 1999), p. 46.
2. A. W. Tozer, *The Pursuit of God* (Lexington, KY: WLC, 2012), p. 13.
3. A. W. Tozer, *The Pursuit of God* (Lexington, KY: WLC, 2012), p. 59.

DAY 5 – RESTORATION

1. Elmer A. Martens, *Cornerstone Biblical Commentary* (Wheaton: Tyndale, 2005), p. 452.
2. Christine Roy Yoder, Kathleen M. O'Connor, E. Elizabeth Johnson, & Stanley P. Saunders (ed.), *Shaking Heaven and Earth: Essays in Honor of Walter Brueggemann and Charles B. Cousar* (Louisville, KY: Westminster John Knox Press, 2005), p. 68.
3. Louis Stulman, *Abingdon Old Testament Commentaries: Jeremiah* (Nashville: Abingdon Press, 2005), p. 268.
4. Louis Stulman, *Abingdon Old Testament Commentaries: Jeremiah* (Nashville: Abingdon Press, 2005), p. 269.
5. Elmer A. Martens, *Cornerstone Biblical Commentary* (Wheaton: Tyndale, 2005), p. 450.
6. Elmer A. Martens, *Cornerstone Biblical Commentary* (Wheaton: Tyndale, 2005), p. 450.
7. Derek Kidner, *The Message of Jeremiah: Against Wind and Tide* (Leicester, England: Intervarsity Press, 1987), p. 109.
8. Elmer A. Martens, *Cornerstone Biblical Commentary* (Wheaton: Tyndale, 2005), p. 455.
9. Kathleen M. O'Connor, *Jeremiah: Pain and Promise* (Minneapolis: Fortress Press, 2011), p. 112.
10. Kathleen M. O'Connor, *Jeremiah: Pain and Promise* (Minneapolis: Fortress Press, 2011), p. 112.
11. J. A. Thompson, *The New International Commentary on the Old Testament: The Book of Jeremiah* (Grand Rapids: Wm. B. Eerdmans Publishing Co., 1980), p. 579.

WEEK EIGHT

DAY 1 – THE FALL OF JERUSALEM

1. G. Campbell Morgan, *Studies in the Prophecy of Jeremiah* (Eugene, Oregon: Wipf & Stock Publishers, 1955), p. 251.
2. J. A. Thompson, *The New International Commentary on the Old Testament: The Book of Jeremiah* (Grand Rapids: Wm. B. Eerdmans Publishing Co., 1980), p. 644.
3. Elmer A. Martens, *Cornerstone Biblical Commentary* (Wheaton: Tyndale, 2005), p. 486.
4. Warren Wiersbe, *Be Decisive* (Colorado Springs: Victor, 2005), p. 151.
5. Walter Brueggemann, *A Commentary on Jeremiah* (Grand Rapids: William B. Eerdmans Publishing Company, 1998), p. 491.
6. Elmer A. Martens, *Cornerstone Biblical Commentary* (Wheaton: Tyndale, 2005), p. 543.
7. John Guest, *The Preacher's Commentary Series, Volume 19: Jeremiah, Lamentations* (Nashville: Thomas Nelson Publishers, 1988), p. 260.
8. Walter Brueggemann, *A Commentary on Jeremiah* (Grand Rapids: William B. Eerdmans Publishing Company, 1998), p. 491.
9. John Bright, **Jeremiah** (New York: Doubleday, 1965), p. 369.
10. Louis Stulman, *Abingdon Old Testament Commentaries: Jeremiah* (Nashville: Abingdon Press, 2005), p. 391.
11. Walter Brueggemann, *A Commentary on Jeremiah* (Grand Rapids: William B. Eerdmans Publishing Company, 1998), p. 372.

DAY 2 – A CHANCE FOR A NEW BEGINNING

1. Elmer A. Martens, *Cornerstone Biblical Commentary* (Wheaton: Tyndale, 2005), p. 490.
2. John Guest, *The Preacher's Commentary Series, Volume 19: Jeremiah, Lamentations* (Nashville: Thomas Nelson Publishers, 1988), p. 270.

ENDNOTES

3. John Guest, *The Preacher's Commentary Series, Volume 19: Jeremiah, Lamentations* (Nashville: Thomas Nelson Publishers, 1988), p. 270.

4. Louis Stulman, *Abingdon Old Testament Commentaries: Jeremiah* (Nashville: Abingdon Press, 2005), p. 327-328.

5. John Guest, *The Preacher's Commentary Series, Volume 19: Jeremiah, Lamentations* (Nashville: Thomas Nelson Publishers, 1988), p. 272.

DAY 3 – EGYPT & JEREMIAH'S LAST WORDS

1. Elmer A. Martens, *Cornerstone Biblical Commentary* (Wheaton: Tyndale, 2005), p. 499.

2. G. Campbell Morgan, *Studies in the Prophecy of Jeremiah* (Eugene, Oregon: Wipf & Stock Publishers, 1955), p. 260.

3. J. A. Thompson, *The New International Commentary on the Old Testament: The Book of Jeremiah* (Grand Rapids: Wm. B. Eerdmans Publishing Co., 1980), p. 671.

4. Derek Kidner, *The Message of Jeremiah: Against Wind and Tide* (Leicester, England: Intervarsity Press, 1987), p. 132.

DAY 4 – WRAPPING IT UP!

1. Elmer A. Martens, *Cornerstone Biblical Commentary* (Wheaton: Tyndale, 2005), p. 204.

2. Matthew Henry, *Matthew Henry's Commentary on the Whole Bible: Volume 4, Isaiah to Malachi* (U.S.A: Hendrickson Publishers, 2000), p. 832.

3. Matthew Henry, *Matthew Henry's Commentary on the Whole Bible: Volume 4, Isaiah to Malachi* (U.S.A: Hendrickson Publishers, 2000), p. 832.

4. Elmer A. Martens, *Cornerstone Biblical Commentary* (Wheaton: Tyndale, 2005), p. 227.

DAY 5 – HOPE

1. Spiros Zodhiates, *Hebrew-Greek Key Word Study Bible: New American Standard Bible: New American Standard Bible* (Chattanooga: AMG Publishers, 1990), p. 624.

2. Spiros Zodhiates, *Hebrew-Greek Key Word Study Bible: New American Standard Bible: New American Standard Bible* (Chattanooga: AMG Publishers, 1990), p. 624.

www.ingramcontent.com/pod-product-compliance
Lightning Source LLC
Chambersburg PA
CBHW080433110426
42743CB00016B/3158